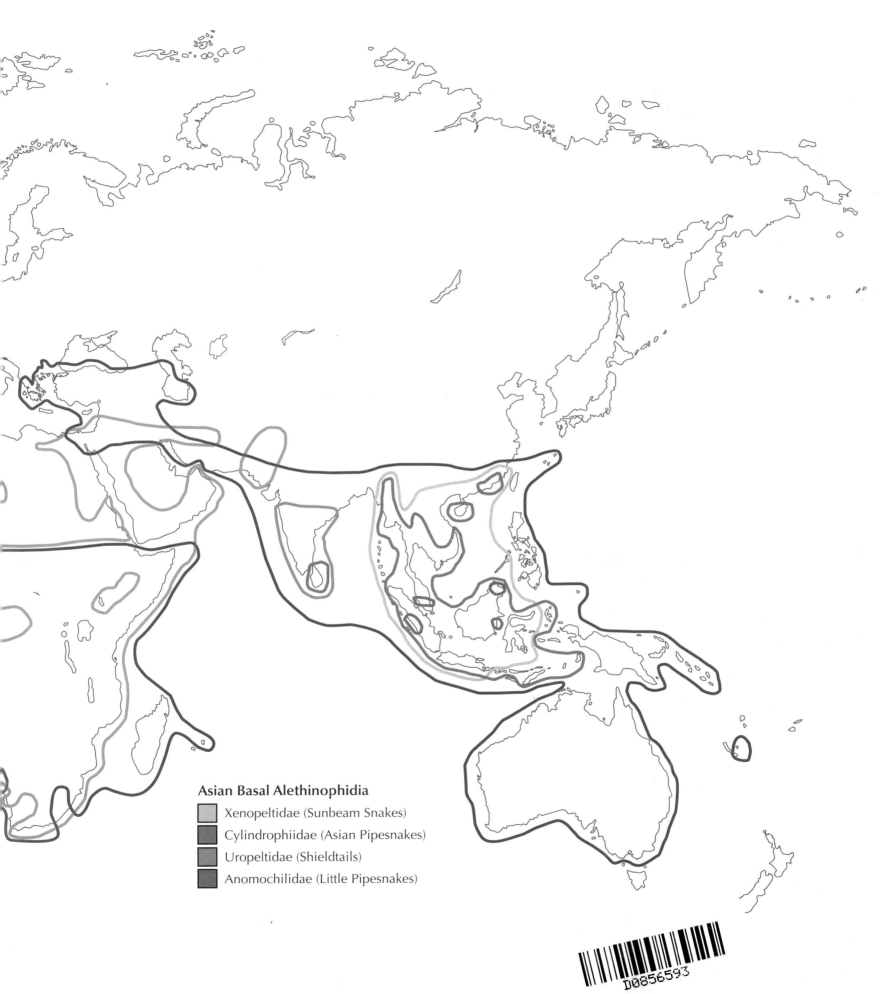

Asian Basal Alethinophidia

Xenopeltidae (Sunbeam Snakes)

Cylindrophiidae (Asian Pipesnakes)

Uropeltidae (Shieldtails)

Anomochilidae (Little Pipesnakes)

BOAS *and* PYTHONS
OF THE WORLD

BOAS *and* PYTHONS
OF THE WORLD

Mark O'Shea

PRINCETON UNIVERSITY PRESS
PRINCETON AND OXFORD

Published in the United States and Canada by Princeton University Press, 41 William Street, Princeton, New Jersey 08540

First published in the United Kingdom and European Union in 2007 by New Holland Publishers (UK) Ltd
London • Cape Town • Sydney • Auckland

Copyright © 2007 in text: Mark O'Shea
Copyright © 2007 in artwork: New Holland Publishers (UK) Ltd
Copyright © 2007 in photographs: see credits on page 160/next to images.
Copyright © 2007 New Holland Publishers (UK) Ltd

All rights reserved. No part of this publication may be reproduced, stored in any retrieval system or transmitted, in any form or by any means, electronic, mechanical, photocopying, recording or otherwise, without the prior written permission of the publishers and copyright holders.

Library of Congress Control Number 2006932790
ISBN-13: 978-0-691-13100-9
ISBN-10: 0-691-13100-7

pup.princeton.edu

Editorial Director: Jo Hemmings
Senior Editor: James Parry
Cover Design and Design: Gülen Shevki-Taylor
Maps: Original artwork by Mark O'Shea, adapted by Bill Smuts
Production: Joan Woodroffe

Reproduction by Pica Digital Pte Ltd, Singapore
Printed and bound in Singapore by Tien Wah Press (Pte) Ltd

10 9 8 7 6 5 4 3 2 1

Photographs: Front cover, main picture: Amazonian Treeboa (*Corallus hortulanus*); Inset: Mark O'Shea with Burmese Rock Python (*Python molurus bivittatus*); Spine: Boa Constrictor (*Boa constrictor*)
Back cover, top: Burmese Rock Python (*Python molurus bivittatus*); below, left to right: De Schauensee's Anaconda (*Eunectes deschauenseei*), Green Tree Python *(Morelia viridis)*, Javelin Sand Boa (*Eryx jaculus*), Royal Python *(Python regius)*
Page 1: Juvenile Green Tree Python *(Morelia viridis)*
Page 2: Brazilian Rainbow Boa *(Epicrates cenchria)*
This page (left): Dumeril's Ground Boa *(Acrantophis dumerili)*
Page 6: (left) Reticulated Python *(Python reticulatus)*; (right) Stimson's Python *(Antaresia stimsoni)*; Page 7: (left) Amazonian Treeboa *(Corallus hortulanus)*; (right) Dumeril's Ground Boa *(Acrantophis dumerili)*

This book is dedicated to my partner Bina Mistry, reluctant snake hunter but aspiring 'jungle girl', who has been at my side through thick and thin, highs and lows, for almost ten years.

Foreword

Mark O'Shea has caught Burmese Pythons in the foothills of Nepal, collected four python species in a single night, evicted a Boa Constrictor from an expedition tent while naked (and made it back to his own tent before colleagues could scramble for their cameras), escaped a near-drowning whilst entangled with a large Amethystine Python, and discovered a new genus of python for New Guinea. These experiences – and many more – have textured the fabric of O'Shea's life as a herpetological field biologist.

Some people choose to pursue herpetology, while others seem to be born with no other desire. Those in this second category are chosen by herpetology, and it guides them, leading them through their entire lives. O'Shea's particular calling became active when he was nine years old, and it has never relinquished its hold on him.

O'Shea serves another master as well – namely, a driving desire for travel and adventure. Early collecting trips to Florida and Borneo further whetted his appetite to see the world, and he has spent a large part of his adult life traveling around the globe, visiting every continent that harbors reptiles.

Few herpetologists have not fantasized about mounting an expedition to a far destination in pursuit of some rare reptile or amphibian. We ourselves have traveled enough on our own herpetological ventures to appreciate O'Shea's dedication and the sacrifices he has made in order to have traveled so extensively. More often than not, a journey far into the field is uncomfortable and beset by logistical problems too numerous to imagine. And once one has arrived – to pole across tropical swamps filled with crocodiles, to clamber over rocky ridges in search of pitvipers, to catch King Cobras, or to grapple with anacondas – these favorite activities of O'Shea add immeasurably to the dangers inherent in any trip, and help is usually a long way off.

Mark O'Shea has sought and found herpetological adventure, and this book is the richer for it. Although several books have been written on the general topic of boas and pythons, this book alone is authored by a herpetologist who has extensive knowledge of these two snake families and has seen many of the species in the wild. Scattered throughout this text are notes and observations made by O'Shea *in situ*, records made from first-hand experience. O'Shea has encountered boas and pythons on every continent where they can be found, and on many islands in the tropical oceans as well.

Beautifully illustrated, O'Shea's book includes many images of rare and seldom-seen species. We, of course, harbor a strong affection for boas and pythons, but it is the information and pictures of the rarely photographed, rarely featured primitive snakes that totally captured our attention, motivating us to sit down and read the book from front to back. This new book will grant you privileged insights into the lives and habitats of these snakes. We salute Mark O'Shea for *Boas and Pythons of the World*, an especially enjoyable and beautiful book, and a valued addition to any library.

Dave and Tracy Barker,
Boerne, Texas, July 2006

INTRODUCTION

This is not simply a volume on the boas (Boidae) and pythons (Pythonidae). Also included within these pages are all the small, secretive families, some of which are known as 'basal snakes' – the blindsnakes, threadsnakes and wormsnakes thought closest to the evolution of snakes from lizards – and all the strange families between the blindsnakes and the more familiar boas and pythons, ie. the pipesnakes, shieldtails, sunbeam snakes, spike-jawed snakes, split-jawed snakes and dwarf boas. This volume therefore contains not only largest snakes in the world, but also the smallest.

As with *Venomous Snakes of the World* (2005), this book is arranged geographically rather than taxonomically. While *Venomous Snakes* included six chapters: Americas, Eurasia, Africa, Tropical Asia, Australasia, and The Oceans, in this book there are no marine boas or pythons to consider, and Eurasia has been combined with Tropical Asia under the heading 'Europe and Asia'. Interestingly, 75 per cent of all boas live in the Americas, while 72 per cent of all pythons are Australasian.

If Europe is poorly represented, then other parts of the world are much richer in boas and pythons than they are in venomous snakes. In the Caribbean, venomous snakes are found on only eight islands, and in *Venomous Snakes* this region received only a single page. In *Boas and Pythons* the reader will discover the rich West Indian diversity, which includes nine species of true boa, two subspecies of boa constrictor, and 17 dwarf boas and woodsnakes. The Indian Ocean islands are absent from *Venomous Snakes* because the great island of Madagascar lacks any front-fanged species, but it is inhabited by three true boas, while two extremely unusual split-jawed boas inhabit Round Island, off Mauritius, although one is now believed extinct. Boas also inhabit far more islands in the southwest Pacific than do venomous snakes.

This geographical approach is, again, not without its complications; the pipesnakes, *Cylindrophis*, and sand boas, *Eryx* and *Gongylophis*, occur in two chapters, the slender blindsnakes, *Leptotyphlops*, and true pythons, *Python*, in three, and the blindsnakes, *Typhlops*, in all four.

A Bibron's Bevel-nosed Boa (Candoia bibroni) *from Fiji, a member of a diverse boa genus distributed around one-fifth of the world's circumference.*

Evolution of Leglessness as an Advanced State

Snakes are generally defined as elongate reptiles with scaly bodies, no ears or eyelids, a forked tongue and – not entirely accurately – no legs. However, leglessness is not only the preserve of boas, pythons and other snakes. There are other reptiles, and even a few amphibians, that also exhibit limblessness and which may serve as examples of convergent evolution with the serpents.

Vertebrates above the level of fishes are placed in the Tetrapoda, literally 'four-legged vertebrates', regardless of whether their legs have subsequently become modified into wings or flippers, or have disappeared entirely, as in snakes. The primitive tetrapod condition is the pentadactyl tetrapod, which means 'five-toed, four-legged'. Any adaptive radiations away from this condition may be considered as an evolutionary advancement, even if that involves a move towards leglessness, the loss of limbs being considered a derived (advanced) character state in the tetrapods.

The reduction or loss of limbs is often associated with elongation of the body, tail shortening, and a fossorial (burrowing) lifestyle. Since many different lineages of reptiles have evolved to occupy subterranean habitats, the reduction and/or loss of limbs has occurred on several occasions in the squamate reptiles. Adaptive radiation therefore provides many excellent examples of convergent (parallel) evolution, with species in the various reduced-limbed families being more closely related to their four-limbed ancestors than to species in parallel legless families. Many of these legless reptiles and amphibians may be mistaken for snakes purely because they lack limbs. It is these non-serpentine tetrapods that I shall be introducing briefly here.

Amphibians

Most of the 6,000 living amphibians belong to the Anura (frogs and toads) or the Urodela (newts and salamanders), both legged suborders. There are also 160 species within the lesser-known suborder, Gymnophiona, and these are the legless caecilians. They resemble earthworms with their cylindrical, annulated, slimy bodies, blunt heads with almost invisible eyes, and short tails. Caecilians are aquatic or subterranean in moist soils, and found throughout the tropics.

Reptiles

Within the reptiles leglessness or limb reduction, and body elongation, is most often associated with the suborder Serpentes (snakes), but it is also the normal condition in the suborder Amphisbaenia (worm-lizards) and is a common factor in the evolutionary adaptation of four out of five lineages within the Lacertilia (lizards).

The Gekkota contains not only 1,000-plus species of agile geckos worldwide, but also the Australasian Pygopodidae, a family of 35 species of elongate lizards lacking forelimbs and with hind-limbs reduced to scaly flaps. Most pygopods prey on ant eggs and soft-bodied invertebrates, as do blindsnakes, but the Australo-Papuan snake-lizards, *Lialis*, have also evolved elongated, highly mobile jaws with which they manipulate and swallow relatively large skinks that may be considered, relative to the snake-lizard's body size, comparable to the prey taken by a python. The secretive, limbless, Indo-Malaysian dart skinks, *Dibamus*, may be mistaken for blindsnakes and require an expert with a hand lens to determine otherwise.

The Scincomorpha contains seven lizard families, including the American teiids, Eurasian-African lacertids and worldwide skinks. Most families contain numerous long-legged species, but each also contains a few snake-like representatives such as the South American bachias, *Bachia*, and African legless-skinks, *Melanoseps*, and African dart-skinks, *Acontias*.

The Diploglossa includes the Anguidae, which contains the legless European Slow Worm, *Anguis fragilis*, American 'glass-snakes', *Ophisaurus*, and the 1.2m-long Balkan Scheltopusik, *Pseudopus apodus*, the longest legless lizard.

The Amphisbaenia, the third suborder of the Squamata, evolved from within the Gekkota. 'Amphisbaenian', from the Greek, means 'to go either way' ie. forwards and backwards. The largest species, the 0.7m Red Worm Lizard, *Amphisbaena alba*, is called 'cobra de duas cabeças' (snake with two heads) in Brazil, due to its identical short rounded head and tail. 140 amphisbaenians are found in South America, the West Indies, southern Florida, sub-Saharan Africa, the Iberian Peninsula, Morocco and the Middle East.

Limblessness has occurred independently many times in amphibians and reptiles, yet legless caecilians, amphisbaenians and lizards number fewer than 350 species compared to the almost 3,000 snakes, which vouch for the fact that limbs are not essential appendages for a successful predator. A fact well proven by the giant anaconda that takes a 1.5m caiman.

ABOVE: *Boulenger's Blind Legless Skink* (Typhlosaurus vermis) *is a reminder that limblessness is not confined to the serpents.*

Anatomy of Snakes

Snakes, lizards and legless amphisbaenians belong to the order Squamata. The Squamata has a sister clade, the Rhynchocephalia, which today only contains two living species, the tuataras, *Sphenodon*, of New Zealand. Together they make up the Lepidosauria, 'the scaled reptiles', as opposed to the Archosauria, 'the ancient reptiles', which include dinosaurs, birds and crocodilians. The turtles and tortoises diverged long before the Lepidosauria-Archosauria split. Snakes can be summarized as elongate, scaled reptiles with a forked tongue and lacking eyelids, external ear openings and, usually, limbs.

BODY SHAPE

Boas and pythons are powerfully muscular, a necessity for constricting large, dangerous prey, but some of the more arboreal species that prey on harmless lizards or frogs are slender and almost aquiline in body shape. Several terrestrial boas are stoutly-built sit-and-wait ambushers of prey, not dissimilar in appearance to the more advanced vipers and death adders (elapids) that adopt the same strategy. The basal snakes are mostly fossorial (burrowers) or at least semi-fossorial, living in the decaying forest leaf-litter. They tend to be slender, often cylindrical, with heads not, or barely, distinguishable from the neck and body, in contrast to the broad-jawed heads of the treeboas and pythons, designed for swallowing broad prey. Sometimes there is a sexual difference in the size of individuals and probably the most extreme example of this is the Green Anaconda, *Eunectes murinus*, of which the males grow to only about 3.5m whereas huge, heavy females may achieve more than twice that length.

Tails, too, provide a clue to the lifestyle of the owner. Agile, arboreal species, especially treeboas and tree pythons, have a long, prehensile tail that serves as a gripping limb. Terrestrial ground boas and subterranean sand boas have short tails that taper rapidly to a point – they have no need to anchor themselves to branches. The highly fossorial blindsnakes also have short tails which terminate in a sharp spine, to assist their progress when burrowing through the soil. The shieldtails have curious, truncated tails covered with spinous 'shields' which collect mud and seal the burrow behind the snake, possibly serving as a rearguard action.

A Peruvian Rainbow Boa (Epicrates cenchria gaigae) *with iridescent patterning and the muscular body coils typical of constrictors.*

EXTERNAL INTEGUMENT

There is a great deal of variation in snake scale shape, size, texture and appearance. Many of the basal snakes are covered in tiny scales almost too small for the naked eye to perceive, the belly scales being virtually identical to those on the back, and the head being enclosed by a few large, transparent scales that almost obscure the miniscule, pigmented eyes. More regular and discernable scales make an appearance in the pipesnakes and other more stout-bodied serpents, and at this level the scales are generally larger, making the counting of rows and identification of species much easier. By the time we reach the pythons and boas we have seen an array of scale types, small and granular in Boa Constrictors, large and distinctly imbricate (overlapping) in the large pythons, but many of the more unusual scale arrangements appear in the more advanced filesnakes (tuberculate scales), seasnakes (hexagonal scales), treesnakes (ridged ventral scales), saw-scale vipers (serrated scales), outside the scope of this book. Amongst the higher snake families are snakes with smooth scales and keeled scales, scales with a longitudinal ridge down the centre which gives them a matt appearance and rough texture. Within the 500-plus snake species, in the 15 families covered by this volume, smooth scales are the norm. Keeled scales are found in fewer than 40 boas, in the broadest sense of the word 'boa', and a single python, *Morelia carinata*.

In terrestrial species, typically pythons and boas, the ventral scales are broader than the ordinary dorsal scales. These enlarged plates are designed to assist in terrestrial locomotion whereas the reduced scales of blindsnakes and pipesnakes are probably sufficient for subterranean movement.

The scales of the head may comprise a mass of small granular scales, indistinguishable from those on the body, or they may comprise a regular arrangement of enlarged, individually named scales known generically as 'scutes'. In the pythons and boas there are species with completely granular head scalation, species with a few recognizable scutes, usually over the eyes and in the internasal region, and species with a complete set of dorsal and lateral head scutes. Examples of species with granular head scalation include the Green Tree Python, *Morelia viridis*, and Boa Constrictor, *Boa constrictor*, while the Water Python, *Liasis fuscus*, possesses well-defined head scutes. Scale type, arrangement and numbers, in particular rows, are so regular and characteristic of particular snake species and genera that they are the single most important factor in determining snake identification. Scale arrangement and number is far more important than variable or relative characteristics such as colour or pattern.

Coloration and patterning in snakes is often highly variable. Many species rely on subdued colours or highly cryptic camouflage to avoid detection, while others use permanent bright warning patterns or temporary flashes of colour to deter interference. The snakes that fall into this latter category are usually venomous and able to back up their show with a dangerous bite. However, some harmless species have patterning that may be mistaken for that of a dangerous species

OPPOSITE: *The sense organs of the Emerald Treeboa* (Corallus caninus) *include a forked tongue, eye with vertical pupil, and thermo-sensory pits in upper and lower lip scales.*

and receive some protection from the confusion. Whether this is intended or accidental is difficult to determine. The South American Pipesnake, *Anilius scytale*, has patterning resembling the highly venomous coralsnakes of genus *Micrurus*, yet it evolved long before the coralsnakes so the mimicry must be incidental in its case. Even within a single species colour and pattern may vary. Clutches of hatchlings, or litters of neonates, may contain differently coloured individuals, the most vivid examples being the yellow, orange or green hatchlings of the Green Tree Python and the red, orange or green neonates of the Emerald Treeboa, *Corallus caninus*. These brightly coloured offspring then undergo an ontogenetic colour change to the green adult livery as they approach maturity. Some species demonstrate sexual dichromatism, ie. the sexes are different colours, and individual Pacific boas of genus *Candoia* are able to change their body hue over time, from light to dark and back again, even managing subtle colour changes in the process. The reasoning and trigger for this behaviour is unclear.

Although lacking eyelids, snakes possess transparent eye coverings known as 'brilles' which are sloughed along with the rest of the upper layer of skin. The replacement of eyelids with brilles is a common characteristic of both snakes and burrowing lizards and is probably a means of protecting the eye at ground level. Skin shedding or sloughing is a regular process for snakes, related to growth, wound healing or as a precursor to laying eggs or giving birth. Snakes sometimes slough their skins in one entire piece, the result being an inverted and colourless 'ghost' of the snake, with only the faintest representation of the original patterning.

INTERNAL ORGANS

Snakes are vertebrates with a skull and jaws, and a backbone to which are attached numerous ribs. They lack a breastbone, the pectoral girdle and forelimbs. However, most of the snakes encompassed in this volume, the pythons and boas and many of the more basal species, even the slender blindsnakes, possess the remains of the pelvic girdle and also cloacal spurs, the remnants of the hind-limbs. These appear, to a greater or lesser degree, as a single, hardened curved spur on either side of the cloaca, the common genital-excretory opening, which is covered by a protective cloacal or anal plate. Spurs tend to be larger in males because, in some species, especially pythons and boas, they use them to stroke the female during courtship. Females, on the other hand, do not use their spurs, they truly are vestigial and redundant, and hence they may be reduced in size, or absent from one or both sides. The presence and size of cloacal spurs is a useful aid in determining the sex of a python or boa. No snakes above the level of those contained within this volume possess either a vestigial pelvic girdle or spurs.

The organs present are the same as in any other vertebrate,

although modified for a cylindrical body. The thoracic organs include a three-chambered heart, compared to the four-chambered heart of mammals or crocodiles; one main lung, which extends for almost half the length of the body, although whether this is the right or left depends on the family concerned; and a reduced second lung.

SENSE ORGANS

The eyes of blindsnakes are reduced to areas of pigmentation under large transparent head scales. All other snakes possess recognizable eyes, although they may be extremely reduced in size since vision is probably not the most importance sense for a burrower or nocturnal leaf-litter inhabitant. Pupils may be round or vertically elliptical, the latter being associated with a nocturnal existence since it enables more light to reach the highly sensitive retina. Snakes can detect motion owing to the structure of the retina, which is armed with more rods rather than cones, and provides vision similar to a mammal's peripheral vision with its 'all or nothing' response. They cannot detect colour or shape. Some snakes seem to possess particularly acute vision, responding to the very slightest movements. It has recently been discovered that some treeboas of the genus *Corallus* possess a *tapetum lucidum*, a mirror-like layer of rods and cones at the back of the retina, and their eyes reflect 'eyeshine' in the same way as the eyes of crocodiles, frogs, nocturnal mammals and birds like nightjars. This is presumably intended to enhance the nocturnal

hunting abilities of these snakes but it has also enhanced my ability to find them using torches at night.

Snakes do not possess external ears so they are 'deaf' to airborne sound as we know it. However, sound causes vibrations to pass through solid material and snakes are adept at detecting vibrations through the ground, via their lower jaws. For those species living on the forest floor the detection of vibrations may be an important warning, and there is some evidence that snakes below ground will exit their burrows rapidly when they detect the vibrations of an earthquake, thereby avoiding the risk of become trapped.

All snakes possess a chemosensory forked tongue to enable them to locate prey and mates and navigate within their home range. The tongue is located in the front of the lower jaws, underneath the extendible airway or glottis, which permits continued breathing during the swallowing process. The forked tongue functions in collaboration with the tubular Jacobson's organ in the roof of the snake's mouth. When faced with a threat a snake will flick its tongue more frequently and more rapidly, in an attempt to determine the identity of the threat. There is no connection between the forked tongue and venom – a snake does not sting with its tongue. Whilst every single one of the 500-plus snakes in the 15 families covered by this volume possesses a forked tongue, not one of them is venomous.

A few snakes, boas, pythons and pitvipers, also possess heat-receptors on their faces, 'pits' containing highly thermosensitive membranes, to enable to them to locate their warm-blooded

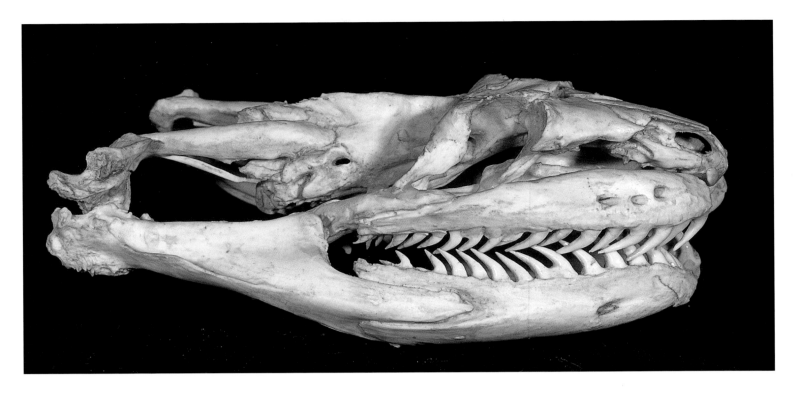

prey. In boas and pythons the pits consist of a series of slit-like openings in the upper and lower lip scales (supralabials and infralabials). These highly sensitive pits provide the snake with instant information as to the location of the prey, both distance and direction, enabling it to make a lightning strike, even in the total dark when vision is virtually useless. Treeboas of genus *Corallus* are able to capture nectar-feeding bats coming to feed on *Parkia* blooms in the total dark of the Amazonian night, purely by the body heat being given off by the bat.

JAWS AND TEETH

The skull and jaws of most snakes are extremely flexible, demonstrating the highest degree of 'cranial kinesis' of any terrestrial vertebrate. Since they lack forelimbs for prey handling, and also lack specialized teeth for reducing the prey animal to smaller, swallowable pieces, a snake has only its mouth and body coils to capture, restrain and swallow its prey. In most advanced snakes, the lower jaw is not united as a single unit, as in mammals, but instead is made up of a right and left half that can move independently because there is no physical link between them at the chin. They can open their mouths extremely wide to swallow prey two, three or more times the width of their own heads, hence the generic term of Macrostomata or 'big-mouthed snakes' (see p.18). These snakes do not 'dislocate' their jaws, a process that would render them ineffectual, they articulate them on the ball and socket joint where the jaw is hinged on the skull. Each side of the lower jaw is also made up of several separate and mobile bones, thereby permitting considerable flexibility in most planes.

Many of the more basal snakes do not possess the same degree of flexibility in their lower jaws and are only capable of swallowing soft prey that can be squeezed into the mouth or elongate prey with a diameter no greater than the snake's

The skull of the Green Anaconda (Eunectes murinus) *contains six rows of sharp recurved teeth but no fangs.*

mouth. The Round Island boas (p.110) are known as the split-jawed boas because they possess a further adaptation of the lower jaw, whereby it is divided into hinged anterior and posterior sections which permit even greater flexibility when dealing with smooth-scaled lizards.

The independent flexibility of the opposing sides of the lower jaw, combined with simple recurved teeth, can be used to draw prey into the throat. The kinesis of the lower jaw replaces the need for other appendages such as hands in prey handling.

As will be seen when visiting the sections dealing with the more basal blindsnakes etc, some snakes possess only a few teeth on either the upper or lower jaws. However, most snakes above the level of the blindsnakes possess six rows of teeth, two in the lower jaw and four in the upper jaw. These are simple recurved 'hooks' to prevent prey escaping and to aid in the directing of prey towards the throat. Some treeboas and pythons have enlarged teeth in the front of the jaw, to capture birds; other species may have enlarged teeth in the rear of the jaw, to puncture frogs, but this is largely the preserve of snakes outside the scope of this book. The curious and very poorly known Malaysian Spine-jawed Snake, *Xenophidion* (p.73), appears to possess a strange spinous, tooth-like projection of unknown purpose in the upper jaw. None of the species in this book is venomous, even in the more recent, broader definition of the term that encompassed many snake species previously considered 'non-venomous'. Since the development and structure of Duvernoy's and venom glands, the composition of venom, and the various arrangements of rear and front-fangs is such a complex subject, outside the scope of this book, I will direct the interested reader to *Venomous Snakes of the World*, pp. 14–22).

Basal Snake Diversity and Distribution

There are almost 3,000 extant (living) species of snakes in the suborder Serpentes (or Ophidia) of order Squamata – the scaled reptiles. They may be divided into three infraorders (if they were superfamilies they would be suffixed with '-oidea'). The. most advanced of these is known as the Caenophidia, literally the 'new snakes' but more accurately termed the 'advanced snakes'. It contains around 2,350 species, in other words the vast majority of all extant species, with 75 per cent (1,700) of them contained within the large and cumbersome family Colubridae, which includes both non-venomous and rear-fanged venomous snakes in its numerous and ever changing subfamilies. The Caenophidia also contains the nonvenomous, aquatic Acrochordidae, from Indo-Australia; the horizontal-fanged venomous Afro-Arabian Atractaspididae; and the two front-fanged venomous snake families, Elapidae and Viperidae. The venomous caenophidians were the subject of a previous volume so I do not plan to expand on them further here.

If the caenophidians are 'advanced', then to refer to the species contained in the other infraorders as 'primitive snakes' would be to do them a disservice since many of them exhibit considerable adaptive radiation in their comparative anatomy, functional morphology and behaviour. It is true that they are closer to the ancestral precursors of early snakes, than are the ratsnakes, cobras and vipers of the Caenophidia, and they retain various primitive characteristics, but that does not necessarily make them primitive, it makes them 'basal'. By definition all snakes are advanced reptiles, the loss of digits or limbs being seen as a derived, or advanced, character state in several lizard families and since this state exists in all snakes and since snakes are considered an advanced offshoot from the lizards, it can be considered that they too are advanced. As already discussed, leglessness is considered an advanced state, at least in reptiles.

This volume concerns the other two infraorders, the Scolecophidia and its sister infraorder, the Alethinophidia, from the latter of which arose the more advanced Caenophidia. Since the relationships of the families within these two infraorders may cause confusion I will attempt to introduce the families here before moving on to deal with representatives of each in more detail in the following chapters. Before embarking on this explanation it should be realized that higher category taxonomy is often the source of dispute and whereas I may refer to two families, another author may consider them merely two subfamilies within the same family. A family can always be recognized by its '–idae' suffix while subfamilies are identified by the '–inae' suffix.

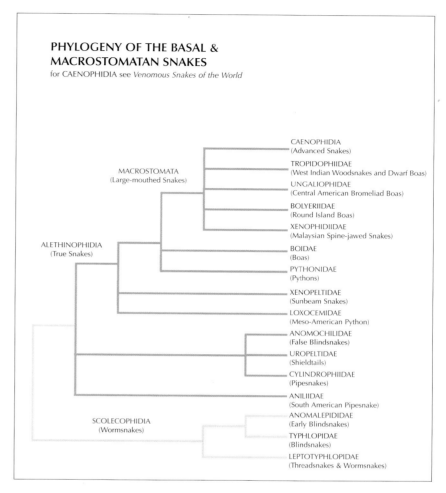

PHYLOGENY OF THE BASAL & MACROSTOMATAN SNAKES
for CAENOPHIDIA see *Venomous Snakes of the World*

CAENOPHIDIA (Advanced Snakes)
TROPIDOPHIIDAE (West Indian Woodsnakes and Dwarf Boas)
MACROSTOMATA (Large-mouthed Snakes)
UNGALIOPHIDAE (Central American Bromeliad Boas)
BOLYERIIDAE (Round Island Boas)
XENOPHIDIIDAE (Malaysian Spine-jawed Snakes)
ALETHINOPHIDIA (True Snakes)
BOIDAE (Boas)
PYTHONIDAE (Pythons)
XENOPELTIDAE (Sunbeam Snakes)
LOXOCEMIDAE (Meso-American Python)
ANOMOCHILIDAE (False Blindsnakes)
UROPELTIDAE (Shieldtails)
CYLINDROPHIIDAE (Pipesnakes)
ANILIIDAE (South American Pipesnake)
SCOLECOPHIDIA (Wormsnakes)
ANOMALEPIDIDAE (Early Blindsnakes)
TYPHLOPIDAE (Blindsnakes)
LEPTOTYPHLOPIDAE (Threadsnakes & Wormsnakes)

INFRAORDER SCOLECOPHIDIA

The Scolecophidia, literally the 'wormsnakes', contains three families of what are more usually called blindsnakes. They are primarily small, slender, smooth-scaled, unicoloured snakes. When lecturing I sometimes comment that the average blindsnake may be described as about the same width as the inside of a 'biro', the same length as the inside of a 'biro', the same colour as the inside of a 'biro', and to most people, about as interesting as the inside of a 'biro'. They are considerably more interesting to herpetologists.

The trouble is, there is no average blindsnake, these tiny snakes may outwardly all look the same but they exhibit some amazing variations, and curious features including subcutaneous and cloacal glands of unknown purpose. The scales are so small, glossy and closely arranged that individual scales cannot be discerned unless illuminated and examined extremely closely under a microscope. Although they look primitive, are frequently mistaken for earthworms, and they do possess a number of primitive features such as the vestiges of the pelvic girdle, and spurs in some species, blindsnakes also demonstrate quite a high degree of adaptation to their subterranean habitat and ecology.

Their skulls are robustly built and designed for burrowing through soil or sand, the scales over the head being larger that

DIVERSITY OF THE SCOLECOPHIDIA			
FAMILY	**GENERA**	**SPECIES**	**DISTRIBUTION**
Leptotyphlopidae Thread, Worm or Slender Blindsnakes	2	96	Americas, Africa & Asia
Typhlopidae Blindsnakes	7	236	Worldwide
Anomalepididae Early Blindsnakes	4	16	South America
TOTAL	13	348	

the body scales and few in number. The largest scale is usually the rostral, at the front of the mouth, which usually extends onto the top of the head and further assists in the burrowing process, especially if it terminates in either a shovel-shape or pointed beak. Even the vertebral column is adapted for a burrowing existence, the various neural spines and hypapophyses present in more advanced snakes and other vertebrates being either reduced in size or absent, although the number of vertebra in blindsnakes can be considerable, one small species possessing over 600 individual vertebrae, the highest number for any snake and more even than in a giant anaconda.

At the other end the tail is short, a common feature of burrowing reptiles including worm-lizards (Amphisbaenia), shieldtail snakes (Uropeltidae), and sand boas (Erycinae). It terminates in a sharp tip, which may be anchored into the ground to aid locomotion through loose soil or along the galleries of termitaria. When handled this sharp point continually explores and harmlessly probes the hand, giving rise to the belief that it is trying to sting, when in truth it is attempting to obtain a purchase and effect an escape.

The burrowing adaptations of the blindsnakes enable them to disappear into the ground so rapidly that they frequently avoid capture unless scooped out onto a hard surface or discovered crossing an impenetrable roadway. Although they spend the majority of their time underground, blindsnakes may be found abroad at night, after rain, and may even be encountered crossing roads or entering houses. They occur in many habitats, from desert to rainforest, and some have adopted an arboreal or subterranean existence, living in the tangled earthy bases of bromeliads and other epiphytes; they may also enter the chambers of Melanesian ant-plants. Blindsnakes have even been observed actually climbing vertical tree trunks in Amazonia.

Being primarily subterranean in existence, they probably have little use for vision beyond being able to determine when they are exposed to daylight. To this end the eyes are either reduced in size, often to a patch of pigmented cells just visible beneath the transparent head scales, or they may absent altogether.

Their tiny mouths are inferior, that is under-slung, and the lower jaw is fused at the front as a single unit, like many other vertebrates but in contrast to more advanced snakes. The arrangement of the teeth is an important characteristic in determining familial identification. Generally teeth are only present on either the upper (maxilla) or the lower jaw (dentary bone) and all three families lack teeth on the pterygoid and palatine bones. Because of the small mouth gap and limited dentition of the blindsnakes, prey is limited to small, soft-bodied invertebrates. Blindsnakes are highly chemosensitive, they have well developed forked tongues and rely on chemicals for seeking mates and for defence. A blindsnake seen twisting and turning vigorously in an ant nest is not writhing in agony from their stings but coating itself with a protective secretion that deflects the attentions of the unsociable, social insects. There is considerable variation in the structure of the male hemipenes and although all known blindsnakes are oviparous, one species is parthenogenetic, existing only in all-female populations that produce fertile eggs without the requirement for a male.

With almost 350 species between the three families, and new species being described, and new genera being defined, with considerable regularity, this is an important infraorder, even if reptile enthusiasts overlook it. There is a great deal still to be learned about the biology, ecology and behaviour of these serpents but sadly there are only a handful of herpetologists actively engaged in their study.

Family Leptotyphlopidae

The characteristics defining the leptotyphlopids centre on their dentition. They are the only snakes to lack teeth on any of the bones of the upper jaw, the only jawbones bearing teeth being the enlarged and bulky dentary bones in the anterior lower jaw. The often applied common names of slender blindsnakes or thread snakes are especially apt because these snakes are typically of very slender build due to a lower number of scale rows around the body than is usually found in blindsnakes from the other two families. Some leptotyphlopids possess the vestiges of pelvic girdles and the remnants of spurs. The Leptotyphlopidae contains almost 100 species, almost all being placed in the genus *Leptotyphlops*. Most are extremely small, the largest specimen on record being around 0.46m in length. A second genus, *Rhinoleptus* from West Africa, is monotypic. The known leptotyphlopid species are split almost equally between the Americas and Afro-Asia, with the bias leaning slightly towards the Americas.

Family Typhlopidae

The largest of the three families, and probably the most diverse, the Typhlopidae contains almost 240 species, split between 6–7 genera and distributed throughout the tropical and subtropical world, only this time the emphasis is on Africa and Asia, with approximately 140 species, while the Americas possess fewer than 40. Unlike the leptotyphlopids, the typhlopids have colonized Madagascar, Southeast Asia, New Guinea and they have speciated widely in Australia, from where some 50 species have been described, many fairly recently from single, remote type-localities. There are undoubtedly many more species that remain to be discovered.

The typhlopids are usually known simply as blindsnakes. Many species are extremely small and, to the naked eye, virtually indistinguishable from leptotyphlopids, but a few species are larger, both in length, and girth due to higher numbers of scale rows around the body. One African species, Schlegel's Blindsnake *Rhinotyphlops schlegeli* (p.96), has been recorded at almost 1.0m in length and may be almost as fat as a human thumb. The most widespread snake in the world is the parthenogenetic Flowerpot Snake or Brahminy Blindsnake, *Ramphotyphlops braminus* (p.66) a species at the other end of the size scale from Schlegel's Blindsnake. The main characters that define the typhlopids as distinct from the leptotyphlopids, apart from the increased number of scale rows around the body, are the presence of teeth on the mobile, downward-protruding maxilla of the upper jaw and a reduction in the size of the toothless dentary bone of the lower jaw.

Family Anomalepididae

The anomalepidids were formerly treated as a subfamily of the Typhlopidae and while they are now recognized as belonging to a separate family, it is not contested that their relationships are much closer to the typhlopids than the leptotyphlopids. Containing only sixteen species, split between four genera, the anomalepidids are confined to tropical South America and are known as 'early blindsnakes' because a combination of primitive characteristics point to them being close to ancestral blindsnakes. The main character that separates them from the typhlopids is the presence of teeth on both jaws, on the moveable maxilla and on the dentary bone, although the dentary bears only 1–3 teeth on either side.

INFRAORDER ALETHINOPHIDIA

The Alethinophidia, the 'true snakes', is the huge sister-taxon of the Scolecophidia. It contains all other living snakes, including the infraorder Caenophidia that arose from within its ranks. Earlier books used the name Henophidia, 'old snakes', in place of Alethinophidia, and defined it as all the snakes between the scolecophidians and the Colubridae, including the filesnake family Acrochordidae, now placed in the Caenophidia.

Within the Alethinophidia are numerous separate snake lineages but they can be roughly grouped into two separate groups. The first of these are the 'Basal Alethinophidians' which

may be characterized as relatively small to medium-sized burrowing snakes with short tails; iridescent, glossy, smooth scales; vestigial pelvic girdles; skulls designed for burrowing; small eyes, and small mouths with fairly inflexible lower jaws which are prevented from articulating widely by connective tissue across the chin.

Family Anomochilidae

The Anomochilidae comprise a single genus with two species from Southeast Asia. They are known as little pipesnakes, and sometimes as false blindsnakes due to a superficial resemblance to the scolecophidians. They may actually not even be alethinophidians but although they seem intermediate between the scolecophidians and the alethinophidians, it would be wrong to consider them as a link between the two superfamilies because that would suggest the alethinophidians arose from within the scolecophidians, whereas current opinion seems to suggest they formed separate lineages. Within the Alethinophidia, the little pipesnakes are probably closest to the Asian pipesnakes of the Cylindrophidae but they differ from those snakes in several respects. Neither species of little pipesnake has been well studied since very few specimens of either have been found.

Family Cylindrophidae

This family, and the Anomochilidae, were formerly included within the Uropeltidae but are now treated as separate families. The Asian pipesnakes are much better documented than the little pipesnakes. Ten species are known, nine from Southeast Asia-Indonesia, including one extremely widely distributed species, and one species from Sri Lanka. The Cylindrophidae also contains an extinct genus, *Eoanilius*, from Upper Eocene France and England, indicating that this family was formerly much more widely distributed.

Family Uropeltidae

With the removal of the Southeast Asian pipesnakes, the Uropeltidae is geographically confined to southern India and Sri Lanka. The eight genera, including five Indian endemics and one Sri Lankan, are represented by 48 species, easily the most in any basal alethinophidian family. These are strange-looking snakes, many having small, sharply pointed heads, for burrowing, and broad, abruptly truncated tails which terminate in a flat, rugose shield, hence the common name 'shieldtails' although they are sometimes also called earthsnakes.

Family Aniliidae

The Aniliidae contains a single species *Anilius scytale*, the South American Pipesnake, but also called False Coralsnake due to its distinctive patterning of alternating red and black bands. Its distribution in Amazonia sets it apart from the three Asiatic families but, like Asian pipesnakes, this is a viviparous species. The Macrostomatan Alethinophidia, literally 'big-mouths', include all snakes above this level ie. the boas, pythons, related smaller families, and the caenophidians. They possess more

DIVERSITY OF THE BASAL ALETHINOPHIDIA			
FAMILY	**GENERA**	**SPECIES**	**DISTRIBUTION**
Anomochilidae Little Pipesnakes	1	2	Southeast Asia
Cylindrophiidae Asian Pipesnakes	1	10	South & Southeast Asia
Uropeltidae Shieldtails	8	48	South India & Sri Lanka
Anilidae South American Pipesnake	1	1	Amazonia
TOTAL	11	61	

mobile, elongate mandibles and distinctive broad ventral scales for terrestrial locomotion, although some marine snakes demonstrate a return to a reduced ventral scale condition for greater swimming ability. It is the Macrostomatan Alethinophidia that is the main subject of this volume.

Family Xenopeltidae

There are two species of Asian sunbeam snakes in the genus *Xenopeltis*, a widespread Southeast Asian species and a southern Chinese species. The name sunbeam snake, and the alternative name of iridescent earth snake, both come about from the glossy, oil-on-water appearance of the smooth scales. Moderately large in size, with a flattened head and blunt, rounded snout, sunbeam snakes are fairly commonly encountered, in contrast to some of the extremely rare basal alethinophidians.

Family Loxocemidae

The monotypic Loxocemidae was created to contain a monotypic genus, *Loxocemus*, which previously was included in the Pythoninae, when the latter was a subfamily of the Boidae, as the only python in the Americas. It has iridescent smooth scales, like the xenopeltids, but the snout is pointed and upturned, rather than bluntly rounded. *Loxocemus* is confined to the Pacific versant of southern Mexico and Central America.

Xenopeltis and *Loxocemus* are more highly adapted than are basal alethinophidians. Their jaw mechanisms are more flexible and they are able feed on larger prey. The presence of enlarged head and ventral scales are also characters more associated with advanced snake families rather than the burrowing basal alethinophidians. Although considered here with the macrostomatans, some authors consider these two families closer to the basal alethinophidians than to pythons and boas.

Family Boidae

The term 'boa' is one that occurs throughout the macrostomatan alethinophidians so those species contained within the family Boidae might be best qualified as the 'true boas'. However, the family is further split into two subfamilies and the term 'true boas' is most applicable to the members of the Boinae, which are distributed throughout Central and South America, the West Indies, Madagascar and the southwest Pacific. Members of the second subfamily, the Erycinae, which includes sand boas and rosy boas, might be better termed 'burrowing boas' due to their secretive fossorial nature. This subfamily is found in western North America, West Africa and in a broad band from North Africa, through East Africa, southeast Europe and Arabia into Asia. As a family the Boidae contains terrestrial, arboreal, fossorial and aquatic species. Subfamily Boinae contains over 30 species in seven genera in habitats ranging from rainforest or swamp to arid tropical islands and although many of its members are medium to large snakes, including the heaviest of all snakes – the Green Anaconda *Eunectes murinus*, the subfamily also contains a few small, delicate species. The smaller subfamily Erycinae, 15 species in four genera, is mostly comprised of relatively small- to medium-sized snakes from hot arid habitats, but there are also tropical rainforest and temperate woodland species, and the northernmost boid in the world belongs to this subfamily. Boas, both subfamilies, retain the vestiges of the pelvic girdles and external spurs, although spurs may be absent in some females. The left lung is well developed while the tracheal lung is absent and both oviducts are present. Many species in the Boinae possess thermosensory labial pits for the location of homoeothermic (warm-blooded) prey, but they are hidden or even absent in some species and genera, and are completely absent in the Erycinae. All boines and most erycines are viviparous.

Family Pythonidae

The 'true pythons' family contains over 30 species in eight genera throughout tropical Africa and Asia but the greatest diversity is found in Australia, New Guinea and the Indonesian islands to the west of New Guinea. Like the Boinae, the Pythonidae contains large species, even giant species including the longest snake in the world – the Reticulated Python *Python reticulatus*, and also small species comparable to some of the smaller island boas. In many aspects of their ecology and behaviour true boas and true pythons mirror each other. Pythons too, are sit-and-wait ambushers possessing thermosensory labial pits for prey location and capture, many species specializing in feeding on mammals. They also possess a well developed left lung, the tracheal lung is absent; the paired oviducts are well developed, and both pelvic vestiges and cloacal spurs are present but a major difference exists in their reproduction, pythons being oviparous. The pythons have been previously included within the Boidae as a subfamily, but that decision may have been based more on a closeness of resemblance than one of relationship, a phenetic rather than phylogenetic classification.

Family Bolyeriidae

The Bolyeriidae contains two species of strange boas, genera *Bolyeria* and *Casarea*, that differ from all other terrestrial vertebrates in the possession of divided and moveable maxillary bones in the upper jaw. They lack any remnants of the pelvic girdle or spurs, have a much reduced left lung while the tracheal lung is absent. Both oviducts are well developed. The Round Island boas are considered a 'primitive' divergence from the boid lineage that have existed in isolation from all other snakes for millennia, on tiny Round Island, northeast of Mauritius in the Indian Ocean. One of these unique species, *Bolyeria multocarinata*, is now feared extinct.

Family Tropidophiidae

The West Indian dwarf boas and woodsnakes, and South American dwarf boas, *Tropidophis* and *Trachyboa*, are small snakes that were formerly included within the Boidae as a subfamily but are now thought to have diverged early in the evolution of the macrostomatans. The family is currently thought to contain 22 species, in two genera, following the removal of the Central American dwarf boas to the following family. Tropidophiids retain the primitive vestigial pelvic girdle in all but one species, with males displaying cloacal spurs, but they also exhibit the derived characteristics of a well-developed tracheal lung with the left lung either reduced or absent, the reverse of the situation in true boas and pythons. Both oviducts are well developed. Thermosensory pits are absent from the lip scales.

DIVERSITY OF THE MACROSTOMATAN ALETHINOPHIDIA (EXCL. CAENOPHIDIA)			
FAMILY	GENERA	SPECIES	DISTRIBUTION
Xenopeltidae Asian Sunbeam Snakes, Iridescent Earth Snakes	1	2	Southeast Asia
Loxocemidae American Sunbeam Snake, Meso-American Python	1	1	Pacific Central America
Boidae (Boinae) True Boas	7	32	Central and South America, Madagascar and Southwest Pacific
Boidae (Erycinae) Burrowing Boas	4	15	Western North America, Africa, Asia and Southeast Europe
Pythonidae True pythons	8	33	Africa, Asia and Australasia
Bolyeriidae Round Island boas, Split-jawed boas	2	2	Mauritius, Indian Ocean
Tropidophiidae West Indian and South American dwarf boas, Woodsnakes	2	22	West Indies and South America
Ungaliophidae Central American dwarf boas	2	3	Central America
Xenophidiidae Spine-jawed snake	1	2	Malaysia
TOTAL	28	112	

Family Ungaliophidae

This small family, containing three curious Central American dwarf boas in *Ungaliophis* and *Exiliboa*, was previously included within the Tropidophiidae as a subfamily, but current opinion suggests that their relationships may not be close and full family status is warranted. These small snakes are anatomically similar to the West Indian dwarf boas but they may still possess a vestigial left lung.

Family Xenophidiidae

The least known family, also formerly contained within the Tropidophiidae as a subfamily, comprising a single Malaysian

ABOVE: *A Diamond Python* (Morelia spilota spilota) *hatching from its egg, aided by the disposable egg-tooth, which is visible in the front of the upper jaw.* BELOW: *A litter of neonate Common Boas* (Boa constrictor constrictor) *emerging from their membranous sac.*

genus, *Xenophidion*, with two species known from only a few specimens. The main characteristic distinguishing these rare snakes is the present of a large canine-like tooth, followed by a diastema, a gap in the teeth, on the front of the dentary bone of the lower jaw, hence the name 'spine-jawed snakes'. They also lack any vestiges of pelvic girdles or spurs.

THE TREND TOWARDS VIVIPARITY

Most reptiles are oviparous. All turtles, tortoises, crocodilians, tuataras, and most amphisbaenians, lizards and snakes lay eggs, but there is a definite trend towards viviparity within the squamate reptiles and this is particularly evident in the snakes with up to 20 per cent of species giving birth to neonates enclosed in a membranous sac. Viviparity has evolved independently 35 times within the snakes including the pipesnake, shieldtail, true boa and dwarf boa families. Amongst more advanced snakes viviparity is found in most of the vipers, a few southern elapids, seasnakes and numerous colubrids. Viviparity is a reproductive trend most suitable for, but not confined to, species occurring at higher altitudes and latitudes, where it is believed to have evolved as a response to cold climates in which abandoned eggs would be vulnerable. A gravid, thermoregulating viviparous snake is able to actively seek out sun-spots to incubate her developing embryos, and then give birth to small replicates of herself, contained in membranous packages. Oviparity, egg-laying, is more basic, the female laying a clutch of eggs in a suitable location and either leaving them to the vagaries of weather and predators, as in most snakes, or actively incubating and guarding them as in the pythons. There is little or no maternal care shown to hatchlings or neonates once they hatch or are born.

Constriction

All snakes are carnivores, although there are generalists and specialists. Snakes prey on a variety of organisms ranging from tiny termites to 1.5m crocodilians, deer-sized mammals and even, albeit rarely, man. The methods adapted to deal with prey depend largely on the risk posed by the prey itself, 'horses for courses' one might say, although I have yet to find a snake that includes horses in its diet.

Blindsnakes seem to do little more than 'absorb' their prey, opening their mouths and swallowing termite eggs, larvae and adults. Those blindsnakes and shieldtails that feed on earthworms also swallow their harmless wiggling prey alive. Pipesnakes feed on smaller snakes like blindsnakes, which are probably easily devoured. With the sunbeam snakes and Meso-American Python we see amphibians and reptile eggs respectively included in the diet, again easy prey to deal with, but beyond this level the prey becomes larger, more difficult and potentially more dangerous.

Small lizards might not seem dangerous prey, although they have small teeth and may bite, but there are snakes that feed on Monitor Lizards, which are certainly dangerous. Birds and mammals have beaks, teeth and claws, and considering the size of some mammals eaten by boas and pythons, the danger can be very real. Choosing to kill and eat a caiman or small crocodile requires some special skills, especially for a predator that lacks any limbs with which to restrain such a powerful adversary.

Snakes preying on potentially dangerous creatures have evolved two main ways to restrain, subdue and kill that prey. The most advanced technique is venom, which probably began as modified saliva that was absorbed through the skin of a frog, diminishing its struggles as it was swallowed alive, but which has evolved into the amazing diversity of toxins described in *Venomous Snakes of the World*.

The other method is constriction and this too may have gone through an evolutionary process, albeit less dramatic. In the absence of hands, it seems reasonable that a snake would use its body coils to pin down and hold a struggling amphibian or small lizard as it attempts to swallow it. This simple restraining technique then graduates to the actual means of dispatching

An African Rock Python (Python sebae) *subduing a Nile Crocodile* (Crocodylus niloticus) *with its powerful constricting coils.*

more dangerous prey prior to swallowing. Constriction is not just the preserve of the boas and pythons – many colubrid snakes use it, including rear-fanged venomous species with fairly slow-acting venoms.

There is a myth about constriction, that the python 'crushes' its prey, breaking all the bones and converting the body into a shapeless, bloodied sausage-shape. It is possible that some bones may break, either in the struggle or during the constriction process, and the python will then also use its coils to assist the prey into its mouth, compressing the body so that the jaws may pass over it, but body-mangling and bone breaking is not the aim of constriction.

The process is as follows: a python, in ambush, launches a strike at its prey aided by a combination of chemosensory forked tongue, thermosensory labial pits, and vision. The strike is successful, the open-mouthed blow bowling the prey off its feet, possibly half-stunning it in the process. As the recurved teeth secure a firm grip on the prey, the python rapidly wraps several body coils around the prey animal. The more the prey struggles, the more coils will be employed and the tighter they become.

The prey quickly becomes unconscious, but constriction continues until death occurs, possibly through respiratory arrest, the rib cage and lungs being compressed so that breathing is impossible, or through circulatory failure as the heart is starved of blood by compression of the circulatory system.

The python is able to determine when the prey's heartbeat has ceased, whereupon it will suddenly slacken its coils and spend a considerable period of time tongue-flicking the entire length of the prey as it seeks out the head end. Ingesting prey headfirst prevents the limbs from creating an obstruction during the swallowing process. This is important since a snake with its mouth full cannot defend itself and is itself vulnerable to predation by man or even small carnivores that would represent prey under normal circumstances.

Following a sizeable meal large pythons and boas may fast for over a year, the stomach shrinking to a fraction of its usual functional size. This ability to go from feast to fast to feast again, with all the necessary metabolic gear-shifts, is an amazing adaptation for survival where prey is often unavailable. Most other animals eating a large meal after a prolonged fast would be in danger of killing themselves, but boas and pythons are designed for this existence.

A Diamond Python (Morelia spilota spilota) *killing and devouring a Crimson Rosella* (Platycercus elegans).

Giant Snakes: Myth or Monster?

One of the most asked questions in herpetology is "Do giant snakes exist and if so, how big do they get?" Stories of giant snakes have peppered travellers' tales for as long as there have been travellers to tell them, and not just in the tropics. Pliny the Elder (23–79 AD) told of a giant 'boa' that ate children, in Italy! We now know there are no giant snakes living in Europe, but what about the remoter tropical jungles of the world, in South America, Africa, Southeast Asia? Surely there must be some credibility in the many stories of huge man-eating serpents lurking in the underground, hanging down from trees, or prowling the murky rivers in the hopes of a human meal.

In the past, one of the most important collecting implements carried by explorers, biologists and natural historians was the firearm. Even Darwin, Wallace and Bates, the pioneering 19th-century biogeo-graphers and naturalists, shot almost everything they encountered, which to our more enlightened, conservation-orientated minds might seem extreme, especially where endangered species are concerned. But of course, most species were not threatened then, although this was the era when the dodo, and some giant tortoises, were exterminated by men with guns. In the case of giant snakes, the idea of 'Shoot first, and ask questions afterwards' was probably also driven by fear, as these were potentially very dangerous animals, especially a large anaconda in deep water. Some of the shot snakes were then measured, with varying degrees of accuracy and reliability, while the lengths of others were simply guessed at, a dangerous practice because these are the sort of measurements that get rounded-up, rarely rounded-down, and then continue to grow, post-mortem, with each telling of the tale.

Where sizeable prepared snakeskins are concerned, it has often been suggested that the original owner of the skin must have been very large indeed, because the skin will have shrunk during the tanning and curing process. On the contrary – the skin will have been stretched considerably during removal from the carcass. Some years ago I put this to the test with a recently deceased Southern African Rock Python, *Python natalensis*,

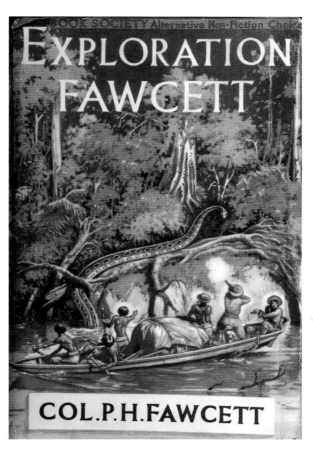

ABOVE: *Percy Fawcett claimed to have shot several giant anacondas. His book,* Exploration Fawcett, *was completed by his son after he and another son disappeared in the Amazon in 1925.*

which measured 3.0m at death. Skinning the snake was a long and laboured process, the connective tissues between the skin and the flesh being so strong that it took some force to separate them. When the skin was finally free it measured 3.65m, a 20 per cent increase on the snake's true length, what I have termed the '20 per cent stretch rule'. These figures agree with those reached by Arthur Loveridge when he carried out the same process on an African Rock Python, *P. sebae*, in 1931, while herpetologist Bill Lamar reported a 40 per cent increase in length when he skinned a 7.35m Green Anaconda, *Eunectes murinus*, and obtained a skin of 10.35m – despite making every effort to avoid stretching. The moral of this story is either not to believe lengths taken from snake-skins or, if you do, be prepared to deduct 20–40 per cent for stretching.

Today we know there are only five snake species that reach lengths in excess of 6.0m. Three species have been recorded to reach maximum lengths of 7.5–8.5m:

- Asian Rock Python (*Python molurus*) to 6.7m, South and Southeast Asia
- African Rock Python (*Python sebae*) to 7.6m, Central and Western Africa
- Australian Scrub Python (*Morelia kinghorni*) to 7.6–8.5m, Queensland, Australia

The longest reliable reports for Asian Rock Pythons are around 6.7m, but it is unclear as to whether these relate to whole snakes or skins. Live specimens of 5.5m are certainly known, and I have caught two of almost 5.0m.

The longest African Rock Python was reported as a 9.8m specimen shot in a hedge in Ivory Coast in 1932, but there is insufficient data available to verify this usually discounted report. There is a reliable record of a specimen killed and skinned on the shores of Lake Victoria in 1927 and subsequently measured at 9.1m by herpetologist Arthur Loveridge, but taking into consideration the '20 per cent stretch rule', that would indicate a 7.6m specimen.

The largest specimens from the Indo-Australian amethystine python complex are those now called Australian Scrub Pythons, from Queensland. Slenderer than the two previous species, there is a 1948 record of a 'scrubbie' killed near Cairns that measured 8.5m and several records of around 7.6m.

The two remaining species are believed to reach greater lengths:
- Green Anaconda (*Eunectes murinus*) 7.5–11.5m, South America
- Reticulated Python (*Python reticulatus*) 10.0–11.55m, Southeast Asia

The record length for the Reticulated Python has not been the source of as much controversy as that of the Green Anaconda. The python is of much slenderer build than the anaconda and does not give the same impression of size so even though this python may be the longest snake species in the world, the anaconda is certainly the heaviest, and if 'largest' is a combination of length, girth and weight, then the green anaconda is also the largest snake in the world.

A Reticulated Python, killed in Malaysia in 1896, was measured at 8.2m before being skinned, when the skin was re-measured at 10.0m. There are numerous specimens reported, both reliably and unreliably, of between 7.6–9.1m, but the generally accepted record length for a Reticulated Python is that of a specimen shot in Sulawesi (then Celebes), Indonesia, in 1912 that measured 10.0m. There is also an interesting report of a specimen that was killed after it had reportedly attacked a man. It was measured at seven Malay fathoms, with one Malay fathom equalling 1.65m, resulting in a total length of 11.55m. This specimen seems to be the largest specimen claimed, even dubiously, in contrast to the super-size claims for the anaconda.

Stories of giant anacondas abound, with almost every 19th- and early 20th-century explorer who ventured into Amazonia coming across at least one of these giant beasts. How disappointed I am then, that after eight separate expeditions

A lithograph from an 1834 magazine showing a fight with a 'boa constrictor' (doubtless a Reticulated Python, Python reticulatus*) in the Sunderbans of India.*

into 'anaconda country', where I have captured 40 anacondas, my largest measured a mere 5.3m, and weighing only 73kg.

Examining some of these stories with a scientific eye can produce different results to those perceived by the romantic traveller. Consider the great coils of an anaconda seen breaking the surface of the water, or an extra-broad snake trail on the river bank. The common conclusion is that some monster of gigantic proportions was responsible. The truth may be far more prosaic, simply that a normal-sized snake has eaten a large meal and left a trail that represents its widest point – the swollen belly – or that digestion has progressed to a point where gases have built up in the stomach and made the coils so buoyant that they float and bob at the surface, while the remainder of a moderately sized snake lies hidden. Colonel Percy Fawcett, the Amazonian explorer and boundary surveyor who disappeared in the Mato Grosso in 1925, was apt to make some amazing claims regarding the lengths of the many anacondas he encountered, and shot. Snakes of 30ft (9.15m) were seemingly very common and he even reports shooting one that he then estimated as measuring 45ft (13.7m) out of the water and 17ft (5.2m) in it, a total of 62ft (18.9m), yet the snake was reportedly only 12inches (30cm) in diameter which means large, but not giant. Numerous other explorers, missionaries, soldiers and engineers made claims that either equalled or exceeded those of Fawcett. Were they all lying, or mistaken, or simply poor judges of size? Fawcett also reported that anacondas possessed luminous eyes, as well as fetid breath, which had a stupefying effect on their victims, and that they uttered weird cries at night during their feeding time. These little snippets of disinformation are probably part of the reason why his natural history reports are not taken very seriously today. But so many stories have come out of the Amazon that one is forced to conclude there must be something there.

It has been suggested that a giant species of anaconda may exist in the remoter parts of the Amazon, one separate from the green anaconda and its smaller relatives. But giant animals do not simply materialize as giants, they have to grow to that size and that means starting out as a juvenile. Even assuming that a giant anaconda species existed it must begin life as a juvenile, albeit a large one, say 2.0m. So why are there no unidentified 2.0m anacondas in the world's natural history museums?

The idea of a separate super-size snake species does not solve the problem. I would make a different suggestion. Most of the anaconda populations studied by herpetologists exist in areas with large populations of snakes that are easy enough to locate. This means most studies have taken place in the flooded savannas of the Venezuelan Llanos and the Brazilian Pantanal and Ilha de Marajo swamps. These areas consist of vast expanses of seasonally flooded grassland and lagoons in close proximity to large rivers. There is also abundant prey, usually wading birds, caiman and mammals to the size of capybara. There are many anacondas, yet there are few reports of them exceeding 7.3m in these habitats. This is possibly because these are seasonally flooded savannas and, for part of the year, are very dry and inhospitable. At this time the anacondas must drag themselves across the mud and retreat to the rivers, or bed down and aestivate in the mud at the bottom of the lagoons and creeks. For part of the year, therefore, the anacondas of these grasslands are neither feeding nor growing.

Now consider from where most of the tales of giant snakes originate: the great, rainforest-shrouded rivers of Amazonia. Prey may be less abundant, but of possibly larger size, so the snakes may not feed as frequently. Could it be that the potentially ever-active anacondas of the non-seasonal rainforest rivers are able to take deer, tapir or jaguar? Is it possible that they can lie in ambush for months, waiting for that chance encounter, and then, having fed, put all that nutrition into growth? These huge snakes can only become so large and heavy because they are aquatic – the water supports their weight – with the more terrestrial pythons forced to retain a slimmer physique for movement over land. What is more, a large anaconda could easily manoeuvre into a position to capture prey without being observed. I once travelled up a river in Venezuela in the dry season for two hours counting caiman. I found 200 individuals, of up to 2.0m in length, in the shallows or on muddy banks and sandbars. After four days of heavy rain I made the same journey and counted only 20. There were still 200 caiman on that stretch of river but they were now floating in deeper water, most of their original basking areas having been submerged. The caiman could easily hide from me, but would have been easy meals for a large and

powerful predator from below. In a river an anaconda could probably feed all year round.

I therefore propose that although the green anacondas of the seasonally flooded savanna and of the rainforest are the same species, those snakes living in rivers can feed and grow all year round and achieve a size where they are adapted to taking larger prey than is generally available to the savanna snakes. The other advantage that a riverine anaconda has over a savanna-dwelling specimen, or the more terrestrial pythons, is that the larger and heavier it gets, the more aquatic it probably becomes. Living in the darkened, murky water, it escapes detection by man much more successfully than a large snake on land, and is less likely to be persecuted. However, this still does not answer how large these anacondas might grow.

When considering maximum snake lengths, it is often an idea to consider fossil records, yet even amongst extinct boids there are no specimens that exceed today's pythons and anaconda. *Madtsoia bai*, 7.0–8.0m, from Paleocene-Eocene Patagonia, and *Gigantophis garstini*, 9.0m, from late-Eocene Africa, belonged to the extinct Boidae subfamily, Matsoidinae. Much later, in Pleistocene southern Australia, lived another extinct boid of smaller proportions, *Wonambi naracoortensis*, 6.1m.

In the early 20th century the 26th President of the United States, and experienced Amazonian explorer, Theodore Roosevelt (1858–1919) put up $5,000 for any giant snake captured, alive or dead, and transported back to the Zoological Society of New York (now the Wildlife Conservation Society) for verification. Over time the reward has risen to $50,000, but it has never been claimed. Finding the snake is one thing, getting it back to New York is another, and in any case, to remove a snake of those proportions from the wild is completely unethical. I believe WCS have withdrawn the prize.

When it comes to determining how long a particular snake species can grow, I believe the longevity of the species is the key. All species have a natural lifespan which is only rarely exceeded, and even then not usually by a great deal. The following are longevity records for the five species in this section: Australian Scrub Python 13 years 10 months; African Rock Python 27 years 4 months; Green Anaconda 28 years 0 months; Reticulated Python 29 years 5 months; Asian Rock Python 34 years 2 months. The longest-lived snake recorded was a Royal Python, *P. regius*, at 47 years 6 months, while a Boa Constrictor, *Boa constrictor*, has been recorded at almost 39 years. These are records of captive snakes that were provided with regular meals and not at risk from predators or humans in the wild, so their lifespans may be artificially lengthened. Assuming a maximum age of over 30 years for an anaconda in the wild, it can only consume so many meals in that time before being overtaken by old age and death.

Readily available meals and growing to a vast size does not enable a species to double its natural life-span, so when one is asked to accept the lengths of 18.0m or even 61.0m claimed by some observers, as genuine wild anacondas, one is forced to question their validity based on what we know about the longevity of the species.

Man-eating Snakes

Surely one of our most ingrained fears is to be eaten by another animal. Man, the most advanced and intelligent creature on the planet, being devoured by a species considered 'inferior' to himself, one over which he is more used to holding the power of life and death. Never is this fear more intense than when the predator is an emotionless, cold-blooded creature like a shark, crocodile, or giant snake.

Being devoured by these cold-blooded creatures, with their alien metabolisms, somehow seems more terrible than being eaten by a warm-blooded furry animal more akin to ourselves. It is probably as near as one could get to becoming the prey of a *Tyrannosaurus rex* or even an intergalactic *Alien*. Even the act of human cannibalism is sanitized, treated with sympathy in the film *Alive*, or as an unseen taboo in *Hannibal*, but film-makers understand that becoming lunch for a cold-blooded creature is a deeply buried fear, and one guaranteed to keep the audience watching. This is why there is a continual stream of films with titles like *Jaws* and *Anaconda*. Being eaten by a big predatory fish or a scaly reptile is too terrible to contemplate, yet too fascinating to ignore.

And of the three, the snake may be the most terrible. Crocodiles and sharks attack their prey and kill it quickly, reducing it to swallowable chunks of unrecognizable flesh and bone. You are possibly not truly human when you go inside. Giant snakes, however, swallow their meals whole, and the process seems so much more gruesome and time-consuming. The struggle for breath as the coils do their work, the jaws advancing over the victim's head and the gradual, laboured process of transporting an intact human body down the length of a reptilian oesophagus to a reptilian stomach, where it remains as a guilty bulge for days.

The fact is that the bulge made by a swallowed human looks much like that made by a pig or a goat, or any other similarly sized mammal. There is no pressing of the body against the side of the snake as the snake swims past, human mouth open, visible,

Often labelled as an anaconda in South America, this apparently genuine case of a snake preying upon a human actually shows a Reticulated Python (Python reticulatus).

silently pleading! That is pure Hollywood. And it is also probably a fact that although crocodiles and, to a lesser degree, sharks are regular predators of man, more people have been swallowed by computer-generated giant snakes in recent times than by real ones. All this despite the gory photographs that appear regularly on the internet or in the press. But beware of photographs that show large snakes with full, but intact, bellies. A photograph of the dead snake split open, human limbs protruding, is likely to syndicate much more widely than a simple photograph of a well-fed snake, so why be content with the latter? Possibly because when the snake was opened up it was found to contain a much less newsworthy animal than a human.

Large python or boa bites are amongst the most unpleasant and bloody delivered by any non-venomous snake. The power and musculature of the neck results in an extremely powerful blow, while the six rows of long recurved teeth will embed deeply, penetrating flesh and muscle and causing extensive bleeding. A blow delivered to the head is likely to stun the victim. If the giant snake is able to coil about its victim and trap the arms, the combined weight of the snake, its tightening grip and the shock of the attack will rapidly cause the victim to fall to the ground, if not already there. It is not necessary for the snake to find an anchorage point for its tail in order to constrict its prey or a victim; simply tightening its coils will apply sufficient pressure to kill, and there is little chance of escape. Clearly, large pythons and anacondas can kill a human but swallowing someone is a more difficult process. It is often believed that the shoulders of an adult male are too broad for a snake to manoeuvre its jaws around, but in truth a 5.0m python or anaconda can probably accomplish this feat. Certainly, children or small adults – of similar proportions to antelope or peccaries – would cause few difficulties for a large snake. On those rare occasions when an attack occurs, it is most likely a case of mistaken identity on the behalf of the snake, and one of wrong place, wrong time, on behalf of the human.

MAN-EATING BOAS – SOUTH AMERICA

The only South American snakes that achieve the proportions necessary to kill and devour a human are the anacondas, amongst which probably only the Green Anaconda, *Eunectes murinus*, is capable. Certainly the Boa Constrictor, *Boa constrictor*, does not reach a large enough size to make it a serious threat to man, the only death I have been able to find attributed to this species being that of a night-club escapologist who was strangled by a juvenile boa whilst performing his act in a coffin. The circumstances of this accident hardly qualify the species as a man-killer!

The Green Anaconda is a large and powerful, semi-aquatic predator of medium to large mammals, and amply capable of killing and potentially swallowing a small human. Attacked in shallow water by a 6.0m anaconda weighing over 100kg, a victim is as likely to die of drowning as constriction, and given that this species feeds on capybara, peccary, deer and caiman, it seems probable that such a snake could articulate its jaws sufficiently to engorge a small human's shoulders (our broadest bony structure). Yet despite this possibility, and the photographs incorrectly attributed to this species (see opposite), attacks by Green Anacondas are extremely rare. Two first-hand and trustworthy accounts of large anacondas attacking from aquatic ambush positions were reported from Colombia and Venezuela in 1978 and 1992 respectively. Clearly the snake was waiting for its more usual prey and mistook the human concerned for a peccary or capybara. However, cases of people actually been eaten are very much rarer and confined to traveller's tales dating from the 19th and early 20th centuries.

It is important to realize that a large anaconda can virtually disappear in relatively shallow water. Much of its habitat consists of turbid, muddy water, where visibility is extremely limited, but even in clear water its body patterning provides excellent camouflage, making a submerged anaconda almost invisible from even a short distance away. Combined with the low human population density of the anaconda's realm, it is extremely unlikely that the disappearance of an unaccompanied fisherman or bather would be noticed for some time, and it would be virtually impossible for searchers to track down the culprit without a witness to locate the scene of the attack. We have interviewed the relatives of people who, they believed, were taken by anacondas, but I believe that in most instances predation by anaconda is a far less likely cause of disappearance than drowning. Unless a body is recovered with signs of a snake-related struggle, it is difficult to blame the anaconda. However, in two Ecuadorian reports, published in 1953, bodies were recovered and anacondas were cited as the cause of death.

MAN-EATING PYTHONS – AFRICA

Unlike the habitually aquatic anaconda, the African pythons are equally at home on land and water. The first report of an African Rock Python, *P. sebae*, eating a human comes from W. Bosman's *A New and Accurate Description of the Coast of Guinea Divided into the Gold, the Slave and the Ivory Coasts*, published in London in 1707, in which a python is reportedly killed and found to contain the body of an African. In the 300 years since there have been various stories, including accounts of a 4.5m Central African Rock Python found with the body of a dead woman in its coils, on an island in Lake Victoria in the late 1920s–early 1930s, and a case of a 13-year-old youth killed and swallowed by a large python in Uganda in 1951, the snake being forced to regurgitate its victim.

Accounts that can be attributed to the Southern African Rock Python, *P. natalensis*, include a famous account from 1979, when a 13-year-old, 45kg goat-herder was ambushed and killed by a 4.5m python. His friend ran for help and the snake was prevented from swallowing the dead boy. Another account features a Portuguese sentry who disappeared in Angola in 1973, when it was still a Portuguese colony. He was later found inside a large python. Strangely, the same story surfaced a little later in Mozambique, also then under Portuguese rule, which demonstrates how the media thrived on these stories even before the advent of global communications and the internet. Other instances include famous photographs of a white doctor examining the body of a black man removed from the stomach of a large python, ostensibly also from Angola. It is possible that the man died of other injuries and the python was merely scavenging, since this was a time of bush wars and conflict in the region. There is also a case of a mineworker who attempted to catch a large python in the Transvaal, but the snake was too large and got the better of him. Despite escaping its coils, he died the following day of a ruptured spleen and damaged kidney.

MAN-EATING PYTHONS – ASIA

Every so often the internet, newspapers or weekly magazines publish a photograph of a poor unfortunate victim, protruding from the mouth or disembowelled stomach of a large snake. Invariably the caption reads something like "Colombian oil worker goes to answer a call of nature and is eaten by giant anaconda". Generally, the victim is not Colombian, and the snake not even a South American anaconda but a Southeast Asian Reticulated Python, *P. reticulatus*, arguably the world's longest snake species, and the species most frequently implicated in cases of human predation. There is a suggestion that one photograph, which shows a male victim spilling out of the body of the dead python lying alongside a hut, may have been faked, but another photograph, involving what appears to be a female victim, is almost certainly genuine (see p.26). The close-up image shows the python in the process of swallowing the person and the fact that the arms are pinned in the coils, the head of the victim is well down the throat of the snake, and there is a considerable quantity of blood on the victim's T-shirt, would suggest that this is a genuine case of a python attempting, but not managing, to ingest an adult human. There are several earlier and apparently reliable reports of Reticulated Pythons eating children in Indonesia, but a photograph of a small Retic, coiled dead in front of a group of World War Two Japanese soldiers, has been variously captioned as an anaconda that ate a Japanese biologist in Amazonia; a python that ate a Japanese soldier in Southeast Asia, and even the devourer of six human babies. It was nothing of the sort: a less publicized photograph of the same snake split open reveals not a human, but the body of a small deer or antelope.

In addition to these accounts from Southeast Asia, there are also several well-documented cases of the keepers of large Reticulated and Burmese Pythons, *P. molurus bivitattus*, being killed, but not eaten, by their pets. All these reports originate from the United States and emphasize that large snakes can be dangerous in captivity as well.

Life Underground

In the previous volume, on venomous snakes, I summarized nine radical adaptations of marine snakes for life in the sea. Seasnakes and sea kraits were not merely land snakes that went for a swim, they had to cope with an array of difficulties and dangers relating to swimming, deep diving, gaseous exchange, water conservation, high salinity and buoyancy. Some of the ways in which they achieved success were remarkable. Burrowing through sand or soil might not pose the same dangers as those faced by a seasnake diving to 100m and returning to the surface, but it is a considerable degree of adaptation that permits an uncovered snake to disappear into the ground so quickly that it is virtually impossible to pursue it, even with both hands digging furiously. Many of the basal snake families in this volume are subterranean inhabitants and even some of the more familiar species, like sand boas, spend the bulk of their lives below ground.

Most snakes are secretive, preferring to hide away and avoid discovery. This is especially the case when they are sleeping, hibernating, aestivating, in pre-ecdysis (approaching a slough), preparing to give birth or lay eggs, waiting in ambush, digesting a large meal, recovering from injury or avoiding enemies, predators, excessive heat, cold or illumination. Being elongate and able to coil due to their highly flexible backbones, and often being fairly small, snakes can fit themselves into some surprisingly small spaces. Even a pet snake, lost in a house, will find somewhere to hide where it may avoid detection for weeks, often only a few feet away from the frantically searching owner. Imagine then, how easy it must be for a snake to 'disappear' in its own environment, an environment full of hiding places, leaf-litter, tree-holes, loose bark, fallen logs with rotten cores, mammal burrows and scatterings of rocks with crevices, nooks and crannies. The snakes that hide here may range from small, insectivorous species to large pythons digesting goats, but in most cases their presence in the hiding place is temporary, they are only sheltering from the heat, the rain, the passing threat, digesting a meal, or waiting to shed their skins, and the time will come when they leave their retreat to hunt, seek a mate or range further afield. The majority of snakes in these situations are shelterers, with no special morphological or physiological adaptations, since sheltering does not require any, apart possibly from disruptive patterning or scale iridescence to break up the body's outline.

However, beyond these shelterers there is another world, the world of the true burrowing or fossorial snake, for whom life underground, in an array of different substrates from fine wind-blown sand to cloying clay, is the norm. They spend most of their time underground, venturing onto the surface at night, only to escape flooding or follow an ant-trail.

The scolecophidians are truly fossorial, and the same can be said for many of the smaller, more primitive basal alethinophidians that prey on invertebrates or other elongate fossorial vertebrates, but as snakes moved into new niches, crawled onto the surface and stayed there, climbed trees, swam in rivers, grew larger and began to prey on more active arboreal, terrestrial or aquatic vertebrates, developing powerful, muscular bodies for constriction, wider jaws for the ingestion of larger prey (became macrostomatans) and an array of acute senses in the process, they moved away from the limitations of truly fossorial life and became shelterers. That does not mean that none of the more advanced snakes are fossorial; there are colubrids and elapids in the Caenophidia that have rediscovered the joys of underground living and re-evolved burrowing adaptations like shovel-snouts or underslung jaws. Although to our eyes the burrowers look primitive, they are often highly evolved for their subterranean existence.

The most obvious reptilian trends towards becoming fossorial are the loss of limbs, a process linked to the elongation of the body; this is discussed in greater detail on p.10. Limbs usually serve little purpose for species living below ground, although some amphisbaenians retain forelimbs that enable them to dig like moles. Body shape is also important for burrowing. An elongate, highly attenuated body might move through the substrate more easily than a short, stout body. Many sand boas, *Eryx*, are short and stout but their locomotion might consist more of shuffling down into an ambush position in a loose substrate, rather than forcing their way through soil,

Hemprich's Shieldtail (Rhinophis homolepis) *demonstrates numerous adaptations for subterranean life. These include a small, pointed head, tiny eyes, small scales and a short, stumpy, soil-collecting tail.*

around stones or down small burrows made by other animals. Those species, blindsnakes, that enter termite or ant nests to feed on their larvae, must be slender enough to pass through the chambers made by their prey, and that requires considerable body attenuation.

Highly evolved tails might appear superfluous to burrowers. They are not required to be long and prehensile for climbing, nor flattened and paddle-shaped for swimming, nor bear a rattle as a warning device. In general, the burrowers have short, rounded tails, some of which even resemble the head of the snake, possibly to distract a predator's attention. Many of the shieldtails (see p.71) possess truncated, thorny tails that collect soil and may serve as a tunnel-blocking defence. Some of the serious burrowers possess a sharp spine on the tail tip that can be used as an anchorage point to force the body forwards in smooth-sided termite chambers. The base of the tail may serve as a fat reserve, and it also contains the sexual organs, especially the long hemipenes of the male, so it is not possible to dispense with the tail entirely. In short-tailed species, the tail of the male may be considerably longer than that of the female.

Most burrowing snakes have smooth scales for ease of movement through the substrate, and these scales are often reduced in size and flush to the body. Since locomotion on the surface is rarely necessary, many basal snakes have not evolved the broad ventral plates known as 'gastrosteges', required by terrestrial and arboreal snakes. The scales of the head consist of a few smooth, large, flush scutes.

The head of a true burrower is usually indistinct from the neck and body, the entire snake being the same diameter for

almost its entire length. The skull is often fairly solidly built, almost armoured, compared to the loosely arranged bones of more terrestrial snakes. The lower jaw is often inferior or underslung, so that the upper jaw protrudes forward. The front of the upper jaw is covered by the rostral scale, which in a burrower is often the most important and distinct scale on the head, since it may be shovel-shaped or pointed to enable the snake to force its head forwards through a particular substrate. The shovel-snout may be more useful when the snake lives in a loose sandy habitat, but a sharp-pointed snout might enable progress through a less forgiving substrate.

A burrower's digging head may be powered by strong neck and anterior body muscles. Even in more advanced colubrids and elapids it is possible to feel the strength in the necks of point-snouted American pinesnakes compared to kingsnakes, or Australian copperheads against tigersnakes.

Shieldtails (Uropeltidae) possess sharply pointed heads, reinforced against compression by the surrounding substrate during burrowing. The muscles of the anterior body operate in a powerful motion that draws the anterior section of the vertebral column into a concertina shape before driving the head forwards against the resistance of the soil. Since the skin is only loosely attached to the musculature, in contrast to that of pythons for example, this concertina-ing of the vertebrae causes the body to expand outwards, widening the burrow, before the head is driven forwards. The anterior body moves forwards and the movement of the vertebral column takes place again, further on, while the posterior portion of the body follows down the widened burrow and the truncated, rough, mud-covered shield-tail blocks it from behind.

The senses relied upon by burrowers may differ slightly from those living on the surface. A snake living within a substrate is likely to be more sensitive to vibrations than a snake living up a tree. Arboreal snakes possess keen vision, albeit confined to movement and monochrome, but in subterranean snakes, only emerging onto the surface at night, vision is of less importance. Many basal snakes have small eyes, while a blindsnake's eyes consist of pigmented areas beneath large transparent head scutes. Probably all the snake wishes to know from its vision is whether or not it is visible to potential predators, so a simple photoreceptive area that reports back 'illuminated, burrow quickly' is probably sufficient. Even the most basal snake possesses a forked tongue, and the ability to use chemosensory detection is especially important for these snakes since they can follow prey trails or locate a mate by following their tongues.

There are many forms of location used by the various families of fossorial or semi-fossorial snakes: sand boas simply shuffle down into the sand; blindsnakes or American pipesnakes can disappear into the earth in a blink of an eye; but space does not permit further discussion here. Any reader interested in pursuing this subject further would be advised to seek the many papers by Carl Gans, or the section on burrowing in Pough *et al* 2004, pp.374–377, and the references therein.

Conservation

Conservation of species and conservation of habitat go hand in hand. It is not sufficient to establish laws protecting a species from international trade if it is being slaughtered wholesale within its native borders, nor is it enough to establish captive breeding programmes with an eye to future reintroduction if the habitat from whence it came is still being destroyed. Habitat loss or alteration is one of the greatest threats to any species; it affects even those specimens which do not physically come into contact with man.

Many of the species in this volume are 'harvested' in large numbers for their skins, meat and gall bladders, which are highly prized in oriental medicine. Huge numbers of pythons are collected in Indonesia, Thailand, Malaysia, the Philippines and other Southeast Asian countries. According to the IUCN (International Union of Nature Conservation), in 1989 alone Indonesia exported almost 556,000 Reticulated Python skins and 71,000 skins from Short-tailed and Blood Pythons. In Africa the large rock pythons are subjected to heavy levels of collection for skins and meat and in South America Boa Constrictors and anacondas are harvested and I have seen specimens of both in Indian markets in Belém (Brazil) and Iquitos (Peru). It is unlikely that the pet trade could equal the skin and meat trade in its proportions, although the trade in Royal (Ball) Pythons from West Africa is very worrying. Today, the interest in unusual, captive-bred colour phases, known as cultivars, may have taken some of the pressure off wild Royal Python populations. However, rarity always adds value, and the rarer pythons and boas are no exception. It is not quantity but quality, and some of the less well-known pythons and boas are much sought after by collectors. Small island populations may be most at risk, such as the Mona and Virgin Island Boas in the Caribbean, the Lesser Sunda Python in Indonesia, or the Bismarck Ringed Python in the islands to the east of Papua New Guinea. Some mainland and large island species are also much sought after: the Madagascan boas, the Angolan Python, the montane New Guinea Boelen's Python, or

The 'Snake Game'. This Papuan Python (Apodora papuana) *has been noosed and dragged onto the highway to be run over.*

The author and Tony Lynam of the Wildlife Conservation Society, with skins of (left) a Burmese Rock Python (Python molurus bivittatus) *and (right) a Reticulated Python* (P. reticulatus) *during a raid on an illegal reptile skin and meat factory near Bangkok, Thailand.*

rare Australian species such as the Rough-scaled Python and the Woma. Wildlife crime does not just involve tanned skins and tiger bones, it also involves trade in small numbers of high value, but highly protected CITES (Convention on Trade in Endangered Species of Wild Flora and Fauna) Appendix I and II species. In fact, sadly, much of the trade in tanned python skins, the thousands and thousands of them, is legal and within annual quotas. Someone who smuggles a pair of rare pythons home, alive, is breaking international law, while someone who kills, skins and exports ten thousand python skins every year, under permit, is acting lawfully.

THREATENED AND ENDANGERED PYTHONS AND BOAS

The following are examples of boas and pythons threatened by man in various different ways, but it is by no means an exclusive list.

• Round Island Burrowing Boa (*Bolyeria multocarinata*), already believed extinct through the ravages of goats and rabbits that stripped the vegetation, allowing the soil to be removed by erosion.

• Cropan's Boa (*Corallus cropani*), confined to a small range

in the threatened Atlantic coastal forests of Brazil.

• Reticulated Python (*Python reticulatus*), as many as half a million harvested for skins, meat and gall in Indonesia each year.

• Short-tailed Pythons (*Python curtus, P. brongersmai, P. breitensteini*), threatened in the same way as *P. reticulatus*.

• Hog's Island Boa (*Boa constrictor imperator*), diminutive island populations threatened with extinction by collection for the pet trade.

• Jamaican, Puerto Rican and other West Indian Boas (*Epicrates subflavus* and *E. inornatus*), threatened by indiscriminate killing and by feral cats and introduced mongooses.

WHAT CAN BE DONE TO CONSERVE SNAKES?

Education is extremely important. People must understand that the majority of snakes are harmless, and many are actually beneficial, removing pests that feed on our crops or carry disease. The conservation of snakes is as important as the conservation of any other species, yet people who would protect a tiger or a giant panda, because it is endangered and furry, need a great deal more convincing to believe that conserving a snake, whether it is venomous or not, is also important. Although many religions vilify snakes, there is no connection between serpents and any 'dark forces' that may or may not exist. Snakes are simply part of the ecological jigsaw. And what use is a jigsaw with pieces missing?

THE AMERICAS

The Americas are ecologically diverse. North America was once part of the Laurasian super-continent that also included Europe and Asia, while South America was part of Gondwanaland, the great southern super-continent that fragmented into South America, Africa, Madagascar, India, Australia and Antarctica. North and South America drifted close together and animal species are believed to have rafted or island-hopped back and forth when the gap closed sufficiently, but when the slender Central American isthmus was formed it permitted much easier radiation between the two land-masses. Theories about how species reached the Caribbean islands range from rafting and island-hopping to the proposal that the Greater Antilles once formed part of an earlier isthmus which linked the two land-masses, before fragmenting and drifting eastwards. However, this latter theory has fallen out of favour.

Boas are a Gondwanan phenomenon. The tropical Americas could be called 'Boa Central', since they are home to 75 per cent of the true boas (Boinae) and 90 per cent of the dwarf boas (Tropidophiidae). The huge swamp- and river-dwelling anacondas are familiar to movie-goers, while the name 'Boa Constrictor' will always, but inexplicably, be linked with the phrase 'man-eating'! Although they are all constrictors, not all true boas are muscle-bound giants. Many feed on small- to medium-sized prey, and the region is home to a fine array of brightly coloured rainbow boas, diminutive eyelash-boas, irascible treeboas, and endangered island boas.

North America, with its deserts and grasslands, is less suitable habitat, but there are boas here also, though in lesser diversity and much reduced size. Two small boas occur from Mexico to California in the USA, and one of these even occurs in southwestern Canada. Boas are found in every mainland American country except Chile, which is two countries more than the rattlesnakes. Boas have taken the Caribbean by storm, unlike front-fanged venomous snakes, which inhabit only a handful of islands, and Cuba is the centre of West Indian boa diversity with 15 species.

Central America is also home to a curious anomaly often referred to as the 'Meso-American Python', although true pythons are actually absent from the Americas.

The Emerald Treeboa (Corallus caninus) *is superficially similar to the Australo-Papuan Green Tree Python* (Morelia viridis).

American Blindsnakes

The basal snakes are the scolecophidians (blindsnakes) and the most primitive members amongst the alethinophidians. The Americas have a rich blindsnake diversity, the Anomalepididae being endemic to the region. However, the basal alethinophidians are poorly represented, only the widespread but monotypic pipesnake genus, *Anilius*, occurring in tropical South America. Four families are represented: Leptotyphlopidae, Typhlopidae, Anomalepididae and Aniliidae.

SLENDER BLINDSNAKES

The slender blindsnakes (family Leptotyphlopidae) are the most widely distributed scolecophidians in the region with approximately 50 species in genus *Leptotyphlops*, including possibly the smallest snake in the world, *L. bilineatus* from the Lesser Antilles, which achieves a maximum adult length of 11cm. Many species are known from only a few specimens and over 30 species are single country endemics or known only from their restricted type localities. Although these tiny snakes are found in the Bahamas and Hispaniola they curiously seem to be absent from Cuba, the largest and the most herpetologically diverse West Indian island.

Plains Slender Blindsnake *Leptotyphlops dulcis*

The northernmost American blindsnake, this species is frequently found in groups known as 'aggregations', often consisting of females with eggs, beneath rocks or inside rotting logs. Being primarily subterranean, they are rarely seen. They may hibernate through cold winters or aestivate during dry periods. Unicolour pink to grey or brown, they inhabit a wide variety of habitats and soil types from sea-level to 2,100m altitude. They also inhabit garden compost heaps but the strangest microhabitat known is the nests of screech owls. Snakes carried to the nest as prey often escape being eaten and continue to survive, feeding on small invertebrates attracted by the decomposing prey remains or the presence of the fledgling

owls. It is believed that fledgling owl survivorship is greater in nests containing blindsnakes since they remove ectoparasites that could otherwise cause infection, anaemia and death.
Range: Kansas, USA, to Hidalgo and Veracruz, Mexico • Max. length: 0.28m • Habitat: Arid grassland and desert fringes • Prey: Ants, termites, also beetles and their larvae, fly larvae and arachnids • Reproduction: Oviparous, 1–8 eggs • Similar species: Western Slender Blindsnake (*L. humilis*)

Seven-striped Slender Blindsnake *Leptotyphlops septemstriatus*

The Seven-striped Slender Blindsnake is easily distinguished from the numerous glossy black blindsnakes of South America by its distinctive yellow-brown dorsal coloration and seven dark brown longitudinal stripes. Although fairly widespread, this does not appear to be a commonly encountered species.
Range: Venezuela, northern Brazil and the Guianas • Max. length: 0.20–0.30m • Habitat: Rainforest and palm-forest Prey: Termites and termite eggs • Reproduction: Oviparous, unknown clutch size

BLINDSNAKES

The blindsnakes (family Typhlopidae) include many small species of similar proportions to the slender blindsnakes but also several larger, more robust species. The typhlopid blindsnakes are common in tropical South America and achieve a greater diversity in the Caribbean than the leptotyphlopids but although they also occur in Central America, they fail to extend further north than southeastern Mexico, suggesting that American species may be less adapted to desert habitats than the smaller leptotyphlopids. There are approximately 25 country endemics amongst the 40 American species of *Typhlops*, many with extremely localized distributions.

Reticulated Blindsnake
Typhlops reticulatus

The Reticulated Blindsnake is a bicoloured species with a white head, tail and venter and a black-brown dorsum, and a sharp transition between dark and light on the flanks. Of stouter build than a leptotyphlopid, this moderately large blindsnake is forced onto the surface after heavy rain and may be encountered crossing roads. The extensive white pigment on the tail may deflect the attention of predators away from the head of the blindsnake. It is one of the most widely distributed and best documented of South American blindsnakes.

Range: South America, east of the Andes • Max. length: 0.2–0.5m • Habitat: Primary and secondary rainforest • Prey: Ants, ant larvae, termites and beetles • Reproduction: Oviparous, to 10 eggs • Similar species: Brongersma's Blindsnake (*T. brongersmianus*)

"The species *Typhlops reticulatus* was easily the largest blindsnake I recorded for the biological reserve of Ilha Maracá during 1987–88. Several specimens fell into my drift fence pitfall traps at night, either forced onto the surface by rain or whilst foraging for ant trails."
Ilha Maracá, Roraima, Brazil

Earthworm Blindsnake *Typhlops lumbricalis*

The Earthworm Blindsnake is a grey-brown species with each scale bearing a darker spot, especially on the back, and a paler snout and slightly paler underbelly. It is also the most widespread and best documented of the Cuban blindsnakes, being found in a wide variety of habitat types, particularly in red soil areas. Occurring in both lowlands and mountains, this snake is curiously feared by locals who believe it to be poisonous. This story may have arisen as a result of the sharp tail-tip, actually a burrowing aid, being used to probe the hand when the snake is handled and its purpose being mistaken for a sting. There are no front-fanged venomous snakes in Cuba, whereas there are scorpions, so possibly villagers did not realize that dangerous snakes bite, they do not sting.

OPPOSITE LEFT: *Plains Slender Blindsnake* (Leptotyphlops dulcis) *with typical blindsnake tiny eyes and mouth, and smooth scales.*

OPPOSITE RIGHT: *The Seven-striped Slender Blindsnake* (Leptotyphlops septemstriatus) *is one of the few non-unicolor slender blindsnakes.*

TOP: *The Reticulated Blindsnake* (Typhlops reticulatus) *is stout with a white tail and head, the latter disappearing underground in this view.*

ABOVE: *Cuban Earthworm Blindsnake* (Typhlops lumbricalis), *the smallest and commonest blindsnake on the island.*

Range: Cuba, Isla de la Juventud and the Bahamas • Max. length: 0.18–0.25m • Habitat: Dry scrub, woodland and agricultural land • Prey: Ants and termites • Reproduction: Oviparous, clutch size unknown • Similar species: Bimini Blindsnake (*T. biminiensis*)

EARLY BLINDSNAKES

The early blindsnakes (family Anomalepididae), sometimes known as 'dawn blindsnakes', are closely related to the typhlopid blindsnakes, from which they are believed to be an early divergence, hence their common name. The 16 known species, in four genera, are endemic to Latin America, being found in southeastern Brazil, the lower Amazon and Guianas, Trinidad, and the Choco region from northwestern Venezuela to lower Central America and coastal Ecuador. Unlike the typhlopid blindsnakes, some species of early blindsnake possess teeth on both upper and lower jaws, but this characteristic is not universal in this small family. Both of the following species have toothless dentary bones.

Central American Early Blindsnake *Anomalepis mexicanus*

Although named *mexicanus*, no specimens have been collected north of Nicaragua. The head of this glossy, brown snake is covered by enlarged scales, which are distinct from the usual small body scales, and the small, vestigial eyes are obscured beneath a pair of large head scales. It is reported to be a leaf-litter dweller, rather than a truly fossorial (burrowing)

species, but its natural history is incompletely documented. **Range: Nicaragua to Panama, also Amazonian Peru • Max. length: 0.18m • Habitat: Tropical rainforest • Prey: Probably ants and termites • Reproduction: Oviparous, clutch size unknown • Similar species: Three other species of** *Anomalepis* **from northwestern South America**

Trinidad Early Blindsnake *Typhlophis squamosus*

Early blindsnakes are poorly known and the Trinidad Blindsnake is no different. Even its common name may be spurious since modern authors no longer consider reports of its occurrence in Trinidad to be based on reliable evidence or actual specimens. Being brown with a pale pink head, it could be confused with the Reticulated Blindsnake, *Typhlops reticulatus*. Unlike other early blindsnakes, the head of *Typhlophis* is covered in numerous small scales. **Range: The Guianas and Para, Brazil, Trinidad record dubious • Max. length: 0.23m • Habitat: Tropical rainforest • Prey: Ant pupae and eggs • Reproduction: Oviparous, 3–4 eggs • Similar species: Reticulated Blindsnake (***Typhlops reticulatus***).**

American Basal Snake

The monotypic South American pipesnake (family Aniliidae) is the most primitive American snake above the blindsnakes, all the other basal alethinophidian families being Southeast or South Asian in distribution. Its presence on the other side of the Pacific raises interesting questions, especially as it occurs on the Atlantic side of South America.

South American Pipesnake *Anilius scytale*

The basal South American Pipesnake, *Anilius scytale*, is a familiar sight in the Amazon Basin countries, although it may be mistaken for one of the highly venomous coralsnakes (*Micrurus* spp, family Elapidae) or the mildly venomous False Coralsnake (*Erythrolamprus aesculapii*, family Colubridae) due to its red and black banded patterning, though the red bands are not complete and give way to off-white ventrally. Whether this patterning is intended to mimic the highly venomous coralsnake is debatable, since the pipesnake is undoubtedly an older species than the coralsnakes. It seems more likely that the sudden flash of colour, when this burrowing snake is unearthed, gives it sufficient time to escape, thereby avoiding capture by a surprised forager. It certainly works when it comes to herpetologists trying to catch a specimen!

tiny eyes. In common with many other basal snakes, the vestiges of the pelvic girdle and a pair of small cloacal spurs represent its ancestral hind limbs. Although it is an accomplished burrower, the pipesnake forages for prey on the surface. Not being a macrostomatan or 'big-mouth', it specializes in elongate prey such as other snakes and amphisbaenians (worm-lizards). Unlike the blindsnakes, the pipesnake is a live-bearer.

The pipesnake exhibits a number of typical burrowing characteristics. It has a short tail, smooth body scales with ventral scales not much larger than the dorsal scales, and a rounded head with

Range: Guianas and Amazonian countries • Max. length: 0.6–0.9m • Habitat: Tropical rainforest and cultivated areas • Prey: Small snakes and amphisbaenians • Reproduction: Viviparous, 7–15 neonates • Similar species: Coralsnakes (*Micrurus* spp.) or False Coralsnake (*Erythrolamprus aesculapii*)

American Macrostomatan Snakes

The macrostomatans are the big-mouthed snakes, which means all snakes above the level of the basal pipesnakes and their small-mouthed relatives. Most American macrostomatans within the scope of this volume are boas, but the region is home to one curious species sometimes referred to as a 'python', but now believed to be related more closely to the sunbeam snakes of Asia.

Meso-American Python
Loxocemus bicolor

Although not a true python, this species – also known as the Mexican Burrowing Python – is certainly more advanced than the pipesnakes and other basal alethinophidians. It is believed to be most closely related to the Sunbeam Snake, *Xenopeltis unicolor*, of Southeast Asia. Both species possess highly iridescent scales, hence the shared name

of 'sunbeam snakes'. Both species achieve similar maximum lengths, inhabit rainforests and forage at night, exhibiting fairly catholic diets when it comes to feeding on small vertebrates. The Meso-American Python, a bicoloured snake, dark grey above and immaculate white below, is not a true burrower even though it is a secretive and rarely observed snake. It inhabits dry tropical forest and thorn scrub, where it feeds on small mammals and reptiles, such as teiid lizards. Specimens have also been observed raiding the nests of sea turtles, Green Iguanas and Spiny-tailed Iguanas, taking both eggs and hatchling iguanas. In the case of the hatchling iguanas, the snakes enter the nest during the night and feed on as many as three hatchlings in a single feeding session. Such depredations could have an adverse effect on the survival of endangered species if more than one snake were involved. *Loxocemus* retains the vestiges of the pelvic girdle and cloacal spurs. In the past two further species have been recognized, but neither is considered valid today, specimens throughout the entire range being referred to as *L. bicolor*.

Range: Mexico to Costa Rica • Max. length: 1.0–1.6m • Habitat: Dry, tropical forest and scrub • Prey: Small mammals, reptiles and eggs • Reproduction: Oviparous, 4 eggs • Similar species: Asian sunbeam snakes (*Xenopeltis* spp.)

OPPOSITE: *The Trinidad Early Blindsnake* (Typhlophis squamosus) *may not even come from Trinidad.*

TOP: The *South American Pipesnake* (Anilius scytale), *is a convincing coralsnake mimic.*

ABOVE: The *Meso-American Python* (Loxocemus bicolor) *is most closely related to the Asian sunbeam snakes* (Xenopeltis).

American Boas

The term 'boa' is applied to the members of the Boidae, Tropidophiidae and Ungaliophidae within the Americas. Some 75 per cent of all boas occur in the Americas, including giant species like the anacondas and diminutive species like the eyelash and dwarf boas. Some of the woodsnakes of genus *Tropidophis* might easily be confused with more advanced members of the Colubridae. Whilst true boas abound, there are no true pythons.

NEOTROPICAL TREEBOAS

Ten years ago the neotropical treeboas genus *Corallus* contained only three species. Now eight species are recognized, from Guatemala to southeastern Brazil. Common characteristics of the

group include a strongly muscular body; long, prehensile tail; bulbous head, with elongate snout; large eyes, with vertically elliptical pupils; enlarged and highly visible labial pits, and elongate curved teeth, especially in the front of the jaws.

As a group, they probably exhibit greater variation in coloration and patterning than any other genus of boas, even demonstrating variation in the same location or litter of neonates. They are primarily arboreal, and found in rainforest or riverine forest habitats, although several species also inhabit dry forest or the Brazilian savanna-woodland known as 'cerrado'.

It might be assumed that the arboreal treeboas prey upon birds, but although they will take avian prey they are mostly nocturnal predators of small arboreal mammals and bats, the latter captured on the wing. The presence of an enlarged, highly sensitive array of heat-sensitive pits along both the supra- and infralabials (upper and lower lip-scales) greatly enhances their ability to locate and capture mammalian prey in the total dark of the rainforest night. The large eyes, with sensitive retinas and vertically elliptical pupils, further assist in making them successful hunters. The eyes of some, if not all, species of *Corallus*, possess a characteristic not reported for any other snakes: they reflect eye-shine (see Amazonian treeboa below).

The most primitive neotropical treeboa is though to be Cropan's Boa (*Corallus cropani*). Formerly known as *Xenoboa cropani*, three specimens of this rare snake were collected near Miracatu, in the mountainous Atlantic coastal forests of São Paulo State, Brazil, in the early 20th century, making it the boa

OPPOSITE TOP: *Cropan's Boa* (Corallus cropani) *is only known from the Atlantic coastal forests of Brazil. This is a preserved specimen.*

OPPOSITE BOTTOM: *Adult Emerald Treeboa* (Corallus caninus), *vivid green with white dorsal markings.*

LEFT: *Juvenile Emerald Treeboas may be orange, red or green, and achieve adult coloration with increased maturity.*

BELOW: *The Northern Annulated Treeboa* (Corallus annulatus) *is named for its banded body patterning.*

with the smallest recorded range, and there have been occasional road-killed specimens since. Cropan's Boa is fairly stout-bodied and is probably a more terrestrial species than typical *Corallus*. All species are viviparous.

Emerald Treeboa *Corallus caninus*

More stoutly built than most other species of *Corallus,* the Emerald Treeboa is believed to be the closest relative of Cropan's Boa. A highly arboreal, generally bright green species, captive specimens are frequently confused with the Green Tree Python (*Morelia viridis,* p.137) of New Guinea and Queensland. The body shape and adult coloration of the two species are not the only characteristics shared by these two arboreal predators. They both adopt the same resting position, whereby the body is looped back and forth over the branch with the head perched in the middle. Both species also demonstrate an ontogenetic colour change – as juveniles they are orange, red or green, taking on the full adult green livery with transverse white vertebral bars, with increased maturity, in the case of Emerald Treeboas when they reach approximately one-third to half full size. It is common for neonates in a single litter to vary in colour from red to green. Emerald Tree Boas can be distinguished from Green Tree Pythons by their supralabial pits, which extend from the snout to well beyond the eye, presenting a sharper appearance than in the python, where the pits are less visible posteriorly. The labial pits are more evident in the Emerald Treeboa than in any other *Corallus* and they are also believed to be the most arboreal species in the genus. The enlarged front teeth are designed to maintain a strong grip on the prey when the boa strikes, preventing it from escaping or dropping from the mouth before the body coils can encircle it. Several distinct geographical forms are recognized, largely based on size and colour variations, but whether they represent

distinct populations has not been determined. These localized colour phases should not be confused with 'cultivars', the colour morphs specifically bred in captivity. Recent research suggests that the Upper Amazonian/Peruvian population may represent a separate species.

Range: Guianas and Amazonia • Max. length: 1.4–1.8m, reports of longer specimens • Habitat: Lowland tropical rainforest with high humidity • Prey: Arboreal mammals, bats, birds and occasionally lizards • Reproduction: Viviparous, 5–12 neonates • Similar species: Green Tree Python (*Morelia viridis*) from New Guinea and Queensland, Australia, and possibly the highly venomous Two-striped Forest-pitviper (*Bothriopsis bilineata*)

Northern Annulated Treeboa *Corallus annulatus*

The Central American member of the genus, the Annulated Treeboa is one of the least known of neotropical boas. It is reported to be secretive, spending its daylight hours hiding under tree-bark or in leaf-litter. I searched a hollow tree in

Costa Rica, that was reputed to be inhabited by a brace of Annulated Treeboas but despite intensive searching, inside and out, I was unable to locate them. The distribution of this species appears to consist of a series of pockets from Guatemala to Colombia. Although former consisting of three subspecies, the Colombian subspecies has been synonymized with the nominate form while the Bolivian population has been elevated to full species status as the Ecuadorian Annulated Treeboa, *C. blombergi*. Annulated Treeboas vary from tan, through the typical red-brown, to dark chocolate with a series of irregular dark ring-markings that earn them their common and scientific names. Although some populations go through an ontogenetic colour change, from red-brown to more subdued adult browns, nowhere is this change as pronounced as that of the Emerald Treeboa. Although agile and arboreal, Annulated Treeboas are reported to hunt terrestrial mammals on the ground.

Range: Caribbean coast of Central America to Colombia and Venezuela • Max. length: 1.2–1.7m • Habitat: Lowland tropical dry forest, rainforest and coastal forest • Prey: Small mammals • Reproduction: Viviparous, 5–16 neonates • Similar species: Ecuadorian Annulated Treeboa (*C. blombergi*) from the Pacific versant of Ecuador

Amazonian Treeboa *Corallus hortulanus*

The Amazonian Treeboa is a confusing species. It was originally known as *Corallus enydris* and two subspecies were recognized, the northern South American Cook's Treeboa, *C. e. cookii*, and the Amazonian or Garden Treeboa, *C. e. enydris* (see the Caribbean Coastal Treeboa account for changes to the status of the northern South American population). The Amazonian Treeboa, as currently recognized and renamed *C. hortulanus*, is the most widespread member of genus *Corallus*, being distributed throughout the Guianas-Amazonian region and across the cerrado (savanna-woodland) of northeastern Brazil to the Atlantic coastal forest strip. In some places it may even be encountered in caatinga (grassland-savanna). One of the smaller members of the genus, the Amazonian Treeboa has an etiolated appearance, with a long, slender, laterally compressed body and prehensile tail and a broad, elongate, distinct head. In coloration and patterning this species is extremely variable and several distinct colour morphs may be found within a single population in a relatively small area. The Amazonian Treeboa is one of the few snakes that can be located by eyeshine. Shining a torch from a distance so that the beam does not illuminate the actual snake or its surroundings will cause the light to be reflected back to the observer by the *tapetum lucidum*, a mirror-like layer behind the rods and cones layer of the retina. This phenomenon has long been known for crocodilians, frogs, some mammals and nocturnal birds, moths and spiders but was only recently discovered for snakes. I have used it to great effect in Guyana and Trinidad, but it would have made my work in the northern Amazon much easier in the 1980s had it been reported in treeboas then.

Range: Guianas, Amazonia and Brazilian Atlantic forests • Max. length: 1.0–1.5m • Habitat: Lowland tropical rainforest, dry forest and riverine forest • Prey: Arboreal mammals, bats and birds including nestlings • Reproduction: Viviparous, 8–19 neonates • Similar species: Caribbean Coastal Treeboa (*C. ruschenbergerii*)

"While working on a research project in northern Brazil, I encountered this treeboa fairly frequently and had additional specimens brought in by the bat team, who found them near their mist-nets at night. The tree-boas were quite common around buildings and also along trails in the dry-forest habitat. This was also the best location for bats, and we assumed that the boas were catching the bats. This fact was borne out by two incidents. On one occasion I was able to examine a treeboa and could tell by the shape of the bulge that it had eaten a bat, one of 49 species recorded on the reserve. On another occasion a researcher told

ABOVE: *The Caribbean Coastal Treeboa* (Corallus ruschenbergerii) *is a large species with a long reach when it strikes.*

OPPOSITE: *An orange Amazonian Treeboa* (Corallus hortulanus). *However, this species may also be red, yellow, light grey or patterned with dark grey reticulations.*

me he had observed a treeboa ambushing a nectar-feeding bat on a *Parkia* tree at night. Among the many specimens I encountered, I noted several distinct morphs, ranging from yellow to red-orange to light grey ground-colour, either patternless, faintly patterned or marked with bold, dark grey reticulations."
Ilha Maraca, Roraima, Brazil.

" A torchlight shone at distant vegetation at night, even when the distance is too great to illuminate actual snakes or their surroundings, will still enable the locations of treeboas to pin-pointed by their eyeshine. A dull red reflection from the retina will be clearly visible to the observer. I found I could locate a treeboa from several hundred feet away at night, purely by its eyeshine. It is extremely satisfying to spot a snake in the darkness from across a river or lagoon and then motor over and illuminate the entire serpent as it weaved its way through the branches."
Iwokrama Forest Reserve, Guyana.

Caribbean Coastal Treeboa *Corallus ruschenbergerii*

Sometimes known as the Black-tail Treeboa, the Caribbean Coastal Treeboa replaces the smaller Amazonian or Garden Treeboa in northern Colombia and Venezuela, Trinidad, Panama and Costa Rica. It was once known as Cook's Treeboa, *C. enhydris cookii*, but *C. cookii*, as a name, is now confined to the population from St Vincent in the Lesser Antilles, while the Grenada Bank Treeboa is also recognized as a separate species, *C. grenadensis*. The large Caribbean Coastal Treeboa is less variably patterned than its smaller southern relative and most specimens are buff to yellow with only limited markings. In aquatic situations, such as swamps, they are important predators of arboreal animals like small mammals and lizards, and they may also take roosting waterbirds.

Range: Pacific Costa Rica and Panama to Venezuela and Trinidad • Max. length: 1.4–2.0m • Habitat: Rainforest, riverine forest, wooded swamps and wooded savanna • Prey: Arboreal mammals, bats and birds, also lizards in island populations • Reproduction: Viviparous, 15–30 neonates • Similar species: Cook's Treeboa (*C. cookii*) and Grenadian Bank Treeboa (*C. grenadensis*) from the Lesser Antilles

" I encountered some very large Caribbean Coastal Treeboas in the dense mangrove swamps. They were easier to find at night, using eye-shine, than during the day using normal search techniques. They were also rather aggressive, so catching and handling them was not easy. These large treeboas had impressive strike ranges."
Caroni Swamp, Trinidad.

RAINBOW BOAS

The rainbow boas are the only mainland representatives of the large boa genus *Epicrates*, all other species being confined to the West Indies. As a genus, *Epicrates* is quite diverse, containing species with maximum lengths of well under 1.0m to more than 4.0m. The mainland rainbow boas achieve lengths somewhere in the mid-range, around 2.0m. While Caribbean species exhibit fairly limited distributions, rainbow boas are widely distributed throughout mainland Latin America. Common characteristics which link the species of *Epicrates*, and cause them to stand apart from other neotropical boas, include the presence of large regular scales on the top of the head, between and in front of the eyes, rather than the usual small granular boid scales. They also exhibit similarities in dentition and vertebral structure, but these are less useful to the fieldworker. Rainbow boas are popularly kept in captivity.

Colombian Rainbow Boa *Epicrates maurus*

Many authors recognize only one species, *Epicrates cenchria*, but there has been a recent move to elevate the subspecies formerly known as *Epicrates cenchria maurus* to specific status. Although it occurs in close proximity to the nominate subspecies *E. c. cenchria* in Colombia, Venezuela and the Guianas, the two boas appear to exhibit different habitat preferences and there are no reports of intergradation (natural hybridization), as occurs between other closely related subspecies elsewhere within the range of *E. cenchria*.

The Colombian Rainbow Boa occurs throughout Costa Rica and Panama and across northern South America to the mouth of the Orinoco, with offshore populations on Trinidad, Tobago and Isla Margarita. This species is also known from the narrow coastal strip of the Guianas (Guyana, Suriname and French Guiana) and specimens very similar to Colombian Rainbow Boas are known from the inland savannas of Guyana-Roraima, Brazil. Whether all these populations, sometimes termed 'Guianan Rainbow Boas', represent the same species has yet to be confirmed, but the Colombian Rainbow Boa as currently recognized appears to be a dry woodland-savanna, rather than rainforest, species. Juveniles are similar in appearance to juveniles of rainbow boas from further south, being marked with a broad brown dorsal stripe containing large cross-vertebral light brown spots, several series of white-edged, black lateral spots, and three dark head-stripes running from the snout to the nape. With maturity most Colombian Rainbows become red-brown to brown with the original pattern obscured, but the iridescent 'oil-on-water' sheen, which earns the snake its common name, is still evident in daylight.

Range: Costa Rica to northern South America, Trinidad and Tobago • Max. length: 1.5–2.0m • Habitat: Savanna and dry savanna-woodland • Prey: Mammals and birds • Reproduction: Viviparous, 6–20 neonates

South American Rainbow Boa *Epicrates cenchria*

The rainbow is a very widespread and variably patterned species. Even after removing the Colombian Rainbow Boa, as many as eight subspecies may be recognized; although the characters that separate some of the described forms are difficult to define, a factor not helped by specimens that exhibit characteristics of more than one subspecies.

Authors are generally agreed that two basic patterning types may be defined. Type A (*cenchria*-type) applies to those forms which bear a dorsal pattern of large, dark, cross-vertebral rings, with light centres, which may form saddles or slightly off-centre S-markings, and lateral markings consisting of a large black ocellus, with a pale crescent in the top sector, with a series of smaller ventrolateral dark spots below. Type B (*crassus*-type) may be defined as those subspecies which bear smaller dark edged, light centred ocelli, which may be described as 'para-vertebral' arranged alongside the vertebral ridge but also crossing it to form fused dumb-bell markings, and several series of smaller lateral spots, often with a light edge to the upper series and often fused to form broken longitudinal stripes.

The best known nominate subspecies with Type A patterning is the Brazilian Rainbow Boa, *E. c. cenchria* (illustrated on p.11), which occurs throughout the rainforests of the Amazon Basin, from its mouth to its Ecuadorian headwaters, and also ventures into Colombia, Venezuela and the Guianas. This is an especially attractive snake, the adult being bright orange-red with bold black vertebral rings and lateral ocelli, each of the latter bearing a pale upturned crescent in its upper centre, and five black longitudinal stripes running off the head. The juveniles start life with very much the same pattern as the juvenile Colombians. The Peruvian Rainbow Boa, *E. c. gaigei*, from the Amazonian

OPPOSITE: *The iridescent-patterned Colombian Rainbow Boa* (Epicrates maurus) *is the northernmost rainbow boa, whereas the Argentine Rainbow Boa* (Epicrates cenchria alvarezi) (BELOW) *is the most southerly representative of the genus.*

headwaters of Peru and the lowlands of Bolivia, closely resembles the Brazilian form, differing only in certain scale counts and the lack of pale centres to each lateral ocelli.

The best known of the Type B patterned subspecies is the Paraguayan Rainbow Boa, *E. c. crassus*, from south and south-central Brazil, Paraguay and northeastern Argentina. It is a red-brown snake with a pair of para-vertebral light centred ocelli, and three rows of dark lateral ocelli. It is found in the savanna-woodland known as 'cerrado' and the seasonally flooded pantanal grassland. The related Argentine Rainbow Boa, *E. c. alvarezi* (illustrated below) occurs in the Andean foothills of northwestern Argentina and southwest Bolivia. Patterning is similar to *E. c. crassus* but the dark borders of the dorsal blotches are fused to form a continuous broad vertebral stripe, and there are also variations in the head scalation.

Within Brazil four further subspecies are recognized by some authors, but even they do not account for all the variations that can be found throughout the range of a species which is probably in need of taxonomic revision. These four subspecies are the Ilha Marajo Rainbow Boa, *E. c. barbouri*, from the large island of that name in the mouth of the Amazon. In appearance is seems closest to *E. c. crassus* from southern Brazil, a distribution pattern seemingly mirrored by the anacondas (see p.53). The Caatinga Rainbow Boa, *E. c. assisi,** inhabits the xerophytic thorn woodland of northeastern Brazil but may occur in close proximity to Eastern Rainbow Boa, *E. c. hygrophilus*, which occurs in the narrow Atlantic coastal forests from Bahia to Rio de Janeiro. The final subspecies, the Central

Highlands Rainbow Boa, *E. c. polylepis*, is described for the elevated country to the north and east of the Brazilian capital, Brasilia. Most of these forms are thought to intergrade with each other, and with *E. c. crassus*, so drawing lines on maps to illustrate their ranges is extremely difficult.

* *E. c. xerophilus* is a much-used synonym of *E. c. assisi*.

Range: North and central South America, east of Andes • Max. length: 1.5–2.0m • Habitat: Lowland tropical rainforest, savanna and savanna-woodland • Prey: Mammals and birds • Reproduction: Viviparous, 6–20 neonates

"On Ilha de Maracá, Brazil, in 1987 I found a 1.8m male Brazilian Rainbow in the forest near the research station, and the next day we encountered a similar-sized female. Then, while driving along the road across the Roraima savanna, I encountered a road-killed specimen with the patterning of a Guianan-Colombian Rainbow and a live juvenile with the same pattern. In Peru, during filming in 2003, we caught two medium-sized adult Peruvian Rainbows within 24 hours, one in an Amerindian village and the other in a garden being prepared for planting. On the Ilha Marajo, in 1999, I found a single small Marajo Rainbow in a pile of cut timber near the house we were using as a base camp.

Ilhas Maracá, Roraima, & Marajo, Pará, Brazil, and Alliance Cristiana, Loreto, Peru

OPPOSITE: *The Brazilian Rainbow Boa* (Epicrates cenchria cenchria) *possesses a vivid pattern of red, orange and blue as an adult.*

BELOW: *The Cuban Boa* (Epicrates angulifer) *is the largest snake in the West Indies, outside Trinidad.*

WEST INDIAN BOAS

There are nine species from the genus *Epicrates* in the Caribbean, compared to only two species on the entire Latin American mainland. They range in size from under 1.0m to over 4.0m and are found throughout the West Indies, excluding the Lesser Antilles. The centres of speciation seem to be the island of Hispaniola (Haiti and the Dominican Republic) and the Bahamian Islands, with three species each, but West Indian boas also inhabit Cuba, Jamaica, Puerto Rico and the Virgin Islands.

Cuban Boa *Epicrates angulifer*

Cuba is the largest island in the Caribbean and the Cuban Boa, the sole member of the genus *Epicrates* present on Cuba, is easily the largest West Indian snake, if Trinidad, with its green anacondas, is treated as a dislodged chunk of South America. Although distributed throughout the island, some of the largest Cuban Boas have been found on the US-controlled Guantanamo Bay, with the record specimen of 15ft 11in (4.85m) reported and historical reports of '5–7yds' (4.8–6.4m). Unfortunately, Cuban Boas are also noted for their irascible attitudes, even neonates launching long, open-mouthed strikes. There is a west to east variation in patterning, specimens from eastern Cuba being paler with faint patterning while those further west are boldly marked with dark brown or black angular dorsal and lateral markings. Cuban Boas are adept predators, ambushing with equal ease rodents and village chickens on the ground and bats at cave entrances, and it is suggested they may even take iguanas, *Cyclura* spp. Juvenile boas certainly take smaller lizards such as anoles, *Anolis* spp. There are also reports of Cuban Boas taking small snakes such as the woodsnake *Tropidophis melanurus* (p.63).

Range: Cuba and Isla de la Juventud • Max. length: 2.0–4.8m • Habitat: Moist and dry woodland and rocky habitats • Prey: Rodents, bats, birds and lizards • Reproduction: Viviparous, 1–7 neonates

Haitian Boa *Epicrates striatus*

The Haitian Boa is the most widespread of the West Indian boas, being found on the island of Hispaniola, comprising French-speaking Haiti and the Spanish-speaking Dominican Republic, and also on the Bahamas to the northwest. Surprisingly, the Haitian Boa is not found on the intervening Turks and Caicos Islands, which are inhabited by the similar-sized Turks Island Boa, *E. chrysogaster*. Three subspecies of Haitian Boa are recognized for Hispaniola and the small off-shore island of Ile de la Tortue, while five are described from the mid-Bahamian Islands (Bimini, Andros, New Providence, Eleuthera, Cat, Exuma and Ragged Islands) and it seems likely that the Bahamian population may deserve specific status. Haitian Boas are blotched snakes, their patterning consisting of regular or irregular dark brown, grey or black blotches on a lighter brown, grey or cream background, but this is really a very variable species. It also occurs in a wide variety of habitats, from dry and moist forests to pinewoods, on Andros Island, and even mangroves.

Range: Hispaniola and Bahamas • Max. length: 1.2–2.5m •

Habitat: Moist and dry woodland, pinewoods and rocky habitats • Prey: Rodents, birds and lizards • Reproduction: Viviparous, 7–51 neonates

Ford's Boa *Epicrates fordii*

Not all West Indian boas are large snakes, several species having a maximum length of less than 1.0m. Ford's Boa, sometimes confusingly called the Haitian Ground Boa, is an example of one of the smaller species. Confined to the island

BELOW: *Haitian Boas* (Epicrates striatus) *are found on Hispaniola and in the Bahamas.*

OPPOSITE TOP: *Ford's Boa* (Epicrates fordi) *is one of the more diminutive West Indian Island boas.*

OPPOSITE BOTTOM: *The Jamaican Boa* (Epicrates subflavus) *has been pushed to the edge of extinction by ignorance and introduced species.*

of Hispaniola, this terrestrial to arboreal snake exhibits quite a disjunct distribution. It is reported from the Ile de la Gonave, off western Haiti, throughout the southern coastal lowlands and offshore islands from Port-au-Prince, Haiti, to Barahona and Bani, in the southern Dominican Republic, as well as isolated locations on the northern coast. Ford's Boa is probably a lowland or coastal species with a preference for the arid *Acacia* and cactus scrub and dry grassland. The habitats in between, the more humid lowland forests of northern Dominican Republic and the Tiburon Peninsula of Haiti, are associated with the more arboreal Haitian Vine Boa, *E. gracilis*. Looking at the distribution maps it is clear there is much still to be learned about the distribution of the three species of *Epicrates* on the pirate island of Hispaniola.

Range: Hispaniola • Max. length: 0.8–1.0m • Habitat: Moist and dry woodland and rocky habitats • Prey: Rodents and lizards • Reproduction: Viviparous, 1–3 neonates • Similar species: Haitian Vine Boa, *E. gracilis*

Jamaican Boa *Epicrates subflavus*
Known as the 'yellowsnake' in its native land, this species has also suffered greatly since European colonization, from active persecution, habitat loss to agriculture, housing and bauxite mining, and most significantly from the introduction of dogs, cats, pigs and especially the

mongoose, to which it has no defence. Various authors, dating back as far as the early 1900s, have suggested the boa may even be extinct on mainland Jamaica, although it is said to survive, ironically, on nearby Goat Island. This species is listed by the IUCN as threatened, and placed on Appendix I of CITES, which provides it with the maximum international protection possible, but does not protect it against domestic threats. The Jamaican Boa is the subject of a concerted international captive breeding programme amongst the world's zoos. A similar situation exists on Puerto Rico, where the endemic Puerto Rican Boa, *E. inornatus*, has also been pushed to the verge of extinction by habitat loss and its collection as a source of snake fat by local people. This species is also protected by CITES and is being

captive bred in institutions.

The Jamaican Boa is an interesting two-tone snake which is olive to yellow on the forebody but with black scale tipping which increases to become broad dark bands by mid-body and eventually a completely iridescent black posterior body and tail.

If the captive breeding programme is ever to move to the reintroduction stage, it will be necessary to educate the people to protect both the snake and its habitat in Jamaica, and eradicate the mongoose. Even then it may not be possible.

Range: Jamaica and Goat Island • Max. length: 1.5–2.3m • Habitat: Moist woodland and limestone habitats • Prey: Rodents, bats and birds, even parrots, also lizards and frogs as juveniles • Reproduction: Viviparous, 3–39 neonates

BOA CONSTRICTOR

The genus *Boa* contains a single neotropical species, *Boa constrictor*. In 1991 the genus was expanded to include the three Madagascan boas formerly contained within the genera *Acrantophis* and *Sanzinia* (see p.108), based on the cladistic analysis of 79 morphological characteristics. However, in 2001 this decision was reversed by a molecular study which demonstrated that, although *Boa* and the Malagasy boas bear a strong phenetic resemblance to one another, *Boa* is phyloge-netically more closely related to *Epicrates* (rainbow and West Indian boas) and *Eunectes* (anacondas), with which it forms a neotropical clade, and to which the Madagascan boas represent a sister-clade.

Boa Constrictor *Boa constrictor*

The Boa Constrictor or Common Boa is one of the most instantly recognizable of all snakes and probably one of the most familiar snake names in the world. Even people living thousands of miles and entire continents away from its range have heard of the boa constrictor. The name 'boa' is very old, having been used by Pliny the Elder (23–79 AD) in *Natural History* Book 8, to describe a snake from Italy which was reportedly so large that it could swallow a child whole, and which fed primarily on milk stolen from cows' udders. Isadore of Seville (c.560–636 AD), in *Etymologies* Book 12, added that the immense boa pursued herds of cattle or oxen, attacked their udders and drained them of milk, thereby killing them and

A typical Boa Constrictor (Boa constrictor constrictor), *ready to defend itself on an island in the mouth of the Amazon.*

OPPOSITE: *A Boa Constrictor* (Boa constrictor constrictor) *from Amazonian Peru, demonstrating the typical saddle markings and dark post-ocular stripe.*

earning the name 'boa' or 'ox killer'. Pliny also credited boas with being able to kill elephants. European herpetology at that time plainly contained more surprises and dangers than today. In view of the ingrained history of this mythical serpent, it is not surprising that Carl Linnaeus, the Swedish father of modern taxonomy, chose to name a genus of real snakes *Boa* in his 1758 publication *Systema Naturae,* although he was not suggesting that the large South American serpents fed on children and milk or possessed a pathological hatred of elephants. Linnaeus also included the Green Anaconda, now *Eunectes murinus*, as *Boa murina*. Although stories of giant Boa Constrictors can be found in the literature of the 19th and early 20th century, the largest specimens discovered and positively identified appear to be less than 5m in length, the report of a 6m-plus specimen from Trinidad having now been attributed to a misidentified Green Anaconda.

The Boa Constrictor is the most widely distributed Latin American boid, being found from northern Mexico to northern Argentina, on the eastern side of the Andes, and to Peru, on the western versant. Although extremely variable in dorsal coloration throughout its range, the general pattern is of a brown or grey snake with a series of broad angular dorsal saddle-markings which may be linked to form a chain pattern down the back, becoming bolder and more solid on the tail. The head is characterized by three dark stripes, a median line, with or without lateral projections, from the snout to the nape, and a lateral stripe on either side which begins as a dark triangle between the snout and the eye, then passes through the eye and angles downwards to the corner of the jaw.

Boa Constrictors have been recorded from most habitats within their extensive range. They are primarily crepuscular or nocturnal, and semi-arboreal, the juveniles being more arboreal than the heavier adults. Specimens in northern Mexico are said to bask, and boas are reported to den together on Dominica. Hunting techniques range from sit-and-wait ambush to active searching. Although a wide variety of prey is taken, mammals make up the bulk of the diet, which is curious since the Boa Constrictor lacks the highly visible thermal pits so evident in rainbow boas and treeboas. Some of the stranger creatures reported as prey include vampire bats, tree porcupines, village dogs, coati mundi, young deer, mongoose (introduced) and an ocelot. A boa was reported to have died in a failed attempt to swallow a tamandua (tree anteater) and another attacked a Brazilian porcupine. Several bird species are reported as prey, and lizards eaten range from small species to spiny-tailed and green iguanas. The only report of a human being killed by a Boa Constrictor concerned a nightclub escapologist strangled by a juvenile boa placed with him in a coffin.

Boas are extremely popular in captivity and they have been recorded as living for 25 to 35 years, with a record just short of 39 years. However, overcollection for the pet trade from small island populations, most notably the Honduran boas from Islas de la Bahia and Cayos Cochinos (Hog's Islands) may have pushed some of these unique insular boas to the point of extinction. On the mainland large-scale harvesting for skins, meat and body parts, combined with active persecution and habitat loss, has also had a disastrous effect on this large and once common species. I have seen Boa Constrictor heads in jars, racks of dried boa tails, and live neonates in sacks for sale in Amerindian markets of Belém, Brazil and Iquitos, Peru. Yet boas are important allies in the control of the disfiguring South American disease, leishmaniasis. The protozoan parasite responsible for this disease in man also occurs in another species, the ubiquitous marsupial opossum, and any blood-sucking sandflies that feed on opossums, and then feed on man, may transfer the disease. Opossums are very common in slums and on rubbish dumps around cities in the Amazon and infection rates can be high. Enter the Boa Constrictor, which feeds well on opossums with no ill effects. Unfortunately, boas are killed by the very people they protect.

Range: North Mexico to north Argentina, including islands off Pacific coast and in Caribbean • Max. length: 2.0–3.0m, occasional specimens to 5.0m, island populations below 2.0m • Habitat: Rainforest, woodland, grassland, semi-desert, tropical islands, agricultural land and plantations from sea-level to 1,000m • Prey: Mammals, bats, birds, lizards • Reproduction: Viviparous, 10–64 neonates • Similar species: Madagascan ground boas (*Acrantophis* spp.)

"One evening, after heavy rain, I captured a very aggressive 2.0m Common Boa on the ecological station. It appeared to have two sharp projections protruding from the top of its head. When I opened its mouth I discovered five imbedded porcupine spines, two of which had penetrated through to the outside world. The only porcupine recorded for the reserve was the Brazilian porcupine, *Coendou prehensilis*. The boa must have struck the porcupine with considerable force to drive two spines through the bones of the skull. After removal of the spines the boa was released, but any similarities to Daniel and his lion were quickly dismissed when the ungrateful snake promptly bit me."
Ilha Maracá, Roraima, Brazil.

Subspecies of *Boa constrictor*

Although the Boa Constrictor is one of the most instantly recognizable of all American serpents, it is also, taxonomically, one of the most confusing. How many subspecies have been described, how many of them are valid, and whether they intergrade (hybridize) naturally, are questions that have yet to find conclusive answers. Even the accurate ranges of the generally accepted subspecies are often open to doubt. I will attempt to summarize the status of the many subspecific names that have been afforded to *B. constrictor* over almost 250 years. The easiest approach is to list them chronologically.

Colombian or Common Boa *Boa constrictor constrictor*

Carl Linnaeus described *Boa constrictor* in 1758, but the exact type locality is unknown because he listed it in error as 'Indiis' (India). The nominate subspecies occurs through much of South America east of the Andes, from Venezuela to southern Brazil, and also on Trinidad and Tobago. The Common Boa is a very variable species which may be dark or light, although most specimens are light fawn or tan with between 15 and 22 dark saddles on the body and a white or yellow underbelly, with few scattered dark markings. The number of saddles and dorsal,

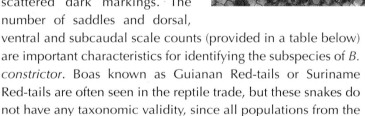

ventral and subcaudal scale counts (provided in a table below) are important characteristics for identifying the subspecies of *B. constrictor*. Boas known as Guianan Red-tails or Suriname Red-tails are often seen in the reptile trade, but these snakes do not have any taxonomic validity, since all populations from the three Guianas are included within *B. c. constrictor*.

St Lucia Boa *Boa constrictor orophias*

Linnaeus also described the full species *Boa orophias* in 1758 but it was reduced to subspecific status in the early 20th century. Subsequent authors have suggested that, since this is an island population existing in reproductive isolation from the mainland or even Trinidad forms, it may warrant recognition as a separate species. The St Lucia Boa has a rich brown dorsal colour, 27–31 narrow saddles down the back and a pale underbelly speckled with black or grey.

Imperial or Central American Boa
Boa constrictor imperator

The Imperial Boa was described by Daudin in 1803, also as a full species *B. imperator*, but it became a subspecies in 1910. It is generally much darker than the Common Boa, grey as opposed to brown, with 22–30 dorsal saddles and scale counts that help to distinguish it from the southern form. Another characteristic used to separate *B. c. imperator* from *B. c. constrictor* is the dark median stripe that runs down the centre

of the head in both subspecies. In the Central American form this stripe bears side projections that extend laterally over the eyes, while the bars are absent in the nominate South American subspecies. The underbelly of the Imperial boa is also more darkly speckled than in *B. c. constrictor*.

B. c. imperator occurs from northern Mexico, on both coasts, southwards through Central America and into South America, west of the Andes to Ecuador. Several island races off the Pacific and Caribbean coasts are recognized as insular populations of *B. c. imperator* despite the fact that they are generally much lighter in colour, smaller in size and less aggressive than wild mainland Central American boas. The best-known populations are from the Bay Islands (Roatan, Guanaja and Utila) and the Cayos Cochinos (Hog Islands) to the north of Honduras, Great Corn Island off Nicaragua and San Andros and neighbouring Mexican Caribbean islands. Many of these small insular populations are threatened with extinction due to persecution, loss of habitat and collection for the pet trade.

Mexican Boa
Boa constrictor mexicana

Described by Jan in 1863 and defined as having a low dorsal scale count and lacking the median dark line on the head, this form was synonymized with *B. c. imperator* 30 years later and is no longer considered valid.

Argentine Boa *Boa constrictor occidentalis*

This form, described as a species by Philippi in 1873 and reduced to a subspecies in 1910, is a very distinctive snake. Black or grey with an irregular reticulated pattern, it is rarely confused with any other taxon. Like *B. c. imperator* at the other end of the range, it has 22 or more dorsal saddles but their edges are irregular and unclear. This is the southern-most subspecies of *B. constrictor*, occurring in Paraguay and northern Argentina.

Peruvian Boa *Boa constrictor ortonii*

Confined to a small area of northwestern Peru, this race was described as a distinct species by Cope in 1878 but relegated to a subspecies in 1943. The population, from the narrow coastal lowlands to 1,000m altitude, is probably the southern-most population of *B. constrictor* west of the Andes. Its background coloration is pale fawn, crossed by 15–19 dorsal

ABOVE: *The Hog's Island Boa* (Boa constrictor imperator), *a dwarf, pastel-coloured island race of the dark mainland Imperial Boa, is threatened with extinction by collection for the pet trade.*

OPPOSITE: *Some Boa Constrictors can be very dark, such as this specimen from the Yavari Valley in Amazonian Peru.*

The Argentine Boa (Boa constrictor occidentalis) *is the southern-most subspecies of the Boa Constrictor and the only one on CITES Appendix I.*

saddles. Many Boa Constrictors possess red tails as juveniles but this coloration diminishes as they mature. In this light-coloured Peruvian Boa the red tail often persists into adult-hood and results in the alternative name of Peruvian Red-tail Boa. Despite its light coloration it is probably closely related to *B. c. imperator* with which it shares a median head stripe with lateral projections over the eyes.

Taboga Island Boa *Boa constrictor sabogae*
Barbour described this race in 1906, but originally placed it in the rainbow boa genus *Epicrates*. Confined to Taboga Island, in the Gulf of Panama off the Pacific coast of Central America, this is the only Central America insular population to be retained as a valid subspecies. The Taboga Island Boa is generally a brown species with widely separated dorsal saddles.

Bolivian Boa *Boa constrictor amarali*
Described in 1932 by Stull, the Bolivian Boa is a light grey race with black or dark grey speckling on the dorsum and venter, at least 19 dorsal saddles and a broad dark median head stripe

that lacks lateral projections. It is distributed from eastern Bolivia to southeastern Brazil and was considered by Stull to be intermediate between *B. c. constrictor* and *B. c. occidentalis*.

Tres Marias Islands Boa *Boa constrictor sigma*
Described by Smith in 1943, from the remote Tres Marias Islands in the Pacific to the northwest of Mexico, this subspecies is usually synonymised with *B. c. imperator* despite its geographical isolation and elevated scale count.

Dominican or Clouded Boa *Boa constrictor nebulosa*
As recently as 1964 Lazell described a second Lesser Antillean island population as a separate taxon from the St Lucia Boa, *B. c. orophias*. Unlike the St Lucia Boa, this is a dark snake with 32 or more irregular edged and indistinct dorsal saddles. Again, given the geographical isolation and therefore possible reproductive isolation of this island population, the Dominican boa may warrant specific status.

Black-bellied Boa *Boa constrictor melanogaster*
Langhammer described the Black-bellied Boa from Amazonian Ecuador in 1983, but chose a non peer-reviewed popular magazine for his description. Subsequent authors believe that the description is flawed and the subspecies if largely discounted. This is a grey or yellow snake with 20–21 dark chocolate brown saddles and a heavily black-spotted or entirely black underbelly.

Long-tailed Boa *Boa constrictor longicauda*
The latest contribution to the list of subspecies of *Boa constrictor*, described by Price and Russo in 1991, is the Long-tailed Boa, from the remote and isolated wet-tropical Tumbes Province of northeastern Peru. Separated from neighbouring boa populations by mountain ranges, the describers refer to it as a black boa and strongly recommend it as a valid taxon, based on several characteristics apart from its isolation, notably its especially long tail and its lower dorsal saddle count (20–21).

MERISTIC VARIATION IN SCALE COUNTS FOR *BOA CONSTRICTOR* SUBSPECIES				
	SADDLES	DORSALS	VENTRALS	SUBCAUDALS
B. c. constrictor	15–22	81–95	234–250	49–62
B. c. orophias	27–31	65–75	270–288	55–59
B. c. imperator	22–30	56–79	225–253	47–69
B. c. occidentalis	22	65–87	242–254	35–58
B. c. ortonii	15–19	57–72	246–252	46–59
B. c. sabogae		65–67	241–247	49–70
B. c. amarali	19	71–79	226–237	43–52
B. c. sigma	30	77	253–260	55–66
B. c. nebulosa	32–35	59–69	258–273	52
B. c. melanogaster	20–21	86–94	237–252	45–54
B. c. longicauda	20–21	60–76	223–247	50–67

ANACONDAS

It may be that the Reticulated Python, *Python reticulatus*, from Southeast Asia is the longest snake in the world, but when it comes to which species is the largest, factors other than length must be taken into consideration, ie. girth and weight. Without doubt, the widest, bulkiest and heaviest snake in the world is the Green Anaconda, *Eunectes murinus*.

Anacondas may be defined as large aquatic South American boas, but the word 'anaconda' is not Spanish, or Portuguese, nor even a native Amerindian name for snake. 'Anaconda' is a Sinhalese word, originating from Sri Lanka, and it means 'python'. It is a dialect name for the Sri Lankan race of the Indian Rock Python, *Python molurus*. The attachment of a Sinhalese word for python to an aquatic South American boa mirrors the way the words 'boa' (a mythological child-eating, cattle-killing Italian snake – see Boa Constrictor, p.48) and 'tarantula' (a large southern European wolf spider) were transported to the neotropics.

Green Anacondas (Eunectes murinus) *are well known for taking mammals and caimans, but a river turtle?!*

The route these names followed can be summed up by the word 'colonization'. They were applied by early travellers, explorers and settlers from Spain, Portugal and Italy who, visiting South America and encountering large snakes and spiders, described them using familiar European names. At that time the Portuguese possessed many far-flung colonies, including the part of Amazonia that is today called Brazil, home to the anacondas, and Taprobane, an Indian Ocean island that later became Ceylon under British control and is now known as Sri Lanka. Clearly the Sinhalese name for python was transposed to the Americas by Portuguese sailors and settlers who had encountered the name applied to large snakes in Taprobane.

Interestingly, in the predominantly black-settled northeast of Brazil the anaconda is called 'aboma'. Again, this is not an Amerindian or Portuguese name, although it also means python. 'Aboma' is a West African name for the African Rock Python, *Python sebae*, and it was probably transported to Bahia and neighbouring states by African slaves destined for the sugar cane plantations.

There is not simply one species of anaconda; up to five species have been described and currently four may be recognized. The Green Anaconda, *E. murinus*, was described by Linnaeus in 1758 as *Boa murina* and over 100 years passed before Cope described a second smaller species from further south, the Yellow Anaconda, *E. notaeus*. In 1936 an unusual and improbable thing happened: two new species of anaconda were described from living specimens at the Philadelphia Zoo. That in itself was not strange, because live specimens were used as type specimens in the past, although it is frowned upon today when an accessioned museum specimen is preferred, but the two new species were unusual in that they were thought to have been collected from the same location, a large island in the mouth of the Amazon, Ilha de Marajo in Para state. The Green Anaconda was already known for Amazonia, including Marajo, so the suggestion that two further species of anaconda might exist in the same location, in the same habitat, stretched credibility.

The two new species were Barbour's Anaconda (*E. barbouri*) which resembled a Green Anaconda, except that the centre of each black ocellus was pale in colour, and De Schauensee's Anaconda (*E. deschauenseei*), named in honour of the original collector of both specimens. This second species bore a strong resemblance to the Yellow Anaconda from much further to the southwest. The status of Barbour's Anaconda was questioned repeatedly in the following years and when specimens of Green Anaconda, from throughout its considerable range, were found with *barbouri*-type patterning it was realized that this was not a valid species and *E. barbouri* was synonymised within *E. murinus*. At the same time, some detractors suggested that De Schauensee's Anaconda was nothing more than a Yellow Anaconda.

However, the isolation of the two populations, with *E. notaeus* in southwestern Brazil and Paraguay, a region known as the Pantanal, and *E. deschauenseei* on Ilha de Marajo thousands of kilometres to the northeast, and its subsequent discovery in the extreme northeastern state of Amapa and neighbouring French Guiana, suggested that, although the two species were extremely alike, they were more likely to be sister-taxa, separated by the Amazon-dwelling Green Anaconda, than two isolated populations of the same species.

Such separation could feasibly have occurred when the Amazon rainforest, in one of its periods of expansion, separated a contiguous population of savanna-dwelling ancestral-Yellow Anaconda into two isolated portions, in much the way that raised sea levels have served to separate island and mainland populations.

Green Anaconda *Eunectes murinus*

The Green Anaconda is the largest and most widespread anaconda species. It is unmistakably patterned dark green above and yellow-green below, with series of large paravertebral black ocelli along either side of the back, which may meet vertebrally, and with several series of smaller, light-centred spots along the lower flanks. A further characteristic of the species is a broad, black-edged, postocular stripe which runs from the eye to the angle of the jaw. Since the early 1800s, two subspecies have been recognized, the nominate Amazonian race, with a stripe the same colour as the general body colour, and a northern race, ranging from Colombia to the Guianas, characterized by its light-coloured, often orange, postocular stripe. However, the stripe colour varies even within specimens from the same location and the subspecies are no longer recognized. These stripes are located on the sides of the head in juvenile anacondas but as the snake matures its head gets wider and both the eyes and the postocular stripes become repositioned on top of the head. This can lead to some interesting interpretations (see *pers. obs.* on p.56).

Green Anacondas occur in seasonally flooded savannas such as the llanos grassland of Venezuela, but they also inhabit the huge Amazon river system. In the seasonally flooded savannas the snakes are subjected to an annual dry season, when the lagoons and grasslands dry out and the snakes are forced either to drag themselves over the mud to deeper water or bury themselves and hope to survive through aestivation. The anacondas in the Amazon Basin are probably not subject to such extremes and may be active all year. Prey availability will also vary for the two habitats. Those anacondas on the grasslands will probably experience seasonal fluxes in prey availability, but when conditions are optimal there is an abundance of small to medium-sized prey species (capybara, wading birds, spectacled caiman), whilst the anacondas inhabiting rivers will probably find prey available all year around but in lower densities.

I travelled up a river in Venezuela for two hours in the dry season and counted 200 caimans up to 2.0m in length, in the shallows or on muddy banks and sandbars. After four days of heavy rain I made the same journey and counted only 20 caimans. There were still 200 caimans on that stretch of river

but they were now floating in deeper water, most of their original basking areas having been submerged. The caimans could easily hide from me but they would be easy meals for a large and powerful predator from below. In a river an anaconda could probably feed all year around. A feeding anaconda is a growing anaconda, so a snake inhabiting the Amazon river system is theoretically likely to grow much larger than a specimen from the seasonally-flooded savannas, where part of the year is lost to aestivation and prey is unavailable.

It has been suggested that the largest savanna-dwelling Green Anaconda might achieve a length of 7.5m but specimens from the deep, dark rainforest rivers further south could grow much larger. Indeed, most of the stories of giant anacondas in the 19th and 20th centuries originate from the deep Amazon in Brazil and Colombia. One theory suggested that the real giants belonged to a different, as yet undescribed, species. However, this idea is easily disputed because nobody has ever collected a juvenile anaconda of the unknown giant species. Far more feasible, if such giants do exist, is the possibility that environmental circumstances, ie. optimum habitat, abundant year-round prey availability, lack of predators, would allow individual animals to achieve huge sizes. Large adult anacondas are almost entirely aquatic. They can avoid overheating and can move and hunt more easily in a medium that supports their massive weight. An aquatic anaconda can achieve a greater girth and weight than a primarily terrestrial Reticulated Python. There are records of 5.0–5.8m anacondas weighing 105–107kg, and a 4.5m anaconda that was as heavy as a 7.4m Reticulated Python. The largest Green Anaconda I have personally captured, from 40 specimens, measured 5.75m and weighed 73kg, and at least two other 5.5m specimens approached the same weight.

Range: Colombia, Venezuela, Trinidad, the Guianas, Brazil, Peru, Ecuador and Bolivia • Max. length: 7.5–11.5m • Habitat: Rainforest rivers and seasonally-flooded savanna • Prey: Mammals, birds, caiman, snakes, occasionally fish • Reproduction: Viviparous, 20–40 neonates, record 82

A proficient predator, the Green Anaconda (Eunectes murinus) becomes more aquatic with size, and it does get very large!

"In 1993 I was asked to join a trip to Guyana to investigate, among other things, a report of a large horned anaconda. I was sceptical, and could think of no reason why an anaconda should have evolved horns. I caught only one 3.0m specimen which lacked horns, but interestingly promptly regurgitated a smaller anaconda, the first record of cannibalism for wild anacondas. Some months later I was viewing some video clips for a film company, including a sequence of a moderately large anaconda swimming towards the camera through shallow water. As the snake approached I realized the origin of the horned anaconda story. The black edges of the post-ocular stripes created a virtual 3-D effect and, when viewed from above, the curved orange stripes appeared to be elevated above the rest of the head. They looked exactly like a pair of curved, pointed horns.
Rupununi River, Guyana and UK

ABOVE: *The Green Anaconda* (Eunectes murinus) *is instantly recognizable with its large black 'ocelli' markings on a green background.*

BELOW: *The smaller Yellow Anaconda* (Eunectes notaeus) *inhabits the seasonally-flooded Pantanal of southern Brazil, Paraguay and northern Argentina.*

Yellow Anaconda *Eunectes notaeus*

The Yellow Anaconda is found in the seasonally-flooded savannas on either side of the Paraguay River from Argentina, north into southwestern Brazil and Paraguay, an area known as the Pantanal. In areas where it occurs alongside *E. murinus*, *E. notaeus* is found in the central swamps while *E. murinus*

De Schauensee's Anaconda (Eunectes deschauenseei) *occurs around the mouth of the Amazon and resembles the Yellow Anaconda* (E. notaeus).

inhabits the peripheral streams. The ground colour of the body is yellow and the paravertebral rows of black spots meet more frequently across the back, to form crossbars or a broken zigzag, than do the large black ocelli of the Green Anaconda. The black markings on the lower flanks consist of a double row of shallow inverted half-moons with small dark spots below. The head bears three broad black converging stripes that form an arrow-head over the snout.
Range: Paraguay, southwestern Brazil, northeastern Argentina and Uruguay • Max. length: 2.5–3.0m Habitat: Seasonally-flooded savanna • Prey: Mammals, bird, caiman, turtles, lizards, occasionally fish • Reproduction: Viviparous, 10–30 neonates, record 37 • Similar species: De Schauensee's Anaconda (*E. deschauenseei*)

De Schauensee's Anaconda *Eunectes deschauenseei*

This species is named in honour of its collector, who sent a specimen to the Philadelphia Zoo in 1924. The collection locality was believed to be the Ilha de Marajo, the largest island in the mouth of the Amazon River and approximately half mangrove swamp and half seasonally-flooded grassland. The anacondas are reputedly found in the grassland alongside

Green Anacondas but, in 1999, when I went to find De Schauensee's Anaconda in the wild, we found only a single recently killed 1.0m specimen and a 5.5m Green Anaconda.

In appearance this species is almost indistinguishable from the Yellow Anaconda, although from the few I have seen the dorsolateral black spots appear broader and the ground colour greener than in its Pantanal relative. De Schauensee's Anaconda has also been recorded from Amapa state and the lower Amazon in Brazil, and from French Guiana to the north.
Range: Ilha de Marajo, Brazil, to French Guiana • Max. length: 2.5–3.0m • Habitat: Seasonally-flooded savanna • Prey: Mammals, birds, fish, probably caiman • Reproduction: Viviparous, litter size unknown • Similar species: Yellow Anaconda (*E. notaeus*)

A new species of anaconda?

The latest potential addition to the portfolio of boas and pythons in the Americas is a new species of anaconda, described by German herpetologist Lutz Dirksen in 2002, from the Beni River system of Bolivia. Named *E. beniensis*, it exhibits characters of both *E. murinus* and *E. notaeus* and Dirksen initially reported it as hybrid between the two established species. Further studies by Dirksen demonstrated several differences of scalation, colouration and patterning which support the recognition of *E. beniensis*. These are summarised in English in Dirksen and Böhme 2005, *Russian Journal of Herpetology* 12(3):223–229.

NORTH AMERICAN ROSY AND RUBBER BOAS

Boas are not generally associated with North America but two species do occur in the United States and one of these even extends its range into Canada. Both species are small, secretive and semi-fossorial and both are popular in captivity. They are also the only New World representatives of the Old World boid subfamily Erycinae, which otherwise contains the sand boas of Africa and Asia and the Calabar Ground Boa of West Africa. The taxonomy of this subfamily has undergone considerable changes in recent years, on both sides of the Atlantic, including the recognition of a single genus, *Charina*, for the two American species and the Calabar Ground Boa, while some authors still prefer to recognize the genera *Lichanura* and *Calabaria* as distinct. I shall take the middle ground and recognize *Calabaria* but retain *Charina* for the two American species.

Rosy Boa *Charina trivirgata*

The Rosy Boa is probably the most popular small boid kept in captivity, possibly because of its placid nature and the variation in its patterning, which has led to the recognition of numerous subspecies within the 'trade' and there is considerable disagreement within taxonomic circles about which subspecies are valid. Up to seven subspecific names are proposed and, whilst most authors only accept three subspecies, they vary as to which three they accept. There are two main body patterns in rosy boas, striped and unicolour. The striped specimens bear three broad red, tan, brown or black longitudinal stripes, one vertebral and two lateral, which are much darker than the white, cream, grey, yellow or light brown ground colour. The unicolour specimens may be brown, yellow-grey or even pinkish red with darker flecking, and frequently the underlying stripes are faintly visible. The head is narrow and pointed, the eyes small and the tail relatively short. Only the males possess visible pelvic spurs, those of even large females hardly piercing the skin. Rosy boas are secretive, nocturnal snakes, which move slowly and which may even be active at cooler times of year. For all their popularity in captivity, they are little studied in the wild.

Range: Southwestern USA and Baja California, Mexico • Max. length: 1.0–1.5m • Habitat: Scrubland, desert fringe and rocky talus slopes • Prey: Small mammals, but also lizards and nestling birds in captivity • Reproduction: Viviparous, 1–12 neonates

The Rosy Boa (Charina trivirgata) *from the southwestern United States and Mexico may be striped or unicolor, often with reddish tinges, hence its common name.*

Rubber Boa *Charina bottae*

This species is the northernmost boa in the world, since it may be found from southern California to south-central British Columbia, Canada. Two subspecies are generally recognized and they may be sufficiently different to be described as separate species. These small snakes are able to survive in much cooler conditions than other boas and they may be found to over 3,000m altitude (compared to 2,000m for the Rosy Boa), hibernating through extremely cold periods at altitude or latitude. Unicolour brown with a small head and tiny eyes, the defensive strategy of these inoffensive little boas involves either freezing or 'balling' – rolling into a ball with the head protected in the centre and the short, stumpy tail protruding as a false head, while it exudes a foul-smelling musk from its cloacal glands. Rubber Boas frequently possess scars on their tails from close encounters with potential predators. Although small in size, Rubber Boas are generally long-lived, over 20 years being recorded in captivity.

Range: Western USA and southwestern Canada • Max. length: 0.7–1.0m • Habitat: Pine-oak woodlands, upland grasslands and desert fringes • Prey: Small mammals, birds, lizards and reptile eggs • Reproduction: Viviparous, 1–10 neonates • Similar species: Indian Sand Boa, *Eryx johnii*, or Calabar Ground Boa, *Calabaria reinhardti*

ABOVE: *The diminutive Rubber Boa* (Charina bottae) *occurs as far north as southwestern Canada and therefore holds the record as the northernmost boa or python in the world.*

BELOW: *The head and tail of the Rubber Boa are very similar in appearance. A defensive Rubber Boa may coil in a ball with its blunt tail protruding like a false head, possibly to deflect unwanted attention away from the head hidden in the centre of the coils.*

EYELASH BOAS

With the removal of the Central American dwarf boas (p.61) from the Tropidophiidae, the genus *Trachyboa*, from Pacific northwestern South America, is the only genus, apart from the West Indian-South American *Tropidophis* (pp.62–63) remaining in this small neotropical family. The two species of eyelash boa are poorly documented in the wild and are difficult to maintain in captivity. The term 'eyelash boas' is not entirely accurate since only one species possesses the enlarged horn-like scales over the eye from which the common name results.

Northern Eyelash Boa *Trachyboa boulengeri*

Specimens of eyelash boa are rare and, although there have been some successes achieved in their captive management, they remain little known in both the wild and captivity. The Northern Eyelash Boa is an inhabitant of the lowland Choco rainforests of Colombia and Panama but some of the early specimens were collected near gold and platinum mines. Whether this is indicative of habitat preference or an artefact of there being Western employees with an interest in natural history in these locations, is impossible to determine. The little Northern Eyelash Boa is an unusual snake, covered in rugous, keeled scales, with a bulbous head and small eyes, over which are several raised eyelash-like scales. It is a brownish snake, with paler irregular saddle blotches. The only colour appears to be a yellow tail-tip, which may suggest caudal luring of prey, a common characteristic of neotropical amphibiophagous snakes (frog-eaters), yet captive specimens have refused most prey offered, except fish (goldfish and guppies) and the occasional small mouse. One of the strange reports about these curious boas is their defensive trait of freezing when handled, regardless of the position they may be in. This is neither the defensive balling found in small boids, nor the thanatosis (shamming dead) of some colubrid hognose and grass snakes, and elapid rinkhals (spitting cobra), but it may be an early precursor to one or both of these behaviours.

Range: Pacific coastal Panama, Colombia and Ecuador • Max. length: 0.4m • Habitat: Lowland tropical rainforest • Prey: Fish in captivity, possibly small mice • Reproduction: Viviparous, 2–6 neonates • Similar species: Southern Eyelash Boa, *T. gularis*, from Pacific coastal Ecuador

The Northern Eyelash Boa (Trachyboa boulengeri) *is a little-known species with raised supraciliary eyelash-like scales around its eyes.*

CENTRAL AMERICAN DWARF BOAS

Three species of Central American dwarf boas, two bromeliad boas (also called banana or vine boas), in the genus *Ungaliophis*, and the monotypic Oaxaca Dwarf Boa, *Exiliboa plicata*, were previously placed in the family Tropidophiidae, with the West Indian dwarf boas, but recent DNA analysis suggests they should be provided with their own family. They are small, secretive snakes whose distribution and natural history are incompletely documented.

Northern Bromeliad Boa *Ungaliophis continentalis*

The Northern Bromeliad Boa is known from a few specimens from Chiapas, southwestern Mexico, and neighbouring Guatemala, but two specimens have also been collected from Honduras. The ground colour is light grey or brown flecked with darker pigment, with a patterning consisting of black-centred, white-edged, ovoid markings arranged in two paravertebral rows, starting as an arrowhead on the head and continuing onto the tail. Rows of smaller black spots are present on the flanks. The iris of the eye is flecked grey or brown like the side of the head, so that it blends in perfectly. Found in lowland rainforests and higher pine forests, these little snakes are reported to inhabit bromeliads and other epiphytic vegetation. An interesting aspect of the reproductive behaviour is the copulatory biting of the female by the smaller male. He uses his spurs to court the female and will then bite her tail while he coils his lower body around her and copulates. Although this snake is small in size, a lifespan of 17 years has been recorded in captivity.

Range: Southern Nicaragua to Colombia • Max. length: 0.4–0.6m • Habitat: Lowland tropical rainforest to montane

The Northern Bromeliad Boa (Ungaliophis continentalis) *is a rainforest snake reported to inhabit epiphytic plants.*

pine forests at 2,000m altitude • Prey: Unknown but captives take lizards, frogs and small mice • Reproduction: Viviparous, 2–10 neonates • Similar species: Isthmian Bromeliad Boa, *U. panamensis,* from southern Nicaragua to Colombia

Oaxaca Dwarf Boa *Exiliboa plicata*

The first specimen of this strange, glossy black boa was discovered in 1967, in the Sierra de Juarez of Oaxaca, Mexico, underneath a large rock in a cloud forest clearing, by the herpetologists J. Stuart Rowley and Charles M. Bogert. Since then a few additional specimens have been collected from close to the type locality but they have proved difficult to maintain in captivity for any length of time and their natural history is poorly known. In captivity they accept small frogs as prey, and museum specimens have been found to contain frogs and salamander eggs in their digestive tracts, and it is therefore assumed that amphibians form the main part of their diet. The Oaxacan Dwarf Boa is distinguished from other neotropical boas by the presence of a single large internasal scale. The only colour on this dark snake is a white spot over the cloacal region, oddly a characteristic also found in the small, cryptically patterned Bevel-nosed Treeboa (*Candoia carinata*) of New Guinea. Defensive behaviour is reported to consist of rudimentary 'balling' and head-hiding, in common with other small boids.

Range: Southern Mexico • Max. length: 0.5m • Habitat: Cloud forest at 2,300m altitude • Prey: Small frogs and amphibian eggs • Reproduction: Viviparous, 8–16 neonates

WEST INDIAN DWARF BOAS AND WOODSNAKES

The diminutive West Indian snakes of the genus *Tropidophis* have long presented a problem for the taxonomist. Are they boas or colubrid snakes? They may superficially resemble small semi-fossorial colubrids, but most species possess vestigial pelvic girdles and the males have small but visible cloacal spurs, both well-documented boid characteristics. The problem was resolved by placing them in their own family, the Tropidophiidae, which is expanded to include the monotypic South American genus *Trachyboa* (see p.60).

The West Indian dwarf boas are also known as woodsnakes, because of their association with woodland habitats and their secretive nature, hiding inside rotten logs and bromeliads. They have vertically elliptical pupils and prehensile tails. Currently 20 species are recognized, 17 from the Caribbean but three extremely poorly documented species from remote locations in Ecuador, Peru and southeast Brazil. Of the 17 West Indian species, 13 are endemic to Cuba and its satellite islands; one is widespread in the Great Antilles (Cuba, Hispaniola and Jamaica); the Bahamas and Cayman Islands are home to two

The Haitian Dwarf Boa (Tropidophis haitianus) *is also found in Jamaica and possibly in Cuba.*

and one endemic species respectively. Most are very small snakes with a maximum size below 0.75m, although one species achieves an impressive 1.0m. Many species are poorly documented with few specimens, natural history notes or field observations. Several of the island populations may be threatened by habitat loss and introduced domestic animals.

Haitian Dwarf Boa *Tropidophis haitianus*

Although commonly known as the Haitian Dwarf Boa, because three subspecies occur in Hispaniola, this is a widespread dwarf boa, being also represented by three subspecies in Jamaica and even a single record from east Cuba. The commonest pattern is tan to brown, with irregular dark brown blotches, but some specimens are unicolour, iridescent slate grey. Habitat preferences are varied, because this little snake inhabits natural rainforest and rocky creek beds, but also adapts well to the detritus of man, moving into coconut husk piles, cocoa trash or under discarded timber. Specimens also turn up

The Cuban Dwarf Boa (Tropidophis melanurus) *is the largest of the dwarf boa-woodsnakes, with a maximum length of over 1.0m.*

inside bromeliads, demonstrating their arboreal habits, and in termitaria. Small vertebrates constitute its main prey.
Range: Hispaniola, Jamaica and Cuba • Max. length: 0.7m • Habitat: Moist woodland, cactus shrub, grassland and rocky areas • Prey: Rodents, lizards and frogs • Reproduction: Viviparous, 4–9 neonates • Similar species: Turks and Caicos Dwarf Boa, *T. greenwayi*

Cuban Dwarf Boa or Woodsnake *Tropidophis melanurus*
The largest member of the genus, the Cuban Dwarf Boa or Woodsnake can achieve a maximum length of a little over 1.0m. This is an extremely variably patterned species, the ground colour ranging from tan to red, brown or grey, overlaid with either blotches, spots or longitudinal stripes. Four subspecies are recognized: a pan-Cuban subspecies, and three isolated subspecies from far-western Cuba, Ile de Juventud, and tiny Navassa Island, a US-controlled island 160km south of Guantanamo Bay. This last population is almost certainly

endangered, because goats have been introduced to Navassa Island.
Range: Cuba and Navassa Island • Max. length: 1.0m • Habitat: Moist woodland, rainforest and rocky areas • Prey: Rodents, birds, frogs and lizards • Reproduction: Viviparous, 8–36 neonates • Similar species: Leopard Dwarf Boa, *T. pardalis*

Brazilian Dwarf Boa *Tropidophis paucisquamis*
None of the three South American *Tropidophis* is well known and they are all widely separated, not only from the West Indian species but also from one another. The Brazilian Dwarf Boa is brown or orange with ill-defined markings, and is recorded from the coastal rainforests from São Paulo to Rio de Janeiro and Espiritu Santo. A specimen collected in the montane forests of Bahia may yet prove to be a new species.
Range: Southeast Brazil • Max. length: 0.5m • Habitat: Coastal rainforest • Prey: Small frogs and lizards • Reproduction: Viviparous, 5 neonates reported • Similar species: Peruvian Dwarf Boa, *T. taczanowskyi* and Ecuadorian Dwarf Boa, *T. battersbyi*

EUROPE AND ASIA

The huge contiguous land mass of Europe and Asia encompasses most of what was formerly the Laurasian supercontinent, with Gondwanan India tacked onto the bottom for good measure. It was the collision between a northward-moving India and generally southward-drifting Eurasia that caused the buckling we now know as the Himalayas. Rather like an extremely slow-motion head-on car accident, the mountains are still rising, but eventually they will slow, stop and possibly start to drop again as the continental plates bounce back off one another.

However, despite its vast size and ecological diversity, from frozen tundra to arid deserts, much of the habitat in Europe and Asia is unsuitable for colonization by pythons and boas. The few species that do occur are found primarily in the more tropical southern fringes.

Several of the more primitive snake families, possible precursors to the pythons and boas, are endemic to this region. All but one family of the basal Alethinophidia occur here (Anomochilidae, Uropeltidae and Cylindrophiidae), as well as several of the more primitive macrostomatans (big-mouthed snakes), for example the sunbeam snakes (Xenopeltidae) and the poorly documented spine-jawed snakes (Xenophidiidae) of Malaysia. Two of the three families of blindsnakes also inhabit the region.

It was always to be expected that Europe would be poorly represented, yet there is a boa in Europe, albeit a very small one confined to the extreme southeastern corner, in Greece and the Balkans. A burrowing species, it belongs to the Erycinae, the primarily Afro-Asian subfamily of the Boidae. More representatives of this subfamily are found scattered across the Arabian Peninsula and the Middle East to India, and they also range into Africa.

Tropical Asia, south and east of the Himalayas, is python country, even though the family achieves its greatest diversity in Australasia. Five species occur within this region, including two of the world's truly giant snake species.

Across the southern half of this huge geographical area we can therefore find species ranging from blindsnakes to small burrowing boas, up to rainforest-dwelling pythons capable of devouring a leopard, or even a man.

Borneo Short-tailed Python (Python breitensteini), *a stout, rainforest-floor species.*

European and Asian Blindsnakes

Two families of blindsnakes are found in Asia, although the Typhlopidae is far better represented than the Leptotyphlopidae, with one species even entering southeastern Europe.

SLENDER BLINDSNAKES

Fewer than ten leptotyphlopid blindsnakes inhabit western Asia from Turkey to India. The most wide-ranging species, the Hook-snouted Slender Blindsnake (*Leptotyphlops macrorhychus*), also occurs across North Africa and has been included in Chapter Three (p.94). Several other species have been synonymised within this single taxon.

Nurse's Slender Blindsnake *Leptotyphlops nursii*

Named in honour of Captain C.G. Nurse, Nurse's Slender Blindsnake is confined to southern Arabia and Yemen and possibly also Oman. It is a light greyish or pink above and yellowish-cream below, with a rounded snout, in contrast to the several other slender blindsnakes in the same region, which have hooked snouts.

Range: Arabian Peninsula and Yemen • Max. length: 0.25m Habitat: Semi-desert • Prey: Termites and their eggs and larvae • Reproduction: Oviparous, clutch size unknown • Similar species: Blanford's Slender Blindsnake (*L. blanfordi*)

BLINDSNAKES

The typhlopid blindsnakes are much better represented in Asia than are the leptotyphlopids and one species even enters southeastern Europe. Five genera are represented: the monotypic *Cyclotyphlops deharvengi* and *Gryptotyphlops acutus*, endemic to Sumatra and India respectively; two species from the African genus *Rhinotyphlops* which occur in Turkey and the Holy Land; eight species from the Australasian-Asian genus *Ramphotyphlops*; and almost 60 from the huge genus *Typhlops*, a total of more than 70 blindsnake species.

Brahminy Blindsnake *Ramphotyphlops braminus*

If a snake could be called global, this is that snake. The Yellow-bellied Seasnake (*Pelamis platurus*) is found across two great oceans, but this little blindsnake has established itself on every continent except Antarctica and Europe, although its presence on the latter cannot be ruled out.

The secret of its success can be partially discovered in its frequently used alternative name of 'flowerpot snake' – this tiny little black serpent will live perfectly happily in the soil surrounding the roots of a plant, and if that plant is transported overseas in a plant pot or simply in the original earth, the tiny snake will travel too. The second part of its success story concerns its reproductive behaviour, the Brahminy Blindsnake being the only known parthenogenetic snake species – it exists

only as a female, no male has ever been discovered, and if the conditions are conducive she will lay fertile eggs which hatch into little cloned females to further increase the colony. Whereas most other animal species colonizing a new shore require a male and a female to meet up before there is a chance of colonization taking place, one adult Brahminy Blindsnake is all that is required to found a new colony.

Originating from India or Southeast Asia, the Brahminy Blindsnake has established itself as far afield as Taiwan, Indonesia and on many Pacific islands (I have found it in Papua New Guinea under oil-drums and paving slabs), northern Australia, Hawaii, USA, Mexico, Guatemala, in Africa from north to south and on Madagascar and most other Indian Ocean islands. Students at the Royal Botanic Gardens at Kew, London, told me of small dark snake-like creatures in the soil, which does not surprise me in the slightest. Perhaps only Antarctica has proved too difficult to colonize. Nor does altitude appear to be a problem, as there are reports from 1,200m in Sri Lanka and 1,500m in Guatemala.

Once the parthenogenesis and distribution of this species have been discussed there is little more to say, other than it is slender, small and glossy black, and it feeds on ant and termite eggs and larvae, which it seeks out with its tiny forked tongue.

One problem does exist regarding the placing of this species

OPPOSITE: *The Brahminy Blindsnake* (Ramphotyphlops braminus) *is the most widely distributed snake in the world. It exists only as a female, capable of laying fertile eggs.*

ABOVE: *Diard's Blindsnake* (Typhlops diardi) *is a common stout-bodied dry-forest blindsnake.*

in *Ramphotyphlops* as opposed to *Typhlops*. These genera are separated on characteristics of the male genitalia, and it does not have any!

Range: Worldwide • Max. length: 0.23m • Habitat: Perianthropic habitats • Prey: Ants and termites eggs and larvae • Reproduction: Oviparous, 1–7 eggs

Diard's Blindsnake *Typhlops diardi*

Diard's Blindsnake was originally a wide-ranging species with two subspecies, one from mainland Southeast Asia as far west as Assam, and one from Malaysia and Indonesia, but now the latter form has been elevated to species status as *Typhlops muelleri*. The range of *T. diardi* has also extended westward, in 1992 I collected the first specimens from far western Nepal and the species is now also known from Orissa in northeastern India. This is a fairly stocky blindsnake with a rounded head and uniform brown coloration, slightly paler below. It spends most of its time below ground, in common with other blindsnakes, only coming above ground at night, especially after heavy rain – I caught the Nepalese specimens by setting drift-fence lines with pitfall traps. Being larger than the average blindsnake, it can probably devour larger prey than can its slimline relatives, which must confine themselves to a diet of ants, termites and their offspring. Diard's Blindsnake is probably large enough to swallow earthworms or other soft invertebrates. The Nepalese specimens were found in dry Himalayan foothill forest known as 'terai'.

Range: Mainland Southeast Asia and Nepal • Max. length: 0.43m • Habitat: Dry forest • Prey: Soft insects, their eggs and larvae, and possibly earthworms • Reproduction: Oviparous, 4–14 eggs • Similar species: Müller's Blindsnake (*T. muelleri*)

European Blindsnake *Typhlops vermicularis*

The only blindsnake to enter Europe, *T. vermicularis* occurs in Greece and the Balkans, on Cyprus, Crete, Corfu and Rhodes, east to Afghanistan and south to Egypt. In coloration it may be brown or pink, pale yellow below. It has an extremely slender body and a rounded head, which suggests it burrows in soft substrates such as loose soil. It favours grassland with scattered stones, and coastal scrub.

Range: Greece, and the Balkans to Afghanistan • Max. length: 0.3–0.4m • Habitat: Grassland and coastal scrub • Prey: Ants, their eggs and larvae, possibly spiders and other soft invertebrates • Reproduction: Oviparous, 4–8 eggs

Asian Basal Snakes

Three unique families of basal alethinophidians are confined to the Oriental region, one of which extends into the western limits of the Australasian region. Many of these snakes are semi-fossorial or fossorial (leaf-litter dwellers or burrowers), secretive and poorly known, others commonly encountered and well documented.

LITTLE PIPESNAKES

The Anomochilidae (little pipesnakes) is a poorly documented family containing one genus and two species in Malaysia and Indonesia. Little pipesnakes can be distinguished from the more widespread and well-known Asian pipesnake of the Cylindrophiidae by the lack of a mental groove, a fold of hidden loose skin running down the centre of the throat. Its lack suggests a snake with a narrow mouth-gape which preys on slender, elongate animals.

OPPOSITE: *The only blindsnake in Europe, the European Blindsnake* (Typhlops vermicularis) *is found in Greece and the Balkans.*

BELOW: *Leonard's Little Pipesnake* (Anomochilus leonardi) *is known from only two specimens collected in Peninsular Malaysia.*

Leonard's Little Pipesnake *Anomochilus leonardi*

Leonard's Pipesnake is recorded from distinctly separate locations. The holotype and paratype were collected from Pahang, at an altitude of 260m in West Malaysia, but the species is also known from two specimens from Selangor, also West Malaysia. A single specimen collected in Sabah, northern Borneo, may be Leonard's Pipesnake or represent an undescribed species. A second species, Weber's Little Pipesnake (*A. weberi*) is known from Sumatra and Kalimantan, Borneo. As with many secretive semi-fossorial snakes, the little pipesnakes, sometimes referred to as 'false blindsnakes', are poorly documented, with few distributional or natural history records. Leonard's Little Pipesnake possesses a yellow bar across the head, in front of the eyes, and a series of large yellow spots extending down either side of the glossy black body. A larger red patch is present under the tail, a common feature of other pipesnakes that roll their tails over defensively to expose their subcaudal coloration and thereby distract attention from the head.

Range: West Malaysian peninsula and Sabah, Borneo • Max. length: 0.4m • Habitat: Lowland rainforest • Prey: Not known, presumed small and cylindrical • Reproduction: Presumed to be viviparous but a female contained four soft eggs • Similar species: Weber's Little Pipesnake (*A. weberi*)

mouth-gape than is possible for the little pipesnakes, they also prey on cylindrical, elongate prey like snakes or eels. They do not exhibit the considerable jaw mobility of more advanced snakes and their prey is therefore limited to what will pass through a fairly small mouth.

ASIAN PIPESNAKES

Ten species of Asian pipesnakes of the Cylindrophiidae are found from Sri Lanka to eastern Indonesia, but the majority of their range within the Southeast Asian region is occupied by one extremely widespread and well-known species, the Red-tailed Pipesnake, *Cylindrophis ruffus*. Another species, *C. maculatus*, the only South Asian member of the genus, is found in Sri Lanka; and two little-known species occur on the island of Borneo. The remaining six species are confined to the islands of eastern Indonesia.

Pipesnakes are semi-fossorial inhabitants of rainforests and other low-lying damp habitats. Although Asian pipesnakes possess mental grooves, folds of skin that permit a wider

ABOVE: *The Red-tailed Pipesnake* (Cylindrophis ruffus) *is the most common pipesnake in Southeast Asia.*

BELOW: *The Sri Lankan Pipesnake* (Cylindrophis maculatus) *rolls its tail in defence, exposing its checkerboard underside.*

Red-tailed Pipesnake *Cylindrophis ruffus*
The Red-tailed Pipesnake is very widely distributed throughout Southeast Asia, from northern Myanmar (Burma) as far south as Sulawesi (Indonesia), and northeast to southern China. A cylindrical snake with smooth scales, its dorsal patterning consists of scattered vertical white to cream, even orange, bars over a glossy black-brown background, the bars of the anterior body extending over the neck as collars and those on the tail, which ends with a sharp spine, being bright red. The undersides are black and cream. Red-tailed Pipesnakes are found in most low-lying humid habitats, either under leaf-litter or in the subsoil, emerging at night to hunt. Prey consists of other snakes, eels, elongate lizards, occasional small mammals and elongate vertebrates such as earthworms and centipedes. The pipesnake's defence consists of rolling its flattened tail over to expose the red underside, possibly mimicking the hood of a small cobra, or distracting attention away from the head.
Range: Southeast Asia • Max. length: 0.5–1.0m • Habitat: Humid lowland habitats • Prey: Snakes, eels and invertebrates • Reproduction: Viviparous, 3–13 neonates • Similar species: Lined Pipesnake (*C. lineatus*) from Borneo

Sri Lankan Pipesnake *Cylindrophis maculatus*
This is the only species in the family occurring outside the Indo-Australian archipelago. It is also probably the most brightly coloured member of the genus, being black-brown above with a series of large orange spots running parallel to the vertebrae, which are neatly marked by a fine black stripe. So large are the orange spots that they almost obscure all the background pigment, except on the head. The underside is chequered black and white.

The pipesnake is an inhabitant of Sri Lanka's central hill region to 1,000m, where it shelters under logs and rocks or in leaf-litter during the day, emerging at night to hunt other snakes including shieldtails (p.71) and small colubrids, in addition to slender invertebrates. It adopts the same defensive display as the red-tailed pipesnake (above) but may even flip over onto its back and remain there, exposing the chequer-board underbelly.
Range: Sri Lanka • Max. length: 0.6–0.7m • Habitat: Lowland paddi-fields and cultivated land • Prey: Snakes and earthworms • Reproduction: Viviparous, 1–15 neonates

SHIELDTAILS

The Uropeltidae is a uniquely South Asian family, containing 48 species in eight genera, including three monotypic genera (*Brachyophidion, Pseudotyphlops* and *Teretrurus*), two, three and four species in *Platyplecturus, Melanophidum* and *Plecturus* respectively, and the remaining species shared between *Rhinophis* (13 spp.) and *Uropeltis* (23 spp.). They are geographically divided between southern India (36 spp.) and Sri Lanka (14 spp.) with endemic genera inhabiting both countries.

Shieldtails, also known as rough-tails, thorntails or earthsnakes, are fossorial (burrowing) snakes. Some species possess small, conically-pointed heads, which end in a keratinized tip or bear a distinct keel to aid excavation. The eyes of these species are extremely small. Other species have more rounded heads and larger eyes. The body is stout, often in contrast to the diminutive head, and in most species the tail terminates suddenly, as if cut through at an oblique angle. This apparent truncation is covered by a variety of caudal shields, depending on the genus. In *Pseudotyphlops* this consists of a flat shield covered in numerous spines; in *Rhinophis* the shield is convex, rounded and rugose; in *Uropeltis* the shield consists of rows of highly keeled, spinous scales and terminates in two points linked by a transverse ridge. The shield collects a cap of mud effectively blocking the tunnel made by the burrowing snake and may act as a form of rear-guard defence.

These highly specialized burrowers range in size from 0.1–0.8m. Despite their subterranean habits, many shieldtails are brightly patterned. Some species are common, others known only from their type specimens. They are inoffensive and rarely bite, preferring to defend themselves by defecation, tail-poking or mouth-gaping. All shieldtails are believed to be viviparous.

BELOW: *The tiny head of Sri Lanka's Hemprich's Shieldtail* (Rhinophis homolepis) *is ideally designed for burrowing.* BELOW RIGHT: *The tail of Large-scaled Shieldtail* (Uropeltis macrolepis) *from India bears a rough scaly plate that collects soil and blocks the burrow behind it.*

Hemprich's Shieldtail *Rhinophis homolepis*

There is some confusion regarding this species, which also goes by the name of Trevelyan's Shieldtail (*R. trevelyanus*), but the name *R. homolepis* has taxonomic priority. This is a common hill-country species, often found in small colonies in gardens, paddi-fields, around cattle-pens and near water-courses. It hunts earthworms at night. The head is sharply pointed, the tail typical of *Rhinophis* with its rounded fleshy shield. The body is dark blue-grey above and yellow below, with the bright pigmentation extending upwards onto the flanks as a series of short triangular bars, the first of which, on the nape, meeting dorsally to form a collar. The entire tail shield is pink with a yellow margin.
Range: Central Sri Lanka • Max. length: 0.2–0.3m • Habitat: Paddi-fields, cattle-sheds and other agricultural areas near water • Prey: Earthworms • Reproduction: Viviparous, 2–4 neonates • Similar species: Drummond-Hay's Shieldtail (*R. drummondhayi*)

Large-scaled Shieldtail *Uropeltis macrolepis*

The head of the Large-scaled Shieldtail is slightly rounded, with relatively large dark eyes. The tail-shield is covered with numerous bi- or tricarinate scales which, when covered by mud, strongly resemble a dirty, scarred wound. Coloration is black above with or without numerous yellow spots, and bright yellow below, with the yellow extending upwards in a series of irregular yellow bars, the anterior-most of which extends forwards onto the nape, throat and lip scales. Two subspecies are recognized, both from the ancient forests of the northern Western Ghats of Maharashtra state, one distributed throughout the west of the state, the other confined to a small area around Mahableshwar. This latter subspecies bears a longitudinal dorsolateral yellow stripe. Nothing is known of the reproductive behaviour, although all shieldtails are presumed to be viviparous.
Range: Maharashtra, western India • Max. length: 0.30–0.33m • Habitat: Presumed paddi-fields and other habitats with loose soil • Prey: Earthworms • Reproduction: Presumed viviparous • Similar species: Elliot's Shieldtail (*U. ellioti*)

Asian Macrostomatan Snakes

The blindsnakes and pipesnakes prey on small, soft-bodied prey or elongate, cylindrical prey. At this level, however, begin the snakes that can feed on prey broader than their own heads, including small mammals and birds. For this they must possess highly adapted jaws and potentially large mouths; these are the Asian macrostomatan or big-mouthed snakes.

SUNBEAM SNAKES

Also known as iridescent earth snakes, the sunbeam snakes are named for the 'oil-on-water' iridescent sheen, which appears when their scales are exposed to natural daylight, a common hologrammic characteristic of nocturnal snakes including the Rainbow Boa (*Epicrates cenchria*, p.42) and the Amethystine Python (*Morelia amethistina*, p.139).

Sunbeam snakes throughout Southeast Asia are treated as a single species *Xenopeltis unicolor*, while those from the southern Chinese coastal provinces and the offshore island of Hainan are recognized as a second species, *X. hainanensis*. The two species can be distinguished by several scalation differences: *X. unicolor* (*X. hainanensis*) postoculars, 2(1); supralabials, 8(7); ventral scales, more than 180 (fewer than 165); pairs of subcaudals more than 25 and distinct from lateral scales (fewer than 20 and similar to laterals). The sunbeam snakes are sufficiently distinct from all other snakes to be placed in their own family, Xenopeltidae, a family considered most closely related to the Meso-American Python (*Loxocemus bicolor*, p.37) in the Loxocemidae.

The Sunbeam Snake (Xenopeltis unicolor) *is also known as the Iridescent Earth Snake, a reference to its oil-on-water coloration in sunlight.*

Sunbeam Snake *Xenopeltis unicolor*

The adult Sunbeam Snake is unicolour light or dark brown above and cream below, although this drab patterning is obscured by the iridescence of the scales. Juveniles possess a white neck-band which fades with age. It has large, smooth, shiny scales, a short tail and a relatively long, dorsally compressed head with small, dark eyes.

This snake can be extremely common, inhabiting rainforests, monsoon forests, gardens, paddi-fields, swampy areas and roadside ditches, especially in the monsoon season. It is a nocturnal snake which adopts a semi-fossorial existence, hiding and hunting beneath leaf-litter. The Sunbeam Snake is a very widely distributed species, occurring from Myanmar (Burma) and Yunnan Province in China, throughout the entire Southeast Asian mainland and on the major islands of Sumatra, Java, Borneo and Sulawesi, as well as the Nicobar Islands, the Philippine islands of Palawan and the Sulu Archipelago, and most intervening smaller islands.

Inoffensive and disinclined to bite, it has a catholic diet which includes lizards, other snakes, frogs, small mammals and ground-dwelling birds, but it appears to have a preference for elongate prey no wider than its own body, and lacks the prey-swallowing capabilities of a similar-sized python.

Range: Mainland and insular Southeast Asia • Max. length: 1.0–1.25m • Habitat: Lowland rainforests, freshwater swamps and paddi-fields • Prey: Elongate reptiles and amphibians, some small mammals and birds • Reproduction: Oviparous, 6–17 eggs • Similar species: Southern Chinese Sunbeam Snake (*X. hainanensis*)

OPPOSITE: *The Malaysian Spine-jawed Snake* (Xenophidion schaeferi) *is known from only two specimens, both from Peninsular Malaysia.*

SPINE-JAWED SNAKES

Both known species of spine-jawed snakes are extremely poorly documented in the wild and only represented in museum collections by their holotypes (the specimens from which they were originally described). The generic name, *Xenophidion*, translates as 'strange snake', a reference to the unusual physical characteristics that characterize the two species, including a spinous projection extending backwards from the upper jaw, only visible by dissection, from which they earn their common name.

The holotype of *X. acanthognathus* was collected in Sabah in 1987, the holotype of *X. schaeferi* on peninsular Malaysia in 1988, but they were not described to science until 1995. Early studies placed them either within the Colubridae, with the legions of other small, striped leaf-litter snakes, or in the Latin American dwarf boa-woodsnake family Tropidophiidae (pp.62–3), but more recent studies have led to the recognition of the separate family Xenophidiidae and the suggestion that they may actually represent the sister-clade to the Round Island boas of the Bolyeriidae (pp.110–11).

The spine-jawed snakes share several characteristics of the skull, and a total lack of the pelvic girdle, with the Round Island boas, and these morphological similarities, combined with their distribution south of the Asian mainland, have led researchers to suggest that both groups may also share a common Gondwanan heritage and ancestry.

Since the species in this obscure family are known only from their holotypes from locations on two separate land masses considerable distances apart, I request that anybody carrying out fieldwork in peninsular Malaysia, Sumatra or Borneo (Sarawak, Sabah, Brunei and Kalimantan) pay particular attention to any small leaf-litter snakes they find. At the moment these two small snakes must be amongst the rarest snake species in the world. It is difficult to be rarer than 'known only from holotype', since one fewer means 'unknown to science'.

Malaysian Spine-jawed Snake *Xenophidion schaeferi*

The holotype was collected and photographed on the borders of the Templer Park, 20km north of Kuala Lumpur, in 1988 and described in 1995. Fortunately, the holotype was photographed in life. The snake appears to be dark brown with a broad, light grey longitudinal zigzag stripe and a dark brown central stripe.

ABOVE: *The Malaysian Spine-jawed Snake* (Xenophidion schaeferi) *is known from only two specimens, both of which came from Peninsular Malaysia.*

OPPOSITE: *The Sunbeam Snake* (Xenopeltis unicolor) *is also known as the Iridescent Earth Snake, a reference to its oil-on-water coloration in sunlight.*

The unusual characteristics of the head scalation include the granulation of all the usual large head scutes posterior to the nasal region, a distinctly uncolubrid-like characteristic. A typical colubrid snake exhibits the 9-scute arrangement of 2 internasals, 2 prefrontals, 1 frontal between 2 supraoculars and 2 parietals, and any variation from this pattern is considered unusual. The complete loss or granulation into much smaller scales of all or most of these scutes is extremely rare in colubrids, though not unknown (ie. neotropical genus *Nothopsis*).

It is probable that this small snake exhibits similar ecological habits to the small colubrids with which it shares its leaf-litter habitat. The female holotype contained several large eggs and it probably fed on worms and/or insect larvae. The characteristic, large *Xenophidion* canine-like tooth on the anterior dentary bone of the jaw may have served the purpose of maintaining a strong grip on slimy prey.

Range: Peninsular Malaysia • Max. length: 0.26m • Habitat: Primary rainforest • Prey: Worms, insects and insect larvae • Reproduction: Oviparous, holotype contained several eggs • Similar species: Schaefer's Spine-jawed Snake (*X. acanthognathus*) from Sabah, north Borneo

Eurasian Sand Boas

The boas of the Old World are not the powerful constrictors of South America but the smaller, much more secretive sand and ground boas of the subfamily Erycinae. These short, stocky snakes possess granular scales, short tails and small heads with diminutive eyes. Distributed through North Africa, the Middle East and South Asia, with one species entering southeastern Europe, they are fossorial (burrowing) inhabitants of sand and earth in arid habitats like semi-desert and coastal scrub. They prey on small mammals and birds, which are ambushed as they pass the boa – buried in the sand – and are killed by constriction. Sand boas are usually nocturnal, although they may also be active during the day.

SAND BOAS

While the genus *Eryx* is sometimes used for all living species, some authors place the three most primitive species in the genus *Gongylophis*, leaving eight species in *Eryx*. The greatest sand boa diversity occurs in the Middle East.

Rough-scaled Sand Boa *Gongylophis conicus*

Also known as the Common Indian Sand Boa, this species is noted for its stout body and short tail, which are covered in rough, keeled scales. Even the posterior scales of the head are rugose, but the most strongly keeled are those on the posterior

body and tail. Coloration and patterning consist of a broad irregular dorsal zigzag of dark brown overlying a pale brown or pale grey background.

Found from Nepal in the north to Sri Lanka in the south (the only sand boa to inhabit that island and sometimes allocated subspecific status) the Rough-scaled Sand Boa is found throughout most of the South Asian peninsula, excluding more humid habitats. Prey includes small mammals, ground-dwelling birds and possibly lizards. The species exhibits considerable sexual dimorphism, the females being several times larger than the males. Although this sand boa resembles other sand boas from further west, it is more likely to be confused, at home, with the venomous Russell's Viper (*Daboia russelii*), a fact exploited by snake charmers, who prefer handling stroppy, but non-venomous, sand boas to lethal vipers.

Range: South Asia • **Max. length:** 1.0m • **Habitat:** Sandy beaches and cultivated land • **Prey:** Small mammals and birds • **Reproduction:** Viviparous, 3–16 neonates • **Similar species:** Russell's Viper (*Daboia russelii*)

Red Sand Boa *Eryx johnii*

The Red Sand Boa, also known as John's Sand Boa, grows slightly larger than the Rough-scaled Sand Boa but in contrast it possesses smooth scales and is generally unicolour brown or red. The two species occupy similar arid habitats across the same range and, although the Red Sand Boa is absent from Sri Lanka, it occurs further west than the Rough-scaled Sand Boa, into Afghanistan and Iran, where the population may warrant subspecific status. Juveniles may be patterned with small, indistinct black spots.

TOP: *The Red Sand Boa* (Eryx johnii) *occupies arid habitats from India to Iran. It has smooth scales, in contrast to the Rough-scaled Sand Boa.*

ABOVE: *The head of the Red Sand Boa is pointed, for burrowing, and the eyes are relatively small.*

LEFT: *Female Rough-scaled Sand Boas* (Gongylophis conicus) *are very much larger than the males.*

Another species popular with snake charmers, the Red Sand Boa is often billed as a 'two-headed snake', but this means one head at either end, since the tail is short, rounded and head-like. True dicephalic (two-headed) snakes are birth defects, with two heads at the same end, in other words Siamese twins. A smaller species with similar patterning has recently been described from southern India: Whitaker's Sand Boa (*E. whitakeri*), named for the highly-respected American herpetologist Rom Whitaker, who has been deeply involved in herpetology and conservation in India for most of his life.

Range: South Asia • Max. length: 1.3m • Habitat: Coastal scrub and semi-desert • Prey: Small mammals, birds and lizards • Reproduction: Viviparous, 6–8 neonates • Similar species: Whitaker's Sand Boa (*E. whitakeri*)

Javelin Sand Boa *Eryx jaculus*

The only boa in Europe, the Javelin Sand Boa also occurs in Africa, north of the Sahara, and across the Middle East, to Saudi Arabia in the south and Iran in the east. In the Middle East and the countries surrounding the Caspian Sea it occurs in sympatry with several other sand boa species, with which it may easily be confused. The Javelin Sand Boa is red-brown or grey-brown with darker brown spots. Less stout and of shorter length than the two previous species, it enters Europe in Greece and the Balkans and also occurs in the Cyclades and on Corfu. Being smaller in size than the other species, this sand boa also includes lizards and invertebrates in its diet. Three subspecies are recognized, of which two occur in Europe.

Range: Southeastern Europe, North Africa and Middle East • Max. length: 0.8m • Habitat: Sandy beaches, arable land and semi-desert • Prey: Small mammals, birds, lizards and some invertebrates • Reproduction: Viviparous, 6–20 neonates • Similar species: Russian or Desert Sand Boa (*E. miliaris*)

ABOVE: *Europe has a boa! The Javelin Sand Boa* (Eryx jaculus) *is found in Greece and the Balkans.*

Asian Pythons

Although only five species of pythons occur in tropical Asia, they are all impressive snakes, either due to their considerable length or formidable girth, and they comprise a very important portion of the herpetofauna. Unfortunately, the pythons of Asia are amongst the most abused of all snakes, many thousands being slaughtered for their skins, meat and gall bladders, despite international control measures to protect them. All the Asian pythons are also popularly kept as pets.

SHORT-TAILED PYTHONS

The three species of python known as blood or short-tailed pythons were long treated as subspecies of a single Southeast Asian species, *Python curtus*. Fairly sedentary in nature and much smaller than the other two Asian pythons, this short-tailed, stout-bodied snake has a reputation for truculence, many of the wild specimens available to keepers in the 1980s living up to the name 'blood python' by drawing as much of it as possible from their keepers. More recently, in 2001, the morphological differences between the three geographical subspecies were reinforced by molecular differences and the recognition of three full species is now fairly universally accepted. Molecular studies

revealed that the Sumatran and Bornean Short-tailed Pythons were closely related, with the distinctive Malaysian Short-tailed, or Blood, Python as their sister-clade, a factor mirrored by the various morphological differences between the three taxa, most particularly the presence or absence of subocular scales. This is a characteristic more important in Asian python taxonomy than the size of these actual scales might suggest (see Asian Rock Pythons, p.81).

It has been suggested that rising sea-levels split the ancestral short-tailed pythons into a mainland Southeast Asian population and a Bornean population. There is a theory that, between 10 and 20 million years ago, when eastern Sumatra was below sea-level, a land-bridge existed between Borneo and southern Sumatra, enabling the Bornean ancestor to cross to the western island. With a later drop in sea-levels, stock from the Malaysian mainland would have been able to invade the newly emerged eastern Sumatra, while the land-bridge between southern Sumatra and Borneo appears to have been broken, separating the two earlier linked populations which evolved into the two

The Sumatran Short-tailed Python (Python curtus) *is confined to western and southern Sumatra, Indonesia.*

closely related species of today. This theory may account for the presence of two species on the island of Sumatra, separated by a central mountain chain that may have inhibited trans-Sumatran gene-flow. The links between the islands of Borneo and Sumatra are strongly evident in the flora and fauna of the two islands, not least in the presence of orang-utans, which are absent from the Malaysian peninsula.

All three short-tailed pythons inhabit lowland rainforests, but they are also associated with man-made habitats such as oil-palm plantations. Their range seems centred in the wet tropical rainforest regions of Malaysia, Sumatra and Borneo. They are notably absent from the drier island of Java, which was already an isolated island at the time the short-tailed pythons were radiating, and their distribution on the Malay peninsular appears to halt in southern Thailand.

Short-tailed pythons are ambush predators of small mammals and ground-living birds, effectively lying hidden in the vegetation due to their cryptic body patterning. There is considerable inter-specific and intra-specific, even ontogenetic, variation in coloration and patterning in the short-tailed python complex. The species can usually be distinguished by their patterning alone, but differences also exist between individuals within a single population and juveniles of some populations may undergo a change in patterning with increased maturity. This variation in coloration and patterning within a population is known as 'polychromatism', and it is common in snakes that exhibit ambush behaviour.

In 1991, CITES (Convention on International Trade in Endangered Species of Wild Flora and Fauna) reported that between 70,000 and 200,000 short-tailed pythons were 'harvested' annually for their skins, meat and gall bladders. These three species could find themselves under threat of at least local extinction in the near future.

The Borneo Short-tailed Python (Python breitensteini) *was named in honour of a German doctor in the Dutch East Indian Army.*

Sumatran Short-tailed Python *Python curtus*

Although the first 'short-tail' (*curtus* means shortened) to be described scientifically, the Sumatran Short-tailed Python, found in southern and western Sumatra, Indonesia and on some of the offshore islands, is the least known of the three taxa. As now defined, it also has the most restricted range and is reportedly the smallest of the three short-tailed pythons.

Sumatran Short-tailed Pythons are dark snakes, black or dark grey with sometimes contrastingly pale-brown, but often equally black heads, a pattern which earns them the confusing and contradictory alternative name of 'black blood python' – they are never blood-red. Body patterning consists of black lateral blotches, with light grey centres and white edges, separated by pale grey spaces. Distinguishing characteristics in their scalation, which serve to separate this species from the Blood Python (*P. brongersmai*) found in the north and east of the island, include a lower ventral scale count (fewer than 166) and a series of up to eight small subocular scales, which serve to prevent contact between the supralabials and the eye itself. The presence of a single supraocular scale, and the anterior parietal scales being either widely separated or only in point-contact with one another, will also distinguish the Sumatran Short-tail from both other species.

Range: Southern and western Sumatra, Indonesia • Max. length: 1.0–1.9m • Habitat: Lowland rainforest and plantations, also offshore islands • Prey: Small mammals and birds • Reproduction: Oviparous, 24–46 eggs

Borneo Short-tailed Python *Python breitensteini*

The Borneo Short-tailed Python was named in honour of its collector, a German doctor who served as a regimental surgeon to the Dutch East Indian army, and who was also a keen collector of the Bornean herpetofauna. Originally described as a separate species, it was relegated by herpetologist Olive G. Stull, in her 1935 *Checklist of Family Boidae*, to a subspecies of the older *Python curtus*, and there it remained until 2001.

Borneo Short-tailed Pythons are pale brown to yellow-brown with dark-edged brown or yellowish-centred lateral blotches, separated by areas of pale cream, but there is considerable variation between specimens from different regions. The scalation of the Borneo short-tail is most like that of the Sumatran Short-tail (*P. curtus*), except that in the Borneo short-tail the anterior parietal scales are in broad contact. The characteristics which separate this species from the Blood Python (*P. brongersmai*) include the lower ventral scale count (fewer than 166) and the presence of a series of subocular scales, which prevent contact between the supralabials and the eye, the same characteristic that separate the Blood Python from the Sumatran Short-tail.

Range: Borneo (Malaysia, Brunei and Indonesia) • Max. length: 1.0–1.6m • Habitat: Lowland rainforest and cultivated land close to water • Prey: Small mammals and birds • Reproduction: Oviparous, 8–24 eggs

Blood Python *Python brongersmai*

The Blood Python, Malaysian Short-tailed Python, or Sumatran Red Blood Python, was described from a Singaporean specimen in 1935 by Olive Stull and named in honour of Leo D. Brongersma, a Dutch zoologist who worked for the natural history museums in both Leiden and London and who contributed greatly to our knowledge of the Indo-Australian herpetofauna.

Although the most recently named species, this is probably the most widespread of the short-tailed pythons, since it occurs from southern Thailand, through the Malaysian peninsula and out to the island of Sumatra, which it shares with the Sumatran Short-tailed Python *P. curtus*, and the intervening islands of Bangka and Billiton, which it does not. Whilst *P. curtus* is distributed through the western and southern parts of Sumatra, *P. brongersmai* occurs in the north and east. Whether the species occur in sympatry has not been determined; they are both primarily lowland snakes and the mountain range running down the centre of the island may serve to separate them geographically, although there are occasional reports of hybrid specimens entering the skin trade slaughterhouses. Reports of this species occurring further north on the mainland, around the Gulf of Thailand into Cambodia and Vietnam, may be in error. The presence of a specimen in the region should be treated with caution, since it may not necessarily indicate a naturally occurring population (see personal observation below).

Blood Pythons may have dark heads, even black that sometimes pales to grey, and their heads may be various shades from bright red to yellow tan, with yellow or orange dorsal markings and dark grey, lighter-edged, lateral blotches, although some specimens may be grey. Those specimens with bright red bodies are the pythons that truly deserve the name 'blood python'. Blood Pythons can achieve considerably longer lengths than the other two species, up to 2.6m in out-sized adult females, and can weigh as much as 22kg. They can also be identified by their greater ventral scale counts (more than 167),

ABOVE: *The Blood Python or Malaysian Short-tailed Python* (Python brongersmai) *is the largest and most variably patterned of the three species.*

OPPOSITE: *An Indian Rock Python* (Python molurus molurus) *photographed in its typical habitat of arid, sandy woodland in northern India.*

and the absence of subocular scales, resulting in direct, broad contact between the supralabial scales and the eye. Both bloods and Borneo short-tails possess anterior parietal scales that are in contact, in contrast to the Sumatran Short-tailed Python.
Range: South Thailand, peninsula Malaysia, Bangka and north and eastern Sumatra, Indonesia • Max. length: 1.5–2.6m • Habitat: Upland and lowland rainforests, and plantations • Prey: Small mammals and birds • Reproduction: Oviparous, 10–22 eggs

" I joined the Thai Wildlife and Forestry Police in a raid on an illegal reptile skin, meat and gall bladder factory, where we found a huge number of dead snakes, snake body parts, and a few live snakes which we rescued. Possibly alerted to the coming raid, the miscreants had thrown large sacks of frozen snakes over a back wall into the vegetation, where we found them. One of the sacks I examined contained several dead Blood Pythons *(P. brongersmai)*, a species only known

from the southern-most provinces of peninsular Thailand. Had these snakes been alive, I was told the authorities would probably have released them in the nearest 'suitable' habitat, rather than transporting them several hundred miles south to their true range. Such releases, outside natural ranges, cannot be considered good policy and specimens of commercially valuable species found outside their known ranges may mislead biologists with regard to the true distribution of that species. As an example, for many years the Burmese Rock Python *(P. molurus bivittatus)* was reported as occurring on the island of Borneo, but it is now thought that the specimens were released/escaped animals belonging to snake charmers from mainland Southeast Asia. Short-tailed Pythons may not suit a snake charmer's purpose but, since they are much in demand in the skin trade, there is likely to be illicit movement of live specimens."
Near Bangkok, Thailand.

ASIAN ROCK PYTHONS

The Asian Rock Python is a widely distributed South and Southeast Asian species and one of the most popular pythons in captivity, yet its exact range and the taxonomic status of some populations have been the source of discussion for over 200 years. One would think that determining the distribution of such a large snake would be a simple matter but, in view of the popularity of this species as a snake charmer's serpent or as a pet, the finding of a specimen in a strange location does not necessarily indicate a natural population. This fact has recently been brought to the fore by photographs and reports of a 'population of Burmese Rock Pythons' living in the Florida Everglades.

For many years three subspecies were recognized: the Indian, *P. m. molurus*; the Burmese, *P. m. bivitattus*; and the Ceylonese or Sri Lankan Rock Python, *P. m. pimbura*, but the insular isolation of this latter form was not sufficient to prevent it being synonymised with the Indian python. Even earlier names, such as *P. m. sondiaca* for the Indonesian population, have not survived the test of time, this name being synonymised with *P. m. bivittatus*. At the time of writing, the Asian Rock Python exists as a single species with two subspecies, *P. m. molurus* and *P. m. bivittatus*, which have been referred to as the 'light-phase Indian Python' and 'dark-phase Indian Python' respectively. These common names have fallen into disuse and I personally feel that these taxa should be allocated separate specific status, for reasons that will become apparent in their respective species accounts.

Although a large species, which may achieve lengths in excess of 5.0m, this is not the longest python species in Asia, though it may be the heaviest since it is much stouter-bodied than a Reticulated Python *P. reticulatus* of the same length.

Prey consists primarily of mammals, from rodents, though monkeys to pigs, goats and deer, and there is even a record of a leopard being killed and eaten. Birds, especially poultry, and lizards, to the size of monitor lizards, are also reported as prey. Although there are reports of humans being constricted and killed there is no authenticated record of anyone actually being eaten by an Asian Rock Python. The recent photographs of a dead Burmese Python, which had apparently killed and eaten an American alligator (*Alligator mississippiensis*) in the Florida Everglades, suggests, if genuine, that this is another species which may prey on small to medium-sized crocodilians. This is an exclusive club with few members, ie. the African and Southern African Rock Python, the Brown Water Python of New Guinea and northern Australia, and the Green and Yellow Anacondas of South America.

Female rock pythons lay large numbers of eggs, sometimes in excess of 100, around which they will coil during the incubation period. These large egg clutches, laid inside hollow trees or under piles of vegetation, would be extremely vulnerable to disturbance, predation or the elements were it not for the protective incubating female.

Throughout much of its range the Asian Rock Python is threatened by collection for skins, meat or gall bladders, or actively persecuted out of ignorance. In Pakistan and Bangladesh it is rare and, even in India, where it is legally

protected, and Sri Lanka, where Buddhist tradition does not permit unnecessary slaughter, it is still under pressure. Populations in Indochina, southern China and Indonesia are also highly threatened. The world is rapidly becoming a dangerous place for large snakes, which cannot hide as easily as their smaller relatives.

Indian Rock Python *Python molurus molurus*

This species was a favourite with snake charmers from the subcontinent and there are numerous late 19th- and early 20th-century postcards of the fakirs draped with these constrictors. Today both snake charming and ownership of pythons in India are illegal, the possession or killing of a python being worthy of one year in jail. Yet pythons are still persecuted, either deliberately or out of ignorance.

The Indian Rock Python can best be described as a heavy-bodied snake with a light grey to grey-brown ground colour overlaid with a dorsal pattern consisting of large, irregular, chestnut brown blotches edged with tan or yellow-brown and a series of pale-centred, dark-edged, lateral blotches running along the flanks. The head is pale brown with faint brown stripes that begin on the snout and extend to the eye before exiting the eye as a broad, pale-brown centred stripe extending to the angle of the jaw, and a second, narrower and shorter, stripe that descends vertically to the lips, directly under the eye. The dorsal pattern extends forwards onto the head as a brown arrowhead, with a pale central stripe. However, this arrowhead fades out completely before it reaches a point level with the eyes, so the anterior dorsum of the head is virtually unicolor. An important

ABOVE: *Head of Indian Rock Python* (Python molurus molurus), *demonstrating contact between the sixth supralabial and the eye.*

OPPOSITE: *A Burmese Rock Python* (Python molurus bivittatus) *in typical habitat, wet, riverine grassland, in northeastern India.*

characteristic in the scalation of the head of this subspecies is the absence of any subocular scales, thereby permitting contact between the 6th and/or 7th supralabials and the eye itself. This is a large species that can achieve lengths of over 7.0m in India, although specimens from Sri Lanka may be smaller, up to 6.0m. **Range: Peninsular India, Pakistan and Sri Lanka • Max. length: 3.0–7.6m • Habitat: Many habitats, but especially dry forest • Prey: Mammals from rodents to deer • Reproduction: Oviparous, 30–100+ eggs**

Burmese Rock Python *Python molurus bivittatus*

Once known as the dark-phase Indian Python and sometimes called the Tiger Python because of its patterning, the Burmese Rock Python is found throughout mainland Southeast Asia from Vietnam and Cambodia to Myanmar (Burma), although its range does not extend far down the Myanmar-Thai peninsula and it is absent from West Malaysia. To the east, this subspecies enters southern China, where it occurs from Yunnan to Fujian, including Hong Kong and Hainan Island, but not Taiwan as reported by earlier authors. To the northwest it enters northeastern India and may be found in the seven little-known states to the northeast of Bangladesh, most notably Assam. This large python does not occur in peninsular Thailand-Malaysia, south of the Isthmus of

Kra, nor on Borneo, where reports of specimens are generally discounted as escaped or released snake charmers' animals. Reports from Sumatra are generally doubted, although it is possible that it occurs in the extreme south of the island, but the python is positively known from the drier islands of Java and Sumbawa, if not the intervening islands of Bali and Lombok. The type specimen is reported to have come from Java, which means that, if the Indonesian population were to receive a taxonomic identity separate from the mainland form, it would retain the name *P. m. bivittatus* and a new name would be required for the popular Indochinese population. This disjunct distributional pattern – present on mainland southeast Asia; absent from the peninsula, Sumatra and Borneo, present again on Java – is mirrored by other snakes, most notably the medically important, highly venomous Russell's Viper (*Daboia russelii*) and Malayan Pitviper (*Calloselasma rhodostoma*). Early records from Sulawesi are also open to question, yet several authors do report specimens from there.

For many years Assam, in northeast India, was believed to represent the westernmost edge of the range of the *P. m. bivittatus*, the entire Indian subcontinent, from Pakistan to Bengal, Nepal to Sri Lanka, being inhabited by *P. m. molurus*. However, in 1992 I found three pythons in remote far western

Head of Burmese Rock Python (Python molurus bivittatus) *from Nepal, with subocular scale preventing contact between the sixth supralabial and the eye.*

Nepal which were clearly specimens of *P. m. bivittatus* and which extended the range of the subspecies 700km westward (see personal observation below). Subsequently this taxon has been discovered in Jim Corbett National Park in India, even further west that my reports. It now seems probable that this Indochinese form is found along the wet Ganges valley to the north of the drier habitats of the Indian subcontinental race inhabiting the Deccan plateau of peninsula India.

The Burmese Rock Python can be distinguished from the Indian Rock Python, *P. m. molurus*, by a combination of the following characteristics. The overall pattern is similar, large, irregular, brown dorsal saddles or blotches separated by yellow pigmentation, and smaller, pale-centred brown lateral blotches, but the background coloration tends towards the brown, rather than the pale grey of the Indian race. In addition, the brown arrow-head on the top of the head is distinct and extends fully to the snout. The most important difference is the presence of one or two subocular scales that separate the 6th and 7th supralabials from the eye. This is an important characteristic that has been instrumental in defining two clades within the short-tailed python complex (p.77) and may be equally important here to separate what I consider to be two distinct species. Further to these morphological differences, I believe the Indian populations of *P. m. bivittatus* may be separated from the northern populations of *P. m. molurus* on the basis of habitat preferences. I suggest that in areas where the two taxa exist in relatively close proximity the Indian Rock Python is found in the dry forests, on

arid sandy substrates, while the Burmese Rock Python inhabits the wet riverine grasslands. If this theory is true it would suggest the two taxa inhabit different habitats and may further warrant specific status under the evolutionary species concept.

Burmese Rock Pythons have long been popular in captivity, the species even being reported to have been bred in the Tower of London Zoo during the reign of King Henry VIII (1507–1547), and they are still popular today. There has been a trend to breed unusual cultivar colour phases and the most popular of these was the albino or Golden Python. Occasionally, unusual colour patterns are reportedly discovered in remote parts of mainland Southeast Asia, such as the Labyrinth Python, which was said to hail from an undisclosed mountain region in Thailand.

Range: Indo–China, northeast India, Nepal, and Java (Indonesia) • Max. length: 3.0–7.0m • Habitat: Many habitats but especially wet forests and grasslands near water • Prey: Mammals from rodents to deer • Reproduction: Oviparous, 30–100+ eggs

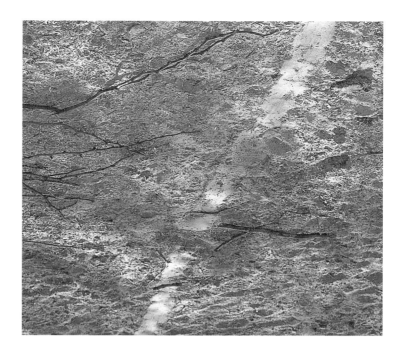

ABOVE: *An Indian Rock Python (Python molurus molurus) trail in Keoladeo Park, northern India. Following this trail led the author to several pythons grouped around porcupine burrows.*

BELOW: *The author (right) and his team in west Nepal with a 4.4m Burmese Rock Python* (Python molurus bivittatus), *one of the first three specimens from the country, the furthest west it has been recorded.*

"Whilst participating in the second of two expeditions (1991–92) to Royal Bardia National Park, located in the terai forests of southern Nepal, my attention was called to the presence of three pythons within a 24-hour period. My team and I investigated each in turn

and were very surprised by what we found. All three were female, the first being a 2.95m specimen with injuries suggesting leopard attack. We travelled to the location on elephant-back due to the large tiger population in the area. The python was found and caught in a shallow pond under a fallen tree. The second specimen, measuring 3.84m, was taken on a pile of riverine driftwood just above the Karnali River, while the third, measuring 4.42m, was captured inside a hollow tree on the river-bank. All three pythons, which were later released, had the yellow-brown background colour and complete dorsal head-arrows of *P. m. bivittatus* and all three possessed subocular scales. I had expected to find Indian Rock Pythons but actually discovered Burmese Rock Pythons, 700km west of their documented range."

Royal Bardia National Park, West Nepal

"We made a film about the feeding dynamics of Asian Rock Pythons in the Indian states of Assam, Chattisgarh, Madhya Pradesh and Rajasthan. Rock pythons are protected in India and in order to handle specimens one requires a licence from the wildlife authorities – I was apparently issued with licence No.1! We found a number of specimens of *Python molurus*, in differing habitats. In Assam we captured two clearly identifiable Burmese Rock Pythons, a small male and a 5.25m female, both in the high elephant grass on the riverine flood plain, a further specimen being found in the Garumara Wildlife Sanctuary.

In Chattisgarh a specimen of Indian Rock Python was found, wedged tightly in a rock crevice, but in the Keoladeo National Park in Rajasthan we encountered one of the highest densities of pythons in India. This former hunting preserve, now a wildlife and waterbird sanctuary, has colonies of Indian Rock Pythons big enough to warrant the title 'Indian Python Central'. India's foremost python expert, Dr S. Bhupathy who, ironically, is not permitted to actually touch his protected study animals, has devoted a great deal of time to this fascinating colony, which lives in the numerous complexes of mammal burrows located in an area of dry thorn forest on an arid sandy substrate."

North and northeast India.

A Burmese Rock Python (Python molurus bivittatus) *is a popular pet species, but owners should realize it can grow to almost 7.0m in length and kill deer.*

RETICULATED PYTHON

Sometimes known as the Regal Python, and not to be confused with the Royal Python (*Python regius*, p.101), the Reticulated Python holds the record for achieving the greatest length of any species, with historical giants reported at 9.0–10.0m, and 7.0m specimens receiving worldwide newspaper coverage today. Yet these fairly slender-bodied species do not achieve the body girth of the other giants, the Green Anaconda, *Eunectes murinus*, African Rock Python, *P. sebae*, and Asian Rock Python, *P. molurus*.

Reticulated Python *Python reticulatus*

This python is distributed over a vast area, from Assam in the northwest, throughout mainland Southeast Asia, excluding southern China, and southeast through the Indo-Malay archipelago from the Nicobar and Mentawai Islands, north and west of Sumatra, to the Lesser Sundas, Tanimbar Islands and Maluku (Moluccan Islands) to the south and southwest of New Guinea. At the southeastern extent of its range the Asian Reticulated Python occurs in sympatry with several of the Australasian pythons, namely water pythons from the *Liasis mackloti-fuscus* complex (p.122), the Lesser Sunda Python *P. timoriensis* (p.147), and several of the scrub pythons belonging to the *Morelia amethistina* complex (p.139). The Reticulated Python is the only python recorded from the Philippines and, although distribution maps show it as

occurring as far north as Luzon, we have found it on the remote island of Itbayat in the northern Batanes islands, which are located closer to Taiwan than Luzon. This constitutes the northeasternmost record for the species. Reticulated Pythons are excellent colonists, adept at crossing the straits between island groups. A Reticulated Python was the first snake recorded in the Krakatau islands, only 22 years after a volcanic eruption extinguished all life in 1883, having clearly reached the archipelago from either Sumatra or Java. Reticulated Pythons are reported from sea-level to over 1,500m altitude. Their habitat is primarily rainforest or monsoon forest, but plantations, swamps and cultivated lands are also inhabited by them, although locations near water are preferred.

Maximum size in 'retics' also seems to be a localized trait, with the largest specimens reported from the southeast of the range, from Sulawesi in Indonesia. Other islands are inhabited by dwarf populations, as would be expected for islands with more limited resources. However, at the time of writing, two island populations have been described as subspecies in the academic literature.*

The Selayar and Tanah-jampea Islands are located, 60km apart, to the south of Sulawesi, but despite the small distances involved these islands are isolated by the prevailing oceanic currents to such an extent that the subspecies described, *P. reticulatus saputrai* and *P. r. jampeanus* respectively, are both morphologically and molecularly distinct from both each other and from Sulawesi and Lesser Sunda Reticulated Pythons. All other populations of Reticulated Python, from Assam to Itbayat, to Tanimbar, are still treated as the nominate race, *P. r. reticulatus*, but there is little doubt that this situation will change as additional distinct populations are recognized and described.

Reticulated Pythons are so named for their reticulate patterning, a characteristic network of browns, greys and yellows presenting a broken, zigzagging dorsal stripe with parallel lateral rows of pale spots, edged with dark pigment. In some populations the elongate heads may be vivid yellow, a colour emphasized by the a black line running right down the centre of the crown, while in others the head colouration, and even the body patterning, may be more subdued. Whereas the overall body shape of African and Asian Rock Pythons is somewhat similar, the Reticulated Python, with its elongate head and slender body-build, appears more similar to some of the pythons of Australasia, namely the Scrub Python complex, Oenpelli Python and Lesser Sunda Python. It is possible that the more slim-line body and long head are more suitable for an island-dwelling python than the heavy-set build of the rock pythons. Reticulated Pythons are expert swimmers.

Preferred habitat is rainforest, but Retics may be found in most habitats within their range, even swimming out at sea. Juvenile Reticulated Pythons are highly arboreal, probably hunting and certainly sleeping aloft. Retics from hatchlings to 2.0m juveniles may frequently be observed sleeping on thin branches overhanging water, a behaviour I found most interesting in Thailand. It is likely that the larger, heavier adults spend an increasing amount of time on the ground, where they are more likely to encounter prey of their preferred size.

The preferred prey of Reticulated Pythons is strongly

ABOVE: *The most widely distributed python in Asia, the Reticulated Python* (Python reticulatus) *may achieve lengths of up to 10.0m.*

OPPOSITE: *The author discovered that young Reticulated Pythons sleep on branches over deep water, into which they will plunge to escape.*

ABOVE: *A large Reticulated Python* (Python reticulatus) *is capable of killing and swallowing large prey, including man on occasion.*

OPPOSITE: *Over half a million Reticulated Python skins are harvested in Borneo and Sumatra each year, threatening the species with extinction, at least locally.*

influenced, as would be expected, by their size. Juveniles prey primarily on small mammals such as rodents, but at 3.0 to 4.0m they adjust their prey preferences upwards towards larger mammals such as pangolins, porcupines, essentially swallowed head-first, monkeys, wild pigs, goats, smaller deer and village dogs, as well as some of the smaller carnivores, such as civets. Frank Buck, the famous 1930s 'Bring 'em Back Alive' animal collector, produced a photograph of a Reticulated Python coiled about a tiger, and also recounted a story in which a leopard was captured, constricted, killed and eaten. If these dated accounts appear far-fetched, a much more recent scientific account (2005) is available, detailing the predation of an adult female sun bear in Borneo. Of course, this is one of the few species of snakes well documented as also preying on humans (p.28). Both juveniles and adults will also take birds, with chickens and other domestic fowl popular prey species, and adults occasionally also feed on monitor lizards.

Female Reticulated Pythons, depending on size, lay from 50 to well over 100 eggs that take from 65 to 105 days to incubate, the hatchlings measuring 0.5 to 0.6m, but the offspring of dwarf insular populations are significantly smaller.

Reticulated Pythons are protected by CITES (Convention on International Trade in Endangered Species of Wild Flora and Fauna) as are all pythons, but these laws are largely designed to prevent or control cross-border international trafficking in wildlife and its derivatives. A great many Retics are harvested for their skins, meat and gall bladders within a nation's boundaries. In 1991 CITES estimated that upwards of half a million Reticulated Pythons were 'harvested' each year in Sumatra and Borneo alone.

* Auliya, M., Mausfeld, P., Schmitz, A. and Böhme, W., 2002, 'Review of the reticulated python (*Python reticulatus* Schneider, 1801) with the description of new subspecies from Indonesia.' *Naturwissenschaften* 89:201–213.

Range: Southeast Asia from Assam to eastern Indonesia and the Philippines • Max. length: 6.0–10.0m • Habitat: Most, but especially rainforest • Prey: Mammals from rodents to deer, birds and lizards • Reproduction: Oviparous, 50–124 eggs

While in Thailand on a film trip, I found 13 Reticulated Pythons in two distinctly different locations. One, a 3.0m specimen with injuries that appeared to have resulted from a barely survived encounter with a leopard or similar predator, was found sheltering inside a fallen tree beside the Phetcha-buri River on the Thai-Myanmar border, but it was the other twelve (1.0 to 2.0m) specimens which we found most interesting. Four of these were also found along

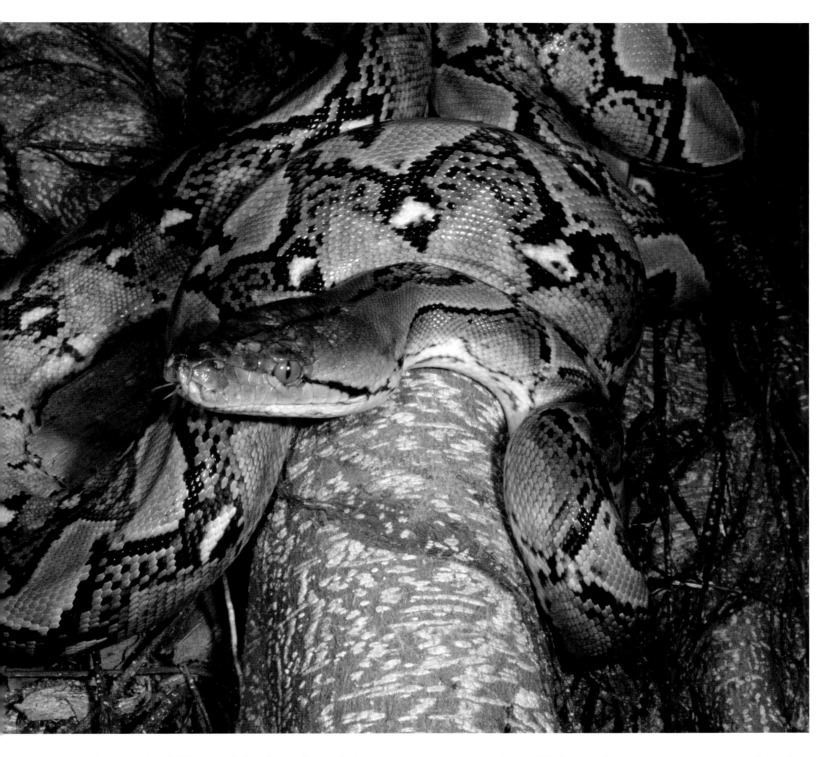

the Phetchaburi River, while the other eight were found along the tidal, mangrove-fringed, Lo Po Creek on Tarutao Island, off the south coast. All these small pythons were resting or sleeping on narrow branches at heights of between 2 and 15m above the surface of the river or creek. If the branch on which they rested was disturbed, they demonstrated a typical escape mechanism – they leapt from the branch and plunged into the water. We were soon able to use this behaviour to our advantage, with a colleague shaking the tree while I stood underneath preparing to catch the plummeting snake. Escape into water is a common behaviour of snakes, but I was left with a question. All the pythons we encountered had positioned themselves over deepish water – on the non-tidal rainforest Phetchaburi River they were over the deeper 'pools' rather than the shallow 'riffles'. And on the tidal Lo Po creek, they were also over the deeper sections, something difficult to gauge at high tide for an animal with good vision, let alone a python resting metres above the water surface. I was wondering how they knew where to rest so that they could escape, not just into water, but into water deep enough to take their dive."

Kaeng Krachen National Park & Tarutao Island, Thailand

AFRICA AND THE INDIAN OCEAN ISLANDS

Sub-Saharan Africa is python territory, with four species of true pythons (Pythonidae) occurring throughout the southern two-thirds of the continent. Two of these are large species, capable of killing and eating large mammals, occasionally even man. Pythons are found in most habitats, from grassland and rocky hillsides to rainforest and coastal forest, but they are absent from extremely arid desert regions. The drier parts of North and East Africa are the preserve of the burrowing sand boas of the Erycinae, which also have relatives in India, the Middle East and southeastern Europe.

West and Central Africa is home to a strange little snake, the Calabar Ground Boa (or is it a python?), which inhabits rainforests and plantations.

Both blindsnakes and slender blindsnakes are distributed throughout sub-Saharan Africa, the slender blindsnakes also being found to the north and east.

Although Africa is python territory, they are absent from the island of Madagascar, the fourth largest in the world and located in the Indian Ocean off Mozambique. Like Africa and India, Madagascar was a fragment of the northward-moving Gondwanaland but, unlike the other two land masses, it never collided with Laurasia or felt the influence of its flora and fauna. Instead of monkeys, Madagascar retains lemurs; instead of the lizard family Agamidae, Madagascar possesses a family known as the Opluridae, related to the Iguanidae of South America; and instead of pythons, Madagascar has three true boas, which represent the sister clade to the boas of South America. Madagascar may be a snapshot of how Africa might have been, had it not crashed into Eurasia with such force that the drawbridge came down and allowed the invaders across.

Finally, there is an island out in the middle of the Indian Ocean known as Round Island. It is, or was, home to two species of extremely primitive boas which warrant their own family, the Bolyeriidae. However, one of these unique species may have become extinct in the last 40 years.

The small and docile Royal Python (Python regius), *called Ball Python in America, is the most popular python or boa in captivity, a fact that almost threatened its continued existence in West Africa.*

African Blindsnakes

Two families of blindsnakes are found in Africa and the islands of the Indian Ocean, almost equally split between the Typhlopidae and the Leptotyphlopidae. However, Africa is also home to numerous genera of legless skinks (lizards), with which these snakes may be easily confused.

SLENDER BLINDSNAKES

The are 40 species of leptotyphlopid blindsnakes known from Africa and the Indian Ocean islands, 39 in the genus *Leptotyphlops* and the monotypic *Rhinoleptus koniagui* from Senegal and Guinea. One *Leptotyphlops* ranges from North Africa, through the Middle East to Pakistan; another, West African, species also occurs on Fernando Po island, off

BELOW: *Hook-snouted Slender Blindsnake* (Leptotyphlops macrorhynchus) *set against a local (Omani) coin to demonstrate its small size and extremely etiolated body shape.*

OPPOSITE: *Bibron's Blindsnake* (Typhlops bibroni). *Note the spine on the tail tip to aid movement through underground burrows.*

Cameroon; while Pemba Island, off Tanzania, has an endemic species; and Socotra, off the Horn of Africa, is home to three further endemics. Slender blindsnakes are extremely etiolated and even more likely to be mistaken for worms than the slightly more heavily built typhlopid blindsnakes.

Hook-snouted Slender Blindsnake *Leptotyphlops macrorhynchus*

This is a widely distributed Afro-Asian species which occurs in scattered locations across all the Saharan countries and then extends through the Middle East to Afghanistan and Pakistan. Slender of body with a protruding rostral scale on its snout for excavation, the Hook-snouted Slender Blindsnake is poorly known despite its wide distribution. It has 14 scale rows around the body, hence it is very slender, and in coloration it is pale red-brown above and whitish below. Preferred habitats include *Acacia* thicket and the roots of savanna grasses.

Range: North Africa to Pakistan • Max. length: 0.22–0.24m Habitat: Semi-desert and arid thicket-savanna • Prey: Termites and their eggs and larvae • Reproduction: Oviparous, 2–4 eggs

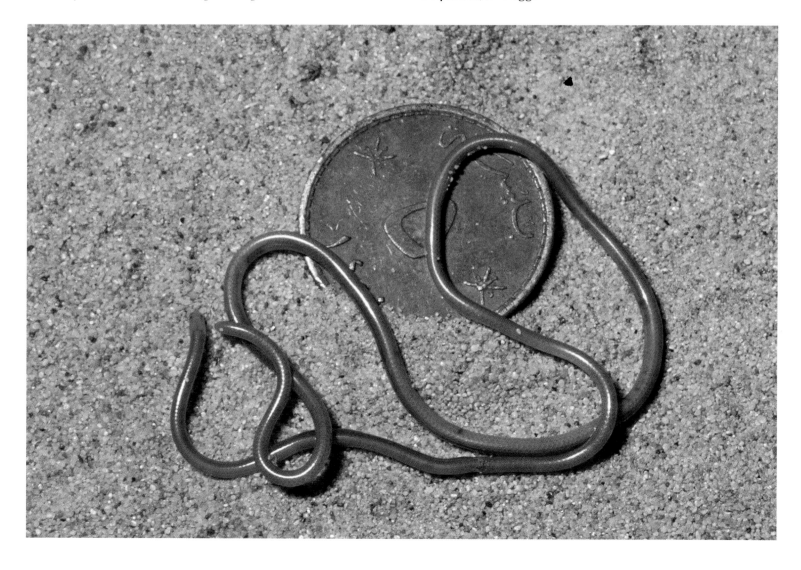

Long-tailed Slender Blindsnake *Leptotyphlops longicaudus*

Occurring from coastal Kenya to Transvaal, South Africa, and Swaziland, the Long-tailed Slender Blindsnake has a much longer tail than most other members of the genus, and also differs from the Hook-snouted Blindsnake in that its snout is rounded. Clearly it lives in softer substrate than its arid habitat relative and has an easier time of digging. Red-brown in colour, this is a species with a distinct preference for coastal habitats. They are preyed upon by other snakes, including centipede-eaters (*Aparallactus* spp.), and even scorpions, and may be confused with some of the slender burrowing legless skinks.
Range: East and southern Africa • Max. length: 0.12–0.25m Habitat: Wet savanna and coastal forests • Prey: Termites and their eggs and larvae • Reproduction: Oviparous, 2–4 eggs • Similar species: Limbless skinks (*Melanoseps* spp.)

BLINDSNAKES

There are approximately 46 species of blindsnakes on the African continent, split almost equally between the two genera *Typhlops* (21 spp.) and *Rhinotyphlops* (25 spp.). In addition, two endemic *Rhinotyphlops* and an endemic *Typhlops* occur on São Tome and Principe, small islands located in the Gulf of Guinea, while the island of Madagascar in the Indian Ocean is home to eight species of *Typhlops* and the endemic monotypic *Xenotyphlops grandidieri*, which is known from only two

specimens. Mauritius, the Comoro Islands, and Socotra, far to the north between Yemen and the Horn of Africa, are each home to an endemic *Typhlops*.

The main difference between *Rhinotyphlops* and *Typhlops* is the broad rostral scale of *Rhinotyphlops* that usually protrudes forwards and downwards as a digging device, the snout of *Typhlops* being more rounded. *Rhinotyphlops* is primarily an African genus, only two species occurring outside the region, from Israel to Turkey, while *Typhlops* is well represented in Asia, America and the Pacific. It is likely that the shovel-snout rostral of *Rhinotyphlops* is a development for excavating through parched African soil and sand, as opposed to damp tropical forest soil favoured by *Typhlops*. All blindsnakes are rarely observed, unless uncovered during digging, or encountered on the surface at night, after heavy rain.

Bibron's Blindsnake *Typhlops bibroni*

Bibron's Blindsnake is found from the Transvaal to KwaZulu-Natal in South Africa, with another population on the Zimbabwe-Mozambique border to the north. It is a fairly stocky species with over 30 transverse scale rows around the body, which is dark brown above and paler below. Females lay a relatively large clutch of eggs, up to 14, and unlike many other snakes they will guard the eggs until they hatch. Although perfectly harmless, the stout-bodied nature of this species could lead to its being confused with the more dangerous Bibron's Stiletto Snake (*Atractaspis bibroni*) or, more seriously, Bibron's

Stiletto Snake being confused with Bibron's Blindsnake.
Range: Eastern southern Africa • Max. length: 0.30–0.48m •
Habitat: Wet savanna, coastal forest and grassland • Prey:
Termites and their eggs and larvae • Reproduction:
Oviparous, 5–14 eggs • Similar species: Bibron's Stiletto
Snake (*Atractaspis bibroni*) or Fornasini's Blindsnake (*T.
fornasinii*)

Delalande's Beaked Blindsnake *Rhinotyphlops lalandei*

This is an extremely slender species of blindsnake, with 26–28
scales transversely around the body but more than 300 rows
longitudinally. It is pink to slate-grey in colour, every scale
edged with lighter pigment to present a chequered effect.
Delalande's Blindsnake is distributed through a broad swathe
of eastern and central southern Africa from Zimbabwe and
eastern Botswana to the Cape and north to Namaqualand, with
isolated pockets in Namibia. In common with other
blindsnakes of its proportions, it feeds on termites and their
eggs and larvae and is itself predated by the small venomous
Spotted Harlequin Snake (*Homoroselaps lacteus*).

Delalande's Beaked Blindsnake (Rhinotyphlops lalandei) *feeds on
termites but is itself preyed upon by other snakes.*

Range: Central southern Africa • Max. length: 0.25–0.35m •
Habitat: Temperate savanna, fynbos, coastal bush and semi-
desert • Prey: Termites and their eggs and larvae •
Reproduction: Oviparous, 2–4 eggs • Similar species:
Schinz's Beaked Blindsnake (*R. schinzi*)

Schlegel's Blindsnake *Rhinotyphlops schlegeli*

This species is large for a blindsnake. It may measure as much
as 1.0m in length and have a body diameter of 3cm (as fat as a
thumb), which puts it on a par with medium-sized semi-
fossorial colubrids and elapids. It is certainly the largest
blindsnake in Africa and probably the largest in the world.
However, the shiny, smooth scales, short-stumpy tail,
protecting sharp snout and diminutive eyes reduced to small
areas of pigmentation under translucent scales, make identification easy for anyone prepared to look more closely.

Patterning can be extremely variable throughout the range of

ABOVE: *Schlegel's Beaked Blindsnake* (Rhinotyphlops schlegeli) *is the largest blindsnake in Africa, possibly in the world.* BELOW: *Head of Schlegel's Beaked Blindsnake, showing large burrowing rostral scale and tiny eyes.*

this species, varying from dark scale edging, resulting in a reticulated appearance, to scattered patches of black or brown scales on a white or pale blue-grey background.

Four geographical subspecies are recognized: from Ethiopia-Somalia; Transvaal-southern Mozambique; Tanzania to Zimbabwe-south-central Mozambique; and northern Namibia-Botswana, although some authors treat these subspecies as full species.

This being a large species, adult females may lay up to 60 eggs, and possibly take a wider variety of invertebrate prey than their smaller, more slimline relatives but, being large, this blindsnake is also high on the list of prey for many of southern Africa's ophiophagous snakes including the purple-glossed snake (*Ambylodipsas* spp.). It is rarely seen on the surface, preferring to burrow deeply, only venturing abroad following

heavy rain. I believe this is the only blindsnake I have ever seen as a road-kill.

Range: Tropical Africa • Max. length: 0.6–1.0m • Habitat: Coastal forest, wet savanna • Prey: Termites and their eggs and larvae • Reproduction: Oviparous, 12–60 eggs • Similar species: Bibron's Stiletto Snake (*Atractaspis bibroni*)

African Boas

Boas are not generally associated with Africa and the mainland does not house any large species comparable to those occurring in the Americas. However, there are relatively small burrowing species in the north of the continent which are closely related to those occurring in the Middle East and South Asia.

SAND AND GROUND BOAS

Sand boas are short, stocky-bodied snakes with tiny granular scales, short tails, small heads and diminutive eyes. They adopt a primarily fossorial (burrowing) existence in the sand or earth of arid habitats like desert, semi-desert or dry grassland. They are predators of small vertebrates, which they capture from ambush and then constrict.

Some authors place all living sand boas in the genus *Eryx*, reserving the genus *Gongylophis* for primitive, extinct, paleontological species. Other authors place three extant species (two African, one Asian) in *Gongylophis*. Accepting the validity of this genus for three living species leaves eight species in *Eryx*. *Eryx* is primarily a Middle-Eastern/Asian genus which includes one eastern Mediterranean species that also occurs in North Africa (*E. jaculus*), and one, possibly two, endemic African species from

The East African Sand Boa (Gongylophis colubrinus) *is a widespread and fairly variable species found from Egypt south to Tanzania.*

the Horn of Africa. Not all African boas inhabit arid desert or savanna habitats – the Calabar Ground Boa is a curious species confined to the rainforest and plantations of West Africa.

East African Sand Boa *Gongylophis colubrinus*

The East African Sand Boa is one of the best known sand boas and a popular species in captivity. Hobbyists tend to recognize two subspecies, the Egyptian Sand Boa (*E. c. colubrinus*) from Egypt and Sudan and west as far as Niger, and the Kenyan Sand Boa (*E. c. loveridgei*) from Kenya, northern Tanzania and the Horn of Africa, but the validity of the subspecies has recently been called into doubt.

The general coloration is white below and orange or tan above, the dorsal pigment being blotched with irregular dark brown spots that in some specimens almost coalesce to obscure the background colour. Once given subspecific rank, this heavily pigmented form is now considered simply a colour

phase. The body is especially stout, the tail short and the head slightly pointed, without an obvious neck.

These sand boas occur from sea-level to 1,500m altitude in a wide variety of arid habitats, and where the ground is too hard for them to burrow they will inhabit small mammal burrows or the loose sand of dry riverbeds. Juveniles ambush lizards while adults prey on small mammals or ground-dwelling birds. Although perfectly harmless, sand boas are feared by local people who believe a bite kills before the victim can walk seven steps, a story probably resulting from confusion with the highly venomous Carpet Viper (*Echis pyramidium*), to which the sand boa bears a passing resemblance. As is the case with many sand boa species, adult females may be twice the length and several times the weight of adult males.

Range: East Africa • Max. length: 0.5–0.9m • Habitat: Desert, semi-desert and arid savanna • Prey: Small mammals, lizards, occasionally birds • Reproduction: Viviparous, 4–20 neonates • Similar species: Saharan Sand Boa (*G. muelleri*) and Carpet Viper (*Echis pyramidium*)

Somali Sand Boa *Eryx somalicus*

First described in 1939, the Somali Sand Boa remains one of the rarest and least studied species, with just seven specimens existing in museum collections. A brown snake with or without dorsal markings, it reportedly exhibits large head scales, and fewer scale rows at midbody than the more widespread East African Sand Boa (*G. colubrinus*). It inhabits the arid centre of the Somali peninsula, to an altitude of 1,050m, where the other species has not been recorded. More recently (2005) another species, *E. borrii*, has been described from Somalia, but its relationships to *E. somalicus* has not been determined. There is clearly much scope for herpetological study in this currently dangerous and war-torn region.

Range: Somalia, Djibouti and Ethiopia, possibly west to Central African Republic • Max. length: 0.4m • Habitat: Sparse thorny woodland and grassland • Prey: Presumed small mammals • Reproduction: Presumed viviparous, no data on clutch size • Similar species: Javelin Sand Boa (*E. jaculus*)

Calabar Ground Boa *Calabaria reinhardti*

The relationships of this species are hard to determine. It was originally described in the genus *Eryx*, the sand boas, before being transferred to its own genus, *Calabaria*, named for the region of Nigeria where it is common. It has been called a python and placed first in the Pythoninae, then in the monotypic Calabarinae, again as a python, before more recently being included in the Rosy and Rubber Boa genus *Charina* as the only non-American species.

The resemblance between the Calabar Ground Boa and an American Rubber Boa is uncanny: they are both cylindrical, with short rounded heads and tails, tiny eyes and the habit of 'balling' defensively with the head protected in the centre of the coils and the head-like tail exposed as a distraction. It seems very likely that the Erycinae is the correct subfamily for this curious snake but I prefer to retain the genus *Calabaria*, rather than include it in *Charina*, as a reflection of the great distances that separate this West African species from the west coast American Rosy and Rubber boas, and the fact that the Calabar Ground Boa is oviparous, a distinctly un-boa trait. This single feature has resulted in the species being called a ground python, rather than a ground boa, yet there are no other pythons in the world that resemble it in body shape. Nor do the eggs resemble those of pythons, which are oval in shape. Rather, they are extremely elongate and, being four times as long as wide, they more resemble ground-nuts than snake eggs.

This species also differs from all the other members of the Erycinae in its preference for rainforest or similar densely vegetated habitat over arid woodland or semi-desert. It occurs in the more vegetated region, to the south of the arid country inhabited by the Saharan Sand Boa *Gongylophis muelleri*, from Sierra Leone to Congo.

In coloration this is a brownish snake with randomly scattered bright red or orange scales, and white bands on the underside of its tail and chin, further confusing which is the head and which the tail end. In this respect it also resembled the pipesnakes

The Calabar Ground Boa (Calabaria reinhardti) *was long considered a python. It differs from other burrowing boas by occuring in forests and by laying eggss.*

(*Cylindrophis*) of Southeast Asia. This really is a most un-African of African snakes. Its prey is believed to consist of nestling small mammals that it hunts in subterranean burrows. It is rarely seen on the surface, except at night or in the early morning after heavy rain.
Range: West Africa • Max. length: 0.6–1.0m • Habitat: Rainforest and plantations • Prey: Small mammals • Reproduction: Oviparous, 1–4 eggs • Similar species: Rubber Boa (*Charina bottae*) or Asian pipesnakes (*Cylindrophis* spp.)

" I have only captured two specimens, both in the early morning on a dirt road cut through an oil palm plantation. The way the road was worn meant that snakes falling into the cutting frequently found it difficult to climb out again and I would walk the road at night or in the early hours looking for them. I caught several interesting species in this fashion, including specimens of the venomous burrowing asps *Atractaspis corpulenta* and *A. reticulatus*, as well as two Calabar Ground Boas."
Plantation bordering Korup National Park, western Cameroon

African Pythons

The vast continent of Africa is only home to four true pythons, two small species and two large. If sand boas dominate the north and east of Africa, then the pythons hold sway in the west and south, although there are areas of overlap where representatives of both families occur in sympatry.

SMALL PYTHONS

The small species are found in the savannas and woodlands of western and central Africa. One species, the Royal Python, has become probably the second most popular snake in captivity after the American Cornsnake, *Pantherophis guttatus*, whilst the other, the Angola Python, is protected and has been largely overlooked.

Royal or Ball Python *Python regius*

In the United Kingdom and much of the English-speaking world this species is called 'Royal Python', from the scientific name, but in the USA the preferred name is 'Ball Python' because of its famous habit of rolling into a ball when it feels threatened, with the head in the centre of the coils for protection. Otherwise the python has little defence; it rarely defends itself by biting and this was probably a factor behind its popularity in captivity. In the late 20th century literally tens of thousands of specimens were exported from their West African homes to Europe and the USA to supply demand for a small, docile python. This trade posed a serious threat to the survival of the species, at least locally, especially because the snakes often arrived diseased and parasitized, and then refused to feed, often fasting to death over a 12- to 15-month period. In my years at the Safari Park I have been brought dozens of Royals that refused to feed for their owners and some of these would not even feed for me. However, the situation has been changing and the Royal/Ball Python looks like becoming the snake pet of choice in the 21st century without causing the extinction of the species in the wild (see below).

It is often thought that this is a rainforest species, but in truth

The ever popular and attractively patterned Royal Python (Python regius). This is a typical specimen with patterning as seen in the wild.

LEFT: *A high-yellow cultivar phase of Royal Python* (Python regius). *These selectively captive-bred phases are more popular with pet keepers than the wild form.*

ABOVE: *The only 'whitesmoke' cultivar phase of Royal Python in the world (at the time of writing). Some of the rarer Royal cultivars are worth up to US$20,000–30,000!*

it inhabits wet or dry savanna and savanna-woodland rather than true tropical rainforest. It has a wide distribution, from Senegal in West Africa, east across the continent to Uganda and just into Sudan and Kenya.

Royal Pythons are relatively slow-moving, adopting the rectilinear motion (caterpillar crawl) more associated with larger, heavier pythons and the Puff Adder (*Bitis arietans*). They are terrestrial in habit though they may climb low shrubs and trees to investigate crevices or holes for prey, which consists mostly of small mammals. They will enter buildings, especially loft spaces, or search mammal burrows during their hunts and rest in such locations during daylight hours.

Apart from the obvious threat from the pet trade, Royal Pythons are also collected for their skins, or killed out of fear by local Africans. The ability to roll into a ball is of little use in these circumstances.

Range: Central and West Africa • Max. length: 1.0–1.5m • Habitat: Dry or wet savanna and savanna-woodland • Prey: Small mammals, occasionally birds • Reproduction: Oviparous, 4–10 eggs

Royal Python cultivars, mutations and colour morphs

After the American Cornsnake (*Pantherophis guttatus*), the Royal or Ball Python has probably become the most popular species of snake in captivity. An entire industry has grown up around this single species, spawning numerous mutations or cultivar colour phases with names like 'super cinnamon pastel-jungle pastel', 'clown pastel', 'desert ghost', 'spider mojave', 'coral glow' and 'woma lesser platinum', and more than a

hundred other stunning creations. Entire books are written about the captive care and selective breeding of this single species and where a normal 'wild phase' python might be worth $80 at the most, some of these induced colour phase specimens are worth up to $20,000 or $30,000 each.

This is indirectly a form of conservation, because the size and docility of this python have made it popular in captivity. Now keepers, both serious herpetoculturists and pet-keepers, desire captive-bred, guaranteed-feeding colour phases and the market for wild-caught, normal-patterned pythons has almost disappeared. In the past, thousands of wild-caught Royal/Ball pythons were exported to the pet trade from West African countries. Then 'ranched' juveniles were imported, ostensibly from captive-bred populations in the native countries but often also taken from the wild, or from gravid females collected in the wild. The modern desire for cultivars should remove the wild population from the picture and provide the reptile-keeping public with 'fancy' pythons in much the same way that the breeding of tropical fish changed aquaculture.

Angolan Python *Python anchietae*

Also known as Anchieta's Dwarf Python, this is the African python with the most restricted range, being found only in southern Angola and northern and central Namibia, where it receives total protection. Believed to be most closely related to the more northern Royal Python (*P. regius*) its pattern is more

ABOVE: *The Angolan Python* (Python anchietae) *is a rare protected species found in Angola and Namibia.*

OPPOSITE: *A young Central African Rock Python* (Python sebae), *a species which grows to be the largest snake in Africa.*

fragmented that that of its relative, consisting of a red-brown background broken by numerous dorsal and lateral dark-edged, pale brown patches. The head is red-brown with similar dark-edged pale stripes running from the snout, through the top of the eye to the back of the head. Its patterning and head shape bear more than a passing resemblance to some of the redder carpet pythons of Australia (*Morelia spilota*, p.131). Like other pythons it is active nocturnally and it will 'ball' like a Royal Python if it feels threatened. Most authors comment on the placid nature of this species, but the only specimens I have encountered, in captivity, have been rather pugnacious. However, being a small species, it is unable to do much damage. Prey consists of desert mammals and ground-nesting birds that are caught and constricted. Nowhere common, an Angolan Python can be considered a real find, though it should not be collected and the finder should be content with photographs.

Range: Southern Angola and northern Namibia • Max. length: 1.3–1.8m • Habitat: Riverine bush, karoo and semi-desert • Prey: Bird and small desert mammals • Reproduction: Oviparous, 4–5 eggs

AFRICAN ROCK PYTHONS

Each of the tropical continents has one or two giant snakes and these are the African representatives. Originally the African Rock Python was one pan-tropical African species with two subspecies, but the differences between the two forms were considered sufficient for them to be recognized as distinct and separate species.

These are often bad-tempered snakes and large examples not only have the capability of easily killing an adult human but there are also several well-documented cases of their eating people (see p.27). In fact, the African Rock Python has a greater reputation for this behaviour than the giant Green Anaconda (*Eunectes murinus*) of South America, for which such stories are difficult to validate, or even the Asian Reticulated Python (*Python reticulatus*), which has been proven occasionally to take humans.

Although large specimens may be seen as a threat, man poses a greater threat to the continued existence of giant pythons in Africa than the python poses to man. Large African pythons are easy to track down owing to their often terrestrial habits (as opposed to the highly aquatic anacondas) in often open or sparsely vegetated country, in contrast to the Reticulated Python's forest habitat in Southeast Asia. In Africa pythons are killed out of fear, for skins, for meat and for ju-ju. Hunters travel great distances to find specimens, and in Mauritania I came across the dried husk of a python, killed and skinned by hide hunters from over the border in Senegal.

Central African Rock Python *Python sebae*

This species occurs from Senegal in the west to southern Sudan and Ethiopia in the east, and Congo and Angola in the south and southwest. Within this range it occurs in most habitats from semi-desert and dry savanna to tropical rainforest and plantation, especially in association with freshwater rivers, lakes and swamps. It can be distinguished from its southeastern relative by the presence of enlarged scutes (shield-like plates) on the top of the head (smaller and more granular in the other species) and more contrasting, brighter head and body markings. The basic pattern is similar, with irregular dark brown saddles and blotches overlying a paler brown background, the edges of the saddles and blotches edged with yellow-brown. The head bears a sharply defined arrow-shaped marking with a pale longitudinal midline.

The maximum length achieved by the Central African Rock Python is open to question. Certainly they may achieve 7.5m, and there are unconfirmed reports of a 9.8m specimen killed in Ivory Coast in 1932. The Central African Rock Python is therefore one of the three longest snake species in the world.

It is usually nocturnal or crepuscular, terrestrial but also aquatic and highly arboreal. A powerful constrictor, it is a dangerous predator, often capturing prey from ambush, sometimes lying in the shallows and launching a crocodile-like strike at unwary animals coming to the water-hole to drink. Juveniles will take small mammals and birds, lizards and frogs but adults are fully capable of killing and devouring (whole)

ABOVE: *The Central African Rock Python* (Python sebae) *can be distinguished from the Southern African Rock Python* (P. natalensis) *by the presence of large scales called scutes, rather than small granulated scales, on the top of the head.*

OPPOSITE: *The Southern African Rock Python was originally treated as as subspecies of the Central African Rock Python.*

small antelope and larger birds. Some of the prey recorded for this species is particularly impressive, including Monitor Lizards, village dogs, domestic goats, wild pigs, medium-sized antelope such as impala to 59kg, porcupines, crocodiles and occasional humans. After a large meal the python is itself extremely vulnerable to being killed, and this is the time when wild dogs, hyenas and man seem most to take advantage of what would otherwise be a formidable adversary.

Large females lay a large clutch of eggs in a termite mound or animal burrow and, coiling about them, will incubate them for approximately 90 days. During this time the female will occasionally leave the eggs to bask and then return to the egg clutch to continue incubation. She is also particularly defensive of her clutch and large females we have maintained have chased members of staff who approached too close to their chosen nesting sites. Angry pythons often raise and coil their tail tips and this should be seen as a warning, especially when accompanied by the long, drawn-out hiss.

Range: Central and West Africa • Max. length: 4.0–7.5m • Habitat: Rainforest, coastal forest, savanna, savanna-woodland, semi-desert, swamps, lakes and rivers • Prey: Small mammals and birds, in juveniles; large mammals, eg antelope, in adults • Reproduction: Oviparous, 16–100 eggs • Similar species: Asian Rock Python (*P. molurus*)

Southern African Rock Python *Python natalensis*

The Southern African Rock Python is found from southern Kenya and Tanzania to Zimbabwe, west to Namibia and south to Transvaal, South Africa and KwaZulu-Natal. Its habitats are similar to those of its northern relative, from which it can be distinguished by the much greater fragmentation of its head scales and less contrasting patterning. The maximum size of the Southern African python is lower than that of the Central African python and its prey capabilities are also slightly less, but antelopes still feature and there have also been cases of human predation by this species in southern Africa. Southern African pythons have been reported to fast for 2.5 years and live for 27 years in captivity.

The most southerly population is located in coastal KwaZulu-Natal, where the species is now afforded total protection owing to its rarity, but a population did exist in the Eastern Cape until the 1920s. Whether any individuals still survive in this area has not been determined.

Although people are fearful of pythons and often kill them on sight, they are important predators of small mammals that would otherwise overwhelm valuable food crops, and they should be protected and encouraged. In 1980 the South African army even went so far as to 'recruit' pet pythons to deal with a plague of rock rabbits on the Botswana-Zimbabwe border and placed an advert to that effect in the press – at the same time stating that pythons were protected and should not be taken from the wild to supply their needs.

Range: Southern Kenya to South Africa and Namibia • Max. length: 3.5–5.8m • Habitat: Coastal forest, savanna, savanna-woodland, semi-desert, swamps, lakes and rivers • Prey: Small mammals and birds, in juveniles; large mammals, eg antelope, in adults • Reproduction: Oviparous, 30–50 eggs

Indian Ocean Boas

The pythons are the dominant constrictors on the African mainland, but the islands of the Indian Ocean are boa country. Madagascar represents a piece of ancient Gondwanaland that never collided with Eurasia and which retains boas rather similar in appearance to those of South America, while Round Island, off Mauritius, is truly a herpetological time-capsule.

MADAGASCAN BOAS

Located 400km east of Mozambique in southern Africa, the island of Madagascar is the fourth largest in the world after Greenland, New Guinea and Borneo. Measuring approximately 1,600km by 570km, it has a surface area of over 587,000 sq km. It forms a fragmented part of what was once the huge, southern supercontinent of Gondwanaland, with Africa, India, Australia, South America and Antarctica, but, unlike Africa and India, it was never in contact with the northern supercontinent of Laurasia and never felt the impact of invasion from Eurasia of monkeys, agamas (lizards) or pythons.

Madagascar has several Gondwanan elements in its faunal composition, including three species of boa. These have been placed in the genus *Boa* with the South American Boa Constrictor, although one species bears a closer resemblance to the neotropical treeboas (genus *Corallus*). The apparent similarity may be more a result of convergent evolution than any actual close relationship, especially since the Madagascan boas have a lower chromosomal count than the Boa Constrictor and other true boas (34 rather than 36). Recently, the Madagascan boas have been returned to their original genera. All three species are nocturnal and possess the typical vertically elliptical pupils of a nocturnal snake.

Madagascan boas are listed on CITES Appendix I, but are only considered 'vulnerable' by the IUCN (the World Conversation Union). They are potentially threatened by local use of their skins and by habitat disturbance and destruction.

ABOVE: *The Madagascan Ground Boa* (Acrantophis madagascariensis) *is a wet-forest species with enlarged scales, known as scutes, on top of its head.*

OPPOSITE: *Dumeril's Boa* (Acrantophis dumerili) *is a dry-forest species with granular head scales.*

Madagascan Ground Boa *Acrantophis madagascariensis*

The larger of the two ground boas, the Madagascan Ground Boa is an inhabitant of the moist forests of the north and northeast of the island. Females produce relatively small litters of very large neonates (over 0.6m) following a lengthy gestation period of eight to nine months. Experts suggest that the production of a small litter of large young is a response to the lack of large mammalian predators on Madagascar.

Both ground boas are nocturnal predators, primarily of small mammals including small lemurs. The Madagascan Ground Boa spends the day in the leaf-litter or underground in burrows. Both species of *Acrantophis* are known as 'do' in Malagasy.

This species is light to medium brown with a series of large dark brown lozenges running along each side, edged above by a yellow-brown stripe and below accompanied by a pair of small whitish spots or a yellowish stripe. The Madagascan Ground Boa has large scales on the top of its head.

Range: Madagascar • Max. length: 1.5–3.2m • Habitat: Moist forests • Prey: Small mammals including small lemurs • Reproduction: Viviparous, 1–8 neonates • Similar species: Boa Constrictor (*Boa constrictor*)

Dumeril's Ground Boa *Acrantophis dumerili*

Dumeril's Boa inhabits the dry forests of west and southwest Madagascar and achieves a slightly shorter maximum length than the related Madagascan Ground Boa. After a slightly shorter gestation period (six to eight months) females usually produce larger litters, of smaller neonates, than do females of the other species. More arboreal than its relative, Dumeril's Boa may include birds as well as small mammals in its diet. Days are spent sheltering in the leaf-litter, down burrows or in holes in trees.

Dumeril's Boa is generally a light brown to grey snake bearing a distinctly 'boa constrictor-like' pattern on irregular dark brown or red-brown saddles and small, granular scales on the top of its head.

Range: Madagascar • Max. length: 1.5–2.0m • Habitat: Dry forests • Prey: Small mammals and birds • Reproduction: Viviparous, 2–21 neonates

Madagascan Treeboa *Sanzinia madagascariensis*

With a chunky head and numerous supralabials separated by deep 'pit' grooves, the Madagascan Treeboa bears a striking resemblance to the neotropical treeboas of the genus *Corallus*. It is also known by the alternative common name of 'Sanzinia',

The Madagascan Treeboa (Sanzinia madagascariensis) *is a highly and variably patterned species which resembles the South American treeboas of genus* Corallus.

which is also the name of the monotypic genus to which it belongs. When transferred to the genus *Boa*, along with the two species of *Acrantophis*, its scientific name was changed to *Boa manditra* to avoid any confusion with *Boa* (*Acrantophis*) *madagascariensis*, its new name originating from the treeboa's Malagasy name of 'manditra'. More arboreal than the ground boas of genus *Acrantophis*, it is widely distributed throughout northwestern, northern and eastern Madagascar and is the most commonly encountered species in most habitats, from rainforest to semi-desert woodland or savanna grassland.

The treeboa is much more variable in patterning than its terrestrial relatives, with localized variations including populations with greenish, brown, red or yellow shading and a series of large dark, light-centred, rhomboid blotches along each flank. In most populations there is a degree of ontogenetic colour change as juveniles mature from their original red coloration into adult livery. Juveniles are also known for their arboreal habits, but adults become increasingly terrestrial, even though they may bask or rest aloft during the day.

Range: Madagascar • Max. length: 1.5–2.5m • Habitat: Dry and moist forest, and savanna grasslands • Prey: Small mammals and birds • Reproduction: Viviparous, 3–16 neonates • Similar species: Neotropical treeboas (*Corallus* spp.)

ROUND ISLAND BOAS

Round Island is a small (150-hectare) island and all that remains of an eroded and submerged 100,000-year-old extinct volcano situated 22km northeast of Mauritius in the Indian Ocean. Its isolation from all other land masses caused it to become a microcosm of endemism, home to a startling array of unique animals and plants, found nowhere else, including two snakes, the only surviving members of the Bolyeriidae. The unusual features of the family include the complete absence of the vestigial pelvic girdle and cloacal spurs so characteristic of other boas and pythons, a much more reduced left lung and a curious mixture of both primitive and advanced skeletal characters of the vertebrae and lower jaw, while the maxilla is divided into two hinged sections, anterior and posterior, believed to be an adaptation to grip smooth-scaled skinks. This unusual characteristic, unique within the tetrapods (all land-living vertebrates), results in the alternative common name of 'split-jawed boas'. Unlike other boas, at least one of the bolyerid boas is oviparous.

The fauna of Round Island existed in isolation until man introduced goats and rabbits in the 19th century. These animals grazed the plant cover, leading to the almost total degradation of the endemic hardwood and palm forests, and the loss through erosion of the island's soil down to the volcanic bedrock.

With the soil went the burrowing animals, and into extinction passed one of the two endemic boas. A recovery programme has been initiated on Round Island. The goats and rabbits have been eradicated and the native flora is being re-established.

Round Island Burrowing Boa *Bolyeria multocarinata*

A fossorial species that suffered from the loss of its habitat through erosion, the Round Island Burrowing Boa has not been seen since 1975, despite extensive searches. It now seems likely that this unique endemic island boa has become extinct.

An early artwork of a specimen of *B. multocarinata* shows a snake with a narrow head, and body patterning consisting of dark reticulations on a pale background.

Virtually nothing further is known of the ecology and biology of this species.

Range: Round Island (presumed extinct) • Max. length: 0.95m • Habitat: Fossorial • Prey: Probably skinks • Reproduction: Unknown

Round Island Keel-scaled Boa *Casarea dussumieri*

This species is more arboreal than its extinct relative but, although it is still extant, numbers are thought to have been as low as 75 specimens in the early 1970s. An intensive rescue programme involving captive breeding and habitat recovery, initiated by the Jersey Wildlife Preservation Trust (JWPT) in 1977 from 11 specimens on loan from the government of Mauritius, has saved the species from extinction. JWPT managed to breed

Back from the brink: the Round Island Keel-scaled Boa (Casarea dussumieri) *and its island habitat are the subject of an intensive recovery programme.*

it in captivity but raising the hatchlings created an additional problem, that of enticing the miniscule 18cm serpents to feed on small mice – the natural lizard prey of the Round Island boa is considered equally endangered. The rescue programme for this species is not before time: Keel-scaled Boas were originally also found on Mauritius, but disappeared following the introduction of rats to the main island, and now only survive in the wild on Round Island, 22km to the northeast.

Coloration consists of grey-brown ground colour with a slightly darker irregular broad longitudinal dorsal stripe. The head is narrow and elongate with a reduced lower jaw and vertically elliptical pupils. It looks very like a West Indian woodsnake (*Tropidophis*) or New Guinea Bevel-nosed Boa (*Candoia carinata*).

Round Island Keel-scaled Boas are nocturnal predators of skinks and *Phelsuma* day geckos, which they actively hunt, approaching close before striking and coiling about their prey, which is then killed by constriction. They shelter in the burrows of shearwaters or under fallen palm fronds.

It seems likely that this species has been saved from extinction at the eleventh hour.

Range: Mauritius (extinct) and Round Island • Max. length: 1.28m • Habitat: Dry forests • Prey: Day geckos and skinks • Reproduction: Oviparous, 3–11 eggs • Similar species: West Indian woodsnakes (*Tropidophis* spp.) and New Guinea Bevel-nosed Boa (*Candoia carinata*)

AUSTRALASIA AND THE PACIFIC OCEAN ISLANDS

The only geographical region capable of rivalling Tropical America with its impressive boa diversity is Australasia, with the difference that the constrictors here are pythons.

The island continent of Australia is 'Python Central', with pythons almost everywhere. They have adapted and evolved to occupy every available terrestrial niche from Gold Coast rainforest to Kakadu swamp, from Hawkesbury sandstone ridges above Sydney to the arid Centralian deserts around Uluru (Ayer's Rock). The only habitats without at least one species of python are located in cooler southeastern South Australia, Victoria and Tasmania.

Mainland Australia is home to 14 python species, three of which have spread north across the Torres Strait into southern New Guinea, while one widely distributed New Guinea species has gone the other way into Cape York Peninsula, Queensland. The island of New Guinea is also home to four endemic python species, with potentially more awaiting description or discovery in its forests, swamps and mountains. The islands of the Bismarck Sea, to the east of New Guinea (New Britain and New Ireland) are home to another endemic, while to the west and southwest lies Maluku (the Indonesian Moluccan islands) with three newly-defined species, and the Lesser Sunda Islands with two species.

In addition to these 25 pythons, the region is also home to boas, with five species distributed westwards from Samoa, one quarter of the way across the Pacific, through the Fijian and Solomon archipelagos to New Guinea, west to Maluku, north to Palau, and south to the Loyalty Islands, off New Caledonia. This is a vast region encompassing thousands of islands, both large and small, offering many varying habitats and opportunity for serpentine colonizers like the Pacific boas.

Although the basal snakes are represented only by the typhlopid blindsnakes, these burrowers are extremely widely distributed through the region, with at least 60 species.

The stunning Boelen's Python (Morelia boeleni), *from the highland regions of New Guinea, is sometimes called the Black Python.*

Australasian Blindsnakes

Although only one family of blindsnakes occurs in the region, that family demonstrates considerable diversity, ranging from lush rainforest to the driest of deserts. New species are being discovered and described with surprising frequency.

BLINDSNAKES

The family Typhlopidae is the only blindsnake family in the Australasian region, where it is primarily represented by the genus *Ramphotyphlops*, with approximately 50 species, mostly in Australia but with a smattering of species in New Guinea, the Solomon Islands, New Caledonia and the neighbouring Loyalty Islands, and an endemic (*R. exocoeti*) on Christmas Island, an Australian territory in the Indian Ocean. The other two genera present in the region have far fewer species. *Typhlops* is strongly represented in the Americas, Africa and

The Southern New Guinea Blindsnake (Ramphotyphlops poly-grammicus) *is also found in northern Australia.*

Asia but only five species occur in the Australasian region, four endemic to Papua New Guinea (PNG) and another species which ranges from West Papua into Maluku (the Moluccan Islands of Indonesia). The Melanesian genus *Acutotyphlops* contains only four species, two PNG endemics and two that range eastwards, from PNG to the Solomons.

Southern New Guinea Blindsnake *Ramphotyphlops polygrammicus*

Known in Australia as the Northeastern Blindsnake, this species was first described from Timor in the Lesser Sundas and, although it ranges through New Guinea to northeastern Queensland, it is possible that more than one species is involved. Fairly large for the genus, the Southern New Guinea Blindsnake is a robust species, purple-grey to grey-brown, with 22 scale rows and an immaculate cream ventral surface. I have caught this species in drift fence pitfall traps in monsoon forest in the southern Trans-Fly region of Western Province.
Range: Indonesia (Lesser Sunda Islands), southern New

Guinea and eastern Queensland • Max. length: 0.25–0.48m
• Habitat: Monsoon forest and rainforests in hills and
lowlands • Prey: Presumably ants and/or termites •
Reproduction: Oviparous, 7 eggs • Similar species: Blackish
Blindsnake (*R. nigrescens*) from New South Wales

Fred Parker's Blindsnake *Typhlops fredparkeri*

This species was described as recently as 1996 and named in
honour of its collector, the patrolling government officer or 'kiap'
Fred Parker, who made a special study of the snakes of Western
Province, PNG. Fred Parker's Blindsnake comes from Korobosea,
near Port Moresby in the narrow coastal strip of savanna and
monsoon forest, and it is most closely related to the Black
Blindsnake (*T. ater*) of West Papua. A slender species, with only
16 scale rows, it is brown above, tan below. The combination of
16 scale rows and a rounded head and snout is unique amongst
Australasian blindsnakes. Only a single specimen is known,
housed in the Museum of Comparative Zoology, Harvard.
Range: Central Province, PNG • Max. length: 0.2–0.5m •
Habitat: Coastal lowland • Prey: Presumably ants and/or
termites • Reproduction: Oviparous, only specimen had one
developing egg in ovary • Similar species: Black Blindsnake
(*T. ater*) of Maluku and West Papua

*The Red Wedge-nosed Blindsnake (Acutotyphlops infralabialis) is
the most widespread member of a recently described genus
confined to the Solomon Islands and the island of Bougainville
(Papua New Guinea).*

Red Wedge-nosed Blindsnake *Acutotyphlops infralabialis*

This blindsnake is found throughout the main islands of the
Solomons and also on the island of Bougainville, which is
politically part of PNG. It is the most widely distributed species
in this small genus, which was described as recently as 1995
and characterized by the possession of a sharp, projecting
rostral scale, presenting a pointed-snout appearance. Reddish-
pink above, yellowish below, it has a relatively high number of
longitudinal scale rows (26–28).
Range: Bougainville, PNG, and Solomon Islands • Max.
length: 0.25–0.35m • Habitat: Presumably forest • Prey:
Presumably ants and/or termites but possibly earthworms
(the prey of the related *A. subocularis*) • Reproduction:
Oviparous, clutch size unknown • Similar species: New
Guinea Wedge-nosed Blindsnake (*A. solomonis*) and
Kunua Sharp-nosed Blindsnake (*A. kunuaensis*), from
Bougainville

Indo-Australian Basal Snakes

Other than the blindsnakes, the only basal snakes to enter Australasia are the pipesnakes, and these Oriental serpents are only represented by a handful of species at the extreme west of the region.

EAST INDONESIAN PIPESNAKES

The Asian pipesnakes or cylinder-snakes are primarily associated with Southeast Asia, with one species occurring in Sri Lanka. Currently the genus *Cylindrophis* comprises one wide-ranging well-documented species, the common Asian Pipesnake *C. ruffus*, and nine much more localized species, several of which are known only from single specimens. The bulk of the range of genus *Cylindrophis* is to be found to the west of the 'Wallace Line'. Named for the 19th-century biogeographer and Darwin prodigy, Alfred Russel Wallace, this is an invisible line through the ocean that separates the Oriental region from the Australasian region, passing through the narrow but deep-water straits between Bali and Lombok, and also separating Borneo and the Philippines on the oriental side from Maluku (the Moluccan Islands) on the Australasian side. Sulawesi, formerly Celebes, is the only island to straddle the Wallace Line. With the exception of the Sri Lankan pipesnake, and a couple of obscure and especially rare Bornean species, the only Asian pipesnake recognized from Southeast Asia, from Borneo and Bali to Burma and southern China, is the widespread *C. ruffus*. Although this species also occurs to the east of the Wallace Line, in Lombok, Flores and Sulawesi, all other populations from the Australasian region are afforded specific status. Six of these species are recorded from Sulawesi and Halmahera; Tanahjampea Island; the Lesser Sundas; Timor and Wetar; the Tanimbar Islands; and the Aru Islands. Given the spread of species it is curious that no pipesnakes have been reported from the Vogelkop of West Papua. Perhaps somebody should look there.

Aru Pipesnake *Cylindrophis aruensis*

The Aru Pipesnake is the species found furthest east, the Aru Islands being a small archipelago located midway between West Papua and northern Australia. It is known from only two specimens, both immature males, and there are no field notes or natural history observations. It seems likely that the habitat and prey preferences are similar to those of its better known eastern relative, *C. ruffus*, which inhabits leaf-litter, preying on elongate vertebrates including burrowing snakes like blindsnakes, and also earthworms and insect larvae. The Aru Pipesnake is a reddish-brown snake with a series of short, pale, transverse bars which neither meet over the back nor pass onto the underside, except under the tail. A pale collar is present around the neck, but this is also broken by the brown vertebral longitudinal stripe, and yellowish spots are also present on the head. This species is separated from most other species in the region by its high midbody scale count (24 including the narrow ventral scale row).

Range: Aru Islands, Indonesia • Max. length: 0.17m (only known from immature specimens) • Habitat: Forest floor leaf-litter • Prey: Probably blindsnakes, other elongate vertebrates and earthworms • Reproduction: Probably viviparous as *C. ruffus* • Similar species: Wetar Pipesnake (*C. boulengeri*) and Tanimbar Pipesnake (*C. yamdena*)

Australasian Pythons

If the Americas are the centre for boa speciation, then Australasia is certainly the hub for python diversity and distribution, with 72 per cent of all species occurring here. Many are widespread throughout Australo-Papua, but others are less well known and more restricted in their distribution. The region is home to some of the rarest, and certainly the smallest, pythons on the planet.

BLACK-HEADED PYTHON AND WOMA

The two slender-bodied but powerful pythons in the genus *Aspidites*, the Black-headed Python and the Woma, are unique within the Pythonidae in that they lack any thermosensitive facial pits. Endemic to Australia, this morphological modification, along with a narrowing of the head, may reflect the dietary preferences of these widespread savanna and desert-dwelling pythons that prey primarily on cold-blooded, slender, even elongate, reptiles.

Unlike most other Australian pythons, the Black-headed Python and Woma also possess enlarged, symmetrical dorsal scutes on the head rather than small granular scales, and the majority of their subcaudal scales under their non-prehensile tails are single. Black-heads and Womas are amongst the most sought after of pythons in captivity and there is considerable interest in localized colour patterns. These species are also popular with Australian aborigines, for the pot!

Black-headed Python *Aspidites melanocephalus*

It is difficult to confuse this species with any other because its most distinguishing characteristic is so evident: the shiny black head that gives the species its common and scientific name. The black pigment actually continues a good head-length onto the back, before terminating in a strongly demarcated line and giving way to the contrastingly light background colour of the remainder of the body and tail. This may be brown, cream, pinkish or yellowish, overlain by numerous irregular, slender, dark bands, although in some specimens these become obscured by a broad longitudinal dark vertebral stripe running back from the head.

The slender-bodied Black-headed Python is a confirmed reptile predator, feeding on dragons (Agamidae), goannas (Varanidae), blue-tongued skinks (*Tiliqua*), and snakes including venomous elapids and even its own species. Mammals make up less than 10 per cent of the diet of this species. Nocturnal and diurnal, the terrestrial Black-headed Python spends a great deal of time underground, even excavating its own burrows; *Aspidites* are the only pythons to do this. Males are reported to enter into vigorous combat in the mating season.

The desert-dwelling Black-headed Python (Aspidites melano-cephalus) *is a python without thermo-sensory labial pits. It does not need them, as it feeds on other reptiles.*

Range: Northern Australia, from the Pilbara to Rockhampton, Queensland • Max. length: 1.5–3.0m • Habitat: Savanna-woodland, savanna, rocky outcrops and both dry and wet forest • Prey: Lizards and snakes, rarely mammals or birds • Reproduction: Oviparous, 6–18 eggs

"Big pythons are often killed on the roads, with slow-moving Black-headed Pythons particularly vulnerable. I caught one adult male specimen crossing a major highway only a few minutes before a 'road-train' thundered past. I obtained another large male from an aboriginal hunter who was planning to eat it. I later released both specimens on a rocky outcrop well away from the road, at opposite ends of the escarpment, mindful of their cannibalistic tendencies."
Warralong, Pilbara, Western Australia.

Woma *Aspidites ramsayi*

Woma, womma or wama simply mean 'python' or 'snake' in Aboriginal dialects. Named in honour of E.P. Ramsay from the Australian Museum, and sometimes called Ramsay's Python, the Woma resembles a Black-headed Python without the black head and neck, the only dark head pigment being a pair of irregular panda-patches over the eyes, which may meet and fuse in the centre of the yellow or brown head, and

dark suturing around the snout scutes. The Woma's head may also be slightly more pointed than its relative, but the body and tail are banded very similarly to the Black-headed Python. There are variations in patterning across the range of the Woma but whether sufficient to qualify for subspecific status is not determined.

In contrast to the Black-headed Python, Womas include a high proportion of mammals in their diet, with introduced rabbits featuring highly. Lizards are taken far more frequently than snakes and cannibalism has not been reported, though it is possible. Prey encountered underground is crushed against the wall of the burrow, since constriction is impossible in a confined space, the same method as used by some large colubrid snakes, for example American indigo snakes and cribos (*Drymarchon* spp.). More Womas than any other pythons lack their tail tips or have tail damage; it has been suggested that this is due to their habit of 'caudal luring' to attract prey within strike range.

Womas are desert pythons, although they also occur in grassland, dry woodland and rocky country and overlap with the Black-headed Python is some areas such as the Pilbara. They are distributed through some of the most inhospitable and least populated regions of Australia and their ecology is incompletely studied. It is suggested that in the southwest of its range the Woma may be endangered, possibly even extinct, due to habitat loss caused by farming and clearance and predation by feral cats and foxes. If it is not too late this population warrants a captive breeding programme and habitat conservation measures.

Range: The coast of Western Australia to the Great Dividing Range • Max. length: 1.5–3.0m • Habitat: Sandy desert and *Spinifex* grassland • Prey: Reptiles and mammals • Reproduction: Oviparous, 5–19 eggs

ABOVE: *The head of a Woma* (Aspidites ramsayi) *showing the dark panda-spots between the eyes.* BELOW: *The Woma preys on rabbits and lizards, captured in the arid centre of Australia.*

OPPOSITE: *The first New Guinea Spotted Python* (Antaresia maculosa) *discovered by the author on an abandoned airfield in Western Province. It may yet prove to be a new species to science.*

CHILDREN'S PYTHONS

The four species of Australian python in the genus *Antaresia* are distributed throughout the continent apart from the south and southeast. These are the smallest pythons in Australia, few specimens achieving 2.0m in total length, with the Anthill or Pigmy Python (A. *perthensis*) of Western Australia, easily the smallest known python in the world, with a maximum length of 0.7m. For many years there was confusion over the distribution and identification of the various populations and all were lumped together within the single species, the Children's Python, named in honour of the English naturalist J.G. Children, not because they were small and suitable as pets for children. These pythons have been kept and bred in captivity for many years and this long-term confusion has unfortunately meant that many captive lineages are hybrids.

These diminutive pythons can be recognized by a combination of characteristics apart from their small size. They possess large dorsal head scutes rather than the fragmented scales common to many other pythons, and numerous loreal scales between the nasal and the preocular scales. The thermosensitive pits are confined to the first supralabials and the last 5–7 posterior infralabials. They are also reported to possess a relatively large number of teeth compared to other pythons.

Nocturnal and primarily terrestrial, these snakes are extremely agile and although their tails are not prehensile, they can climb well. They are especially common around termitaria, hence 'Anthill Python', and rocky outcrops.

Spotted Python *Antaresia maculosa*

The Spotted Python was long considered an eastern population of the very similar Children's Python (A. *childreni*) but it is now regarded as a separate species. Also known as the Eastern Small-blotched Python and Banded Rock Python, this species occurs east of the Great Dividing Range from the New South Wales border to the tip of Cape York Peninsula, Queensland, and has now been recorded from southern New Guinea.

Like most *Antaresia*, this is a variably patterned species but the general markings consist of ragged-edged, dark spots or blotches over a light brown background, the bold para-vertebral rows often meeting over the back to form a broken zigzag, and numerous smaller lateral spots which may coalesce to form short vertical bars, the spots persisting into adulthood.

Spotted Pythons are found in habitats ranging from forest to open savanna and rocky country. On Mount Etna, near Rockhampton, Queensland, a very large population of Spotted Pythons is known to feed on the resident Bent-winged and Ghost Bat populations. Caves, rocky fissures, hollow logs and abandoned termitaria all provide retreats for this adaptable species. Although not usually exceeding 1.0m in length, specimens from Tully, Queensland, are reported to achieve 2.0m.
Range: East and Northern Queensland, and southern New Guinea • Max. length: 0.8–1.0m, reports of 2.0m specimens • Habitat: Savanna-woodland, coastal and dry forest, cane fields and rocky outcrops • Prey: Small mammals including bats, birds, lizards and frogs • Reproduction: Oviparous, 4–18 eggs • Similar species: Children's or Northern Brown Python (A. *childreni*)

"In 1996 I wrote *A Guide to the Snakes of Papua New Guinea*, which included all eight species of New Guinea pythons between its covers. In 2001 Robert Sprackland and I were in Western Province, Papua New Guinea, searching for Salvador's monitor lizard (*Varanus salvadori*) when we discovered two small shed snake skins between sheets of long-abandoned corrugated sheeting on the edge of a disused airfield. A further search revealed a small python, which I initially mistook for a juvenile Amethystine Python *(Morelia amethistina)*, but then considered might be a juvenile Water Python *(Liasis fuscus)*. On discounting both species I realized we had actually captured something very important, both physically and on film.

Starting with the basics (it was certainly a python) I worked out that I was holding a

BELOW: *Stimson's Python* (Antaresia stimsoni)*, a widespread member of the Children's Python complex.*

OPPOSITE TOP: *Head of Stimson's Python. This species is also known as the Large-blotched Python.*

OPPOSITE BOTTOM: *Confusion reigns over identication of the Water Pythons. This is a specimen from the Sunda Islands which is sometimes called a Freckled Python* (Liasis mackloti).

specimen from the genus *Antaresia*, until that moment a genus considered endemic (confined) to Australia. The surrounding habitat was very similar to Cape York habitat, savanna-woodland with scattered termitaria, and there are strong faunal similarities between the two land masses. The little python may ultimately turn out to be a new and fifth species of Antaresia but, being in possession of a single specimen, we only felt justified in reporting it as a range extension for the spotted python from Cape York. We had discovered the ninth species of python for New Guinea, the island's first new python for almost 50 years. The find was reported in *Herpetological Review* 35(3) 2004."
Weam, Western Province, Papua New Guinea

Stimson's Python *Antaresia stimsoni*
Named in honour of Andrew F. Stimson, a highly respected herpetologist at the British Museum of Natural History, *A. stimsoni* is the most widely distributed species in the genus. It ranges from the coast of Western Australia, across a great swathe of central Australia, to the western slopes of the Great Dividing Range. Western and central-eastern subspecies are recognized, largely separated by scale characteristics, although the eastern may achieve the greater length of the two subspecies. An alternative common name is Large-blotched Python, which describes the species well because the pattern

does consist of several series of very large dark blotches, over a yellow, red or light brown background, which may be fused to form bold transverse bars across the back or down the flanks, the patterning in some specimens resembling that of a Carpet Python, *Morelia spilota*. Although found throughout a major proportion of western and central Australia, Stimson's Python is not thought to inhabit extreme desert, preferring rocky outcrops where it can prey on geckos, skinks and small mammals.

Range: Western and central Australia, all mainland states except Victoria and ACT • Max. length: 1.0–1.5m • Habitat: Savanna, dry savanna-woodland, and open rocky country • Prey: Small mammals, lizards and birds • Reproduction: Oviparous, 6–15 eggs • Similar species: Carpet Python (*Morelia spilota*)

WATER PYTHONS

Water Pythons are found in northern Australia (Northern Territory, Queensland and the islands of the Torres Strait), southern New Guinea (Papua New Guinea and West Papua, formerly Irian Jaya) and the Indonesian Lesser Sunda islands (Timor, Wetar, Sawa, Semau and Babar). Today these large and small land masses are separated by the Arafura Sea, Timor Sea and the Gulf of Carpentaria, so before it is possible to understand current opinions regarding the taxonomic status of the water pythons of Australasia it is necessary to understand the biogeographical history of the region over the last 50,000 years, as summarized by Rawlings *et al* 2004.*

Today the Torres Strait, between Queensland and New Guinea, is 12m deep, the Gulf of Carpentaria is 70m deep while the Arafura Sill, where the Arafura Sea meets the Indian Ocean, is over 53m deep. New Guinea and Australia sit on the shallow water Sahul Shelf that was exposed as a land-bridge when sea-levels were at least 50m lower than they are today. This occurred during the frequent ice-ages, the last of which peaked 20,000–18,000 years ago, when much of the world's water was locked up in the extensive polar ice-sheets. At the same time what is now the 70m-deep central depression in the Gulf of Carpentaria was a huge freshwater paleo-lake into which flowed the rivers of the region. A wide river is also believed to have flowed westward, out of Lake Carpentaria to the edge of the Arafura Sill and into the Indian Ocean, effectively separating northwestern Australia from New Guinea and preventing gene flow, whereas a land bridge remained to the east, between

Queensland and New Guinea, until 8,000–6,000 years ago when sea-levels rose again, the Torres Strait was formed and the link was broken.

Now a wide expanse of ocean separates northern Australia from the Indonesian Lesser Sunda Islands but at times of lowered sea-level, when more land would have been exposed to the northwest of Australia, this gap may have been less than 100km, possibly narrow enough to permit rafting, and therefore gene flow between the populations of northwest Australian and Lesser Sunda archipelago.

Taking the above historical interpretations into consideration it may be easier to understand the proposals put forward by Rawlings et al, which are summarized in the species account below.
*Rawlings, L.H., Barker, D.G. & Donnellan, S.C., 2004, 'Phylogenetic relationships of the Australo-Papuan *Liasis* pythons (Reptilia: Macrostomata), based on mitochondrial DNA'. *Australian Journal of Zoology* 52(2):215–227.

Water Pythons *Liasis mackloti* and *Liasis fuscus*

There has been much discussion about the correct name for the water pythons of this region, some authors favouring *L. mackloti* for Indonesia and New Guinea and *L. fuscus* for Australia, others (myself included in the past) confining *L. mackloti* to Indonesia and referring to all Australian and New Guinea specimens at *L. fuscus*. All these opinions were based on scale counts, patterning and other morphological characteristics, but the development of mitochondrial DNA (mtDNA) analysis has greatly enhanced our ability to understand what is going on and, combined with a knowledge of biogeography, habitat and climate over the past 50,000 years Rawlings et al seem to have come up with the most persuasive argument so far. However,

the authors admit that there are still questions to be answered about the relationships of the various water python populations.

They suggest that New Guinea and Queensland water pythons are closely related, more closely related than Queensland and Northern Territory (NT) pythons, which may have become separated by an area of dry forest habitat south of Carpentaria unsuitable for swamp-dwelling water pythons. They are unsure about the exact relationships between NT water pythons and those from the Lesser Sundas, but indicate that they may be related. Although they avoid applying names to the various populations they suggest that the eastern clade (Queensland and New Guinea) might be known as *L. fuscus*, since the type specimen is from Queensland, while the western clade (NT and Indonesia) could warrant the name *L. mackloti*.

The Indonesian situation has been further complicated by the recognition of subspecies, *L. mackloti dunni* from Wetar and *L. m. savuensis* from Sawu. In recent years these subspecies have largely fallen out of favour with taxonomists although 'Savu pythons' are popular in herpetocultural circles. Rawlings and his colleagues seem to support the herpetocultural viewpoint that these island races are valid subspecies and should be recognized as distinct from the Roti-Semau-Timor-Babar population which would become *L. m. mackloti*.

Many Australian and New Guinea water pythons are fairly unicolour snakes above, being black-brown to olive-brown, without any markings other than a shimmering 'oil-on-water' iridescence, and white to yellow beneath. Specimens from Indonesia, where the names Macklot's or Freckled Python have been applied, may be more variable and mottled and sometime bear a dark stripe between the eyes. These are fairly slender, but very powerful, pythons with their thermo-sensory pits confined to the first supralabial and 3–4 posterior infralabials. The tail is non-prehensile. Spending the bulk of their time in freshwater, they prey primarily on other vertebrates inhabiting or visiting watercourses and they are one of only a handful of species recorded to prey on crocodilians, albeit only hatchling freshwater crocodiles (*Crocodylus johnstoni*). Waterbirds and their eggs are also included in the diet of adults while juveniles are reported to take frogs, fish and lizards.

In parts of Kakadu National Park, NT, water pythons are so commonly encountered, often every ten minutes, that the idea of python safaris has been proposed. However, I think the enthusiasm of even the most ardent of snake enthusiasts might become jaded by the discovery of numerous examples of the same relatively small species, and some emphasis on other species may be required to make this a viable and exciting proposition for the eco-tourist.

Range: Lesser Sundas, Indonesia, northern Australia and southern New Guinea • Max. length: 1.0–2.0m, rarely 3.0m • Habitat: Swamps, lakes, wet forest and flooded grasslands • Prey: Mammals, waterbirds, lizards and hatchling crocodiles • Reproduction: Oviparous, 6–23 eggs • Similar species: Olive Python (*L. olivaceus*) and White-lipped Pythons (*Leiopython* spp.)

OPPOSITE: *A specimen of fairly typical northern Australian Brown Water Python* (Liasis fuscus).

BELOW: *The Australian Olive Python* (Liasis olivaceus) *that tried to devour a rare Rough-scaled Python* (Morelia carinata).

OLIVE PYTHONS

There are two olive pythons. The Australian species, *Liasis olivaceus*, is considered the sister taxon to the water python complex (*L. fuscus/mackloti*), while the New Guinea species, once treated as a subspecies of the Australian Olive Python, is now allocated its own monotypic genus, *Apodora*, which is considered the sister taxa to the genus *Liasis* (*L. olivaceus* and *L. fuscus/mackloti*). The olive pythons are stout-bodied, non-prehensile tailed, predators of mammals, birds and reptiles and while reports exist of longer scrub pythons in the *Morelia amethistina* complex (most notably *M. kinghorni*, p.142), these are fairly slimline snakes compared to the stout-bodied olive pythons. One could almost make a comparison with the stout *Python molurus* and the lengthy but more slender *P. reticulatus* in Asia.

Australian Olive Python *Liasis olivaceus*

Two subspecies of Australian Olive Python are recognized, separated by scale counts, maximum size (see below) and geographical distribution, and supported by mtDNA analysis. The nominate race, the Olive, or Eastern Olive, Python (*L. o. olivaceus*) is found from Broome and the Kimberley region of Western Australia, through the Top End, around the Gulf of Carpentaria to central Queensland and the western half of Cape York Peninsula, while the Western Olive Python (*L. o. barroni*) is confined to the Pilbara region of Western Australia (WA), over 600km southwest of Broome, and also reportedly the Dampier archipelago off the WA coast.

Olive pythons are large snakes capable of overpowering large marsupials like wallabies but they are just as adept at

swallowing elongate prey like other snakes. In many respects Olive pythons look like large water pythons, though they may be less iridescent and possess proportionally longer heads. Unicolour brown or olive dorsally with a paler yellow-cream underside and lip scales, they are most frequently encountered in rocky habitats and gorges associated with water courses, although they may also move into forests or onto savannas.

Range: Northern Australia (*L. o. olivaceus*) and the Pilbara, WA (*L. o. barroni*) • Max. length: 2.0–3.0m, occasionally 4.5m (*L. o. olivaceus*) or 6.5m (*L. o. barroni*) • Habitat: Rocky watercourses and gorges but also forest and savanna • Prey: Mammals, birds and reptiles including other pythons • Reproduction: Oviparous, 14–31 eggs • Similar species: Water pythons (*L. fuscus, L. mackloti*) and King Brownsnake (*Pseudechis australis*)

" I once accompanied John Weigel, of the Australian Reptile Park, on a search for the Rough-scaled Python (*Morelia carinata*, p.135). One of John's team, Alf Britton, called me to help him high on the cliff-face. He was holding a male Rough-scaled Python that he had rescued from the mouth of a large olive python, which was now pouring itself down a hole in the rocks. It took me a good 20 minutes, with both arms down the hole, to extricate my first wild Australian Olive Python, a specimen over 2.0m in length."
Hunter River, Kimberley, Western Australia.

Papuan Python *Apodora papuana*

Formerly known as the Papuan Olive Python, the trend has been to shorten the name to Papuan Python, thereby avoiding confusion with the Australian species which is often known simply as the Olive Python. While Papuan Pythons I have seen from Western Province, Papua New Guinea (PNG), appear to be unicolour olive-green, those from Central Province, across the Gulf of Papua, are not really olive, possessing brown backs, yellow-brown flanks and grey-brown heads where every single scute and scale is edged with black presenting an extremely handsome appearance. This is a widespread species and I am certain there are specimens elsewhere equally stunning but for now I consider the Central Province olives among the most subtly beautiful of all New Guinea pythons.

These are large predators capable of devouring large prey, a 22.7kg wallaby having been reported, but like their Australian relative they also feed on other snakes, particularly pythons (see below). Whether the Papuan Python or the New Guinea Amethystine Python (*M. amethistina*) is the largest New Guinea snake is a source for some discussion. A python of 4.3m was collected from Astrolabe Bay in the 1930s and described as *Liasis maximus*. This specimen, now lost, may have been a Papuan Python, but another specimen of *A. papuana*, collected in Milne Bay Province, measured in at 4.78m.

Range: New Guinea • Max. length: 1.4–3.6m, occasionally more than 4.0m • Habitat: Lowland monsoon forest, savanna-woodland and savanna • Prey: Mammals, birds and reptiles including other pythons • Reproduction: Oviparous, 10–20 eggs

"The 'Snake Game' is an unpleasant pastime in parts of PNG. A snake is noosed in the bush, clubbed and dragged onto the highway, where it is run over by passing vehicles. I have seen many snakes, post-game, string still around the neck, including a very large (4.0–5.0m) Papuan Python encountered stretched across the Ramu Highway (see photograph on p.30). Why do people kill pythons? These snakes control the disease-carrying, garden-raiding rodents."
Nadzab, Morobe Province, PNG.

"In 1986 I removed a drowned 2.0m Papuan Python from a fisherman's gillnet in the Binaturi River. The dead snake had a large bulge which contained an Amethystine Python *(M. amethistina)* of the same length, but lesser girth, than itself. I have also observed keratophagy in this species, a specimen that ate its own shed skin – this python is a snake-eater!"
Kunini, Western Province, PNG.

OPPOSITE: *The attractive Papuan Pythons (Apodora papuana) from Central Province, PNG, have grey heads with black scale-edges.*

BELOW: *Northern White-lipped Pythons* (Leiopython albertisi) *have chestnut bodies and glossy black heads with black and white lip barring.*

WHITE-LIPPED PYTHONS

Originally a single species, the White-lipped Python has a long head, fairly stout body and non-prehensile tail. Across its extensive range, this species exhibits considerable variation in coloration and physical size. For anyone who has seen specimens from different parts of New Guinea, one fact seems obvious: there is more than one species involved here. Yet only now is a truly detailed study of the genus *Leiopython* nearing completion. The alternative common name of D'Albertis Python may not now be entirely appropriate when applied to the entire *Leiopython* complex, since *Leiopython albertisii* will become just one of several species within the genus. The White-lipped Python is found throughout New Guinea and also on many of the coastal islands. Its closest relative is believed to be the Bismarck Ringed Python from New Britain and New Ireland to the east, an archipelago from which the White-lipped Python appears to be virtually absent, yet it is present again on the remote St Matthias archipelago, New Ireland Province, to the north of the Bismarck Archipelago. Apart from the Northern and Southern White-lipped Pythons featured in this account, it seems there could be 4–5 scattered highland and island populations that also warrant specific status. What was for so long, a single species, could soon become six or seven valid species based on their external morphology and mtDNA analysis.

Northern White-lipped Python *Leiopython albertisi*

This is the original D'Albertis Python, named in honour of Italian naturalist and 19th-century Papuan explorer Luigi

Maria D'Albertis and described from specimens collected in the Vogelkop (Bird's-Head) and Onin Peninsulas of West Papua. Although the name was applied to White-lipped Pythons from throughout New Guinea and surrounding islands, *L. albertisi* is now reserved for specimens collected from western and northern West Papua and the lowlands of the northern and northeastern Papua New Guinea (PNG). Mainland Northern White-lipped Pythons are medium-sized snakes with iridescent chestnut brown backs that become lighter yellow-brown on the flanks and immaculate cream below. This body colour, which has earned them the name 'golden phase', contrasts sharply with the glossy black head

and the bold black and white barred supralabials. Within the lowland parts of its range this may be the most common python species (see below), a position occupied in the south by the Carpet Python, *Morelia spilota*. Prey consists primarily of small mammals. Subspecies of *L. albertisii* may be recognized for some of the islands to the north of New Guinea, including the isolated St Matthias Group which are separated from mainland PNG populations by the range of the Bismarck populations of *Bothrochilus boa* (p.129).

The Northern White-lipped Python (Leiopython albertisi) *is the commonest python in northern Papua New Guinea.*

Range: Northern New Guinea and off-shore islands • Max. length: 1.0–1.8m • Habitat: Many habitats but a preference for coastal rainforest • Prey: Mammals and birds • Reproduction: Oviparous, 10–14 eggs

" O n good nights road-cruising the North Coast Highway, from Madang to Alexishafen and beyond, I could expect to find *Morelia amethistina, M. viridis, Apodora papuana*, but this was the python I encountered most frequently. Northern White-lipped Pythons were found in most habitats – dense coastal forest, sparse secondary growth, especially along creeks, and in coconut plantations. The only snake I found inside a coconut husk pile on the mainland was a pre-slough White-lipped Python. Unfortunately, I also met with numerous dead pythons, either killed on the road or thrown over telephone cables. These pythons adopt the small boid defensive of 'balling', hiding the head in the centre of the coils, when they feel threatened."

North Coast Road, Madang Province, PNG.

Southern White-lipped Python *Leiopython* sp.

The Southern White-lipped Python is quite different from the chestnut brown northern race, and if it were not for the shiny black head and black and white barred supralabials it would probably have been described as a separate species long ago. Not only is the southern race much darker, the body colour is an iridescent blue-grey which almost blends into the black head and neck, which results in this form being called the 'black phase'. Although I have previously used the name Southern D'Albertis Python for this form, that name no longer seem appropriate now that it has achieved specific status.

The Southern White-lipped Python is found throughout the southern lowlands from Timika, West Papua, to Central Province, PNG, and is officially included in the herpetofauna of Australia due to its presence on several of the Australian-controlled Torres Strait islands, although their location, only a few kilometres offshore from Western Province, makes them faunistically Papuan. Reports of specimens from Cape York Peninsula may infact result from misidentifications of water pythons (*Liasis fuscus*). Prey includes bandicoots and rats,

probably of a larger size than those taken by its smaller northern relative.

Range: Southern New Guinea and northern islands of the Torres Strait (Australia) • Max. length: 1.5–2.5m • Habitat: Lowland monsoon forest and riverine forest • Prey: Mammals and birds • Reproduction: Oviparous 9–16 eggs • Similar species: Brown Water Python (*Liasis fuscus*)

" I found the Southern White-lipped Python much rarer than its smaller and more ubiquitous northern relative, but I have captured a number of specimens along rivers entering the coastal monsoon forest in Western Province and crossing roads under 'rain trees', where creeks intersect the dry Central Province savannas. I never observed 'balling' in the large specimens I encountered."
Binaturi River, Western Province, and Goldie River, Central Province, PNG.

PAPUAN ARCHIPELAGO PYTHONS

Most New Guinea pythons are mainland species which have spread to the smaller islands off the coast, but the islands of the Bismarck Archipelago (New Britain and New Ireland) are sizeable islands in their own right. They are home to an endemic island python which does not occur on the mainland.

Bismarck Ringed Python
Bothrochilus boa

This species is a Papua New Guinea endemic and confined to the Bismarck Archipelago. The western-most record for this python is Umboi Island, Morobe Province, across the Vitiaz Strait from the Huon Peninsula, once itself an island. From Umboi, the ringed python is widely distributed throughout the large islands of New Britain, New Ireland and New Hanover, in addition to many of their satellite island clusters, with the exception of the isolated St Matthias Group to the north, where *Leiopython albertisi* is known to occur. The easternmost record for the Ringed Python comes from the Nissan Atoll, in the Green Islands Group, part of North Solomons

(Bougainville) Province located between New Ireland and Buka Island. Reports from Bougainville Island itself are unsubstantiated.

This is a small to medium-sized, fairly slender snake, with a narrow, almost pointed head and non-prehensile tail. It starts life as a bright orange and black-ringed snake with glossy black head. Although brightly patterned when juvenile, the rings may become less distinct, even completely obscured by brown pigment with increasing maturity.

It is unlikely to be confused with any snakes within their known geographical range, although the venomous New Guinea and Solomons Small-eyed Snakes may also be banded. They are found in similar habitats to the ringed python but in different parts of Melanesia, so confusion is unlikely.

Like many of the snakes from the archipelagos to the east of New Guinea, this is a poorly documented species in the wild and little is known about its ecology or natural history. Secretive, and the most semi-fossorial of all New Guinea pythons, its prey consists of small mammals and terrestrial lizards, but speaking with people who have worked in New

OPPOSITE: *Southern White-lipped Pythons* (Leiopython *sp.*) *are dark blue-grey to black snakes, larger and less frequently encountered than their northern relatives.*

TOP: *A true island python, the Bismarck Ringed Python* (Bothrochilus boa) *is confined to the Bismarck Archipelago of Papua New Guinea.*

BOTTOM: *The bright orange and black banding of the Ringed Python may fade with increasing maturity.*

Britain and New Ireland, it seems that the Ringed Python also eats snakes.

Range: Bismarck Archipelago, Papua New Guinea • Max. length: 1.0–1.8m • Habitat: Little documented, forests and coconut plantations • Prey: Small mammals and lizards (skinks), possibly snakes • Reproduction: Oviparous, 9 eggs • Similar species: New Guinea Small-eyed Snake (*Micropechis ikaheka*) from Karkar Island and mainland New Guinea or Solomons Small-eyed Snake (*Loveridgelaps elapoides*) from Solomon Islands, see O'Shea, 2005, p.133–135

CARPET PYTHONS

The head is broad, a shape emphasized by the distinctly narrow neck and allowing a wide mouth-gape. The dorsal head scales are fragmented with few enlarged scutes remaining, and thermo-sensory pits are present on the rostral, anterior supralabials and most of the infralabials. These snakes are highly adapted, homeothermic predators of mammals and birds, although as juveniles they include a fairly high proportion of lizards in their diet. They are agilely arboreal, when necessary, and possess highly prehensile tails.

Centralian Python *Morelia bredli*

Also known as Bredl's Python, named for South Australian herpetologist Joe Bredl, the Centralian Python was long considered a subspecies of the widespread Carpet Python complex and was known as the Central Carpet Python. Its specific status was established in 1981, based on its considerably higher scale counts, in almost every direction, than those found in the carpet pythons. Since its body proportion and size are not dissimilar to those of the carpets, these greater scale counts are due to the Centralian Python possessing much smaller scales, a reflection of its desert adaptation – desert snakes frequently exhibit smaller scales and subsequently high scale counts compared to species from less arid environments. Centralian Pythons are vividly marked snakes with broad, broken red-orange bands overlying a yellowish-cream background, although this pattern is reported to degrade to shades of brown in captivity, away from direct UV light. Although the dorsal head scales of this python are greatly fragmented, a few slightly enlarged scutes remain over the snout, and the frontal scale, between the eyes, is two to three times larger than the surrounding scales.

Centralian Pythons are found in a relatively localized area, in the MacDonnell ranges of southern Northern Territory, in the vicinity of Alice Springs. They are to be found in the gorges and dry drainages of the Todd and Charles Rivers, both in the trees and on the escarpments. Activity depends on the season and, although nocturnal during the summer months, the pythons become more crepuscular, even diurnal, during spring and autumn when night-time temperatures are too low for a poikilothermic reptile to function efficiently. Prey consists of tree-hole nesting birds, marsupials ranging from possums to rock wallabies, and even feral cats. Rabbits may also be taken, since large specimens have been seen around rabbit warrens.

Range: Southern Northern Territory, Australia • Max. length: 1.5–2.6m • Habitat: Rocky outcrops and ridges and sparse *Acacia* **woodland along creek-beds • Prey: Mammals and birds • Reproduction: Oviparous, 13–47 eggs**

Carpet Python *Morelia spilota*

The Carpet Python complex has been the source of considerable confusion and argument relating to its geographical distribution and taxonomic status. As the most widely distributed Australian python, it occurs across most of northern, eastern and southwestern Australia, although it is absent from Victoria and Tasmania, the southern half of the Great Dividing Range (GDR) and the central and western deserts of Western Australia, Northern Territory and South Australia. Carpets also occur across the Torres Strait, in southern New Guinea, and are even reported from northwestern New Guinea.

With the exception of the Diamond and Jungle Carpet Pythons (*M. s. spilota* and *M. s. cheynei* – see below) most Carpet Pythons are patterned with a series of red or brown, dark-edged, irregular blotches over a paler, yellow to light brown background. The blotches may cross over the back and meet dorsally, or fuse laterally to form broken stripes. Several stripes of the same colour pass forwards onto the head, laterally passing through the eye to the snout, and dorsally curving down to above the eye. At one time all the current subspecies, except the nominate *M. s. spilota,* were treated as a single subspecies, *M. s. variegata.* It is highly likely that further study and collection of specimens from remote locations, particularly in New Guinea, combined with advances in DNA analysis, will lead to the description of further forms. However, the intensive captive hybridization to produce 'attractive' designer morphs could greatly reduce the value of these gene pools when it comes to maintaining breeding groups for threatened populations.

In Australia, Carpet Pythons are generally known simply as carpet snakes, while in PNG there are grouped with all pythons as 'moran'.

OPPOSITE: The Centralian Python (Morelia bredli) *prefers arid habitats and in particular the dry gorges and escarpments around Alice Springs.*

BELOW: The Diamond Python (Morelia spilota spilota) *is the nominate species of Carpet Python but is limited in its distribution to coastal New South Wales and northern Victoria.*

Range: Northern and eastern Australia, also southwestern Australia and New Guinea • Max. length: 1.4–2.8m, occasionally >4.0m • Habitat: A wide variety of wet and arid habitats, savanna to woodland, forest and rocky outcrops • Prey: Mammals and birds, also lizards, especially when juvenile • Reproduction: Oviparous, 11–28 eggs (12–54 in larger subspecies)

Photo by David G. Barker, VPI

Subspecies of *Morelia spilota*

Originally only two subspecies were recognized, but up to eight have been proposed. Today six are generally accepted, while the validity of the Papuan subspecies is controversial.

Diamond Python *Morelia spilota spilota*

The nominate subspecies is easily recognized. The background colour is yellow to cream, overlaid with a striking pattern of black reticulations and scale edging. The overall appearance is a cream snake with every scale heavily edged in black and four longitudinal rows of cream lozenges or diamond markings, boldly outlined in black. The Diamond Python has a limited distribution, down the coast of New South Wales and just into Victoria, making it the world's southernmost python. Separated from other Carpet Pythons to the west by the Great Dividing Range, Diamond Pythons encounter Coastal Carpets (*M. s. mcdowelli*) only at the extreme northern tip of the Diamond's range, and here the two forms are reported to intergrade.

Habitats frequented by Diamond Pythons, in this relatively cool part of Australia, range from dry forests to steep sandstone precipices and escarpments, and owing to the greatly varying seasonal conditions they vary their activity and habitat use

ABOVE: *The Northwestern Carpet Python* (Morelia spilota variegata) *is found throughout the northern half of Australia.*

accordingly, often overwintering in north-facing rocky crevices away from the southern cold. Since this species occurs near an area of high human population, Diamond Pythons even move into gardens and overwinter in attics.

Prey is primarily mammalian, but lizards and birds also feature, especially in the diets of juvenile Diamond Pythons.

" In May 2001, I was with Australian herpetologist Jonathan Webb, searching for Broad-headed Snakes *(Hoplocephalus bungaroides)* on the steep Hawkesbury sandstone escarpments to the west of Sydney, when we made a surprising discovery. On a narrow and precarious ridge near the top of a knoll we encountered a large Diamond Python which had obviously just emerged from a crevice to begin basking. It was a very exciting find for me as I had never before seen a Diamond Python in the wild."
Morton National Park, New South Wales

Northwestern Carpet Python *Morelia spilota variegata*

Originally all carpets, other than the Diamond Python, were considered to belong to this subspecies, but today its range is restricted to those Carpet Pythons found from Broome and the Kimberley in Western Australia, through Northern Territory, around the southeast of the Gulf of Carpentaria, including those islands located in the Gulf, to a point midway up the western coastline of Cape York Peninsula. They are inhabitants of savanna-woodland, monsoon forest and dry forest, in contrast to the Papuan specimens across the Arafura Sea, formerly included within this subspecies, which show a distinct preference for open savanna habitats.

Southwestern Carpet Python *Morelia spilota imbricata*

This is the only mainland taxon of Carpet Python which does not have contact with any other subspecies; it was recognized as the third subspecies in 1981. Occurring in a diverse array of habitats, from grassland to wooded hillsides, the Southwestern Carpet Python is confined to southwestern Western Australia. The region is often known as the wheat belt, and the intensive monoculture and habitat destruction resulting from these farming techniques may be a threat to the survival of this isolated subspecies. Certainly the conservation status of the Southwestern Carpet Python is of concern to environmental groups in Australia.

A number of scalation differences stand to separate this subspecies from more eastern forms, but it differs also in coloration, being more subdued and darker than its relatives.

An isolated population of Southwestern Carpets is also found on the tiny, windswept Isle of St Francis, off South Australia. The habitat is heathland and stunted trees, the climate foggy and damp. The pythons here are small, less than 1.5m, and demonstrate some curious scalation characteristics, including fusion of the scales on the head or over the tail. The island conditions might be suitable for the resident tigersnake population, a live-bearing elapid, but would seem unsuitable for an egg-laying python. Perhaps the presence of the species is entirely dependent on the population of burrow-digging mutton birds which would provide shelter, a place to lay eggs and abundant prey for a few weeks each year. Young pythons and tigersnakes would have to survive on a diet of lizards if there are no small mammals present. This is certainly a population in need of study and protection.

Coastal Carpet Python
Morelia spilota mcdowelli

The Coastal Carpet Python is named in honour of Samuel McDowell, the American herpetologist responsible for intensive studies of Melanesian snakes. This subspecies is distributed from northeastern New South Wales (NSW) to far northern Cape York Peninsula, to the east of the Great Dividing Range (GDR), although in central Queensland the subspecies is also found to the west of the GDR in the black-soil country.

Coastal Carpets can be large snakes, the usual maximum length being 1.8–2.7m, with specimens over 4.0m reported. Prey size increases with the larger body proportions, and cats, bandicoots and possums are all commonly taken. Water dragons are reported taken and fruit bats are also potential prey. Preferred habitat appears to be woodland and forest.

Jungle Carpet Python *Morelia spilota cheynei*

The Jungle Carpet Python is one of the most sought-after phases for keepers and some specimens can only be described as spectacular, but it is hard to determine just how much of that is due to selective breeding and how much is natural. Many Jungle Carpets look like brighter examples of Coastal Carpets, but a few may be intensely patterned with bold black bars over a brilliant yellow background, or even with broad black longitudinal stripes overlying the yellow beneath to the extent that only fine yellow stripes remain.

Wild Jungle Carpets inhabit the smallest range of any of the recognized Carpet Python subspecies. Their home range is located in the drainages that run off the Atherton Tableland in the southeastern portion of Cape York Peninsula, an area in the middle of the range of the widely distributed Coastal Carpet Python (*M. s. mcdowelli*), although the two are not thought to occur in the same locations. Jungle Carpets inhabit the lush subtropical rainforest of the region, particularly along the creeks, but this habitat has seen considerable degradation and little remains of the original forest.

The Jungle Carpet Python (Morelia spilota cheynei) *is the most stunning carpet python, and also the one with the most restricted range.*

specimens from Western Province are especially stoutly built, with broad heads, unlike the more slender Central Province specimens I have seen. This is the most frequently encountered python on the savannas around Port Moresby.

Inland Carpet Python *Morelia spilota metcalfei*

To the west of the GDR can be found the widely-distributed and variable Inland Carpet Python, which occurs from central Queensland to the NSW-Victoria border region and the southern coast of South Australia from Adelaide to the Eyre Peninsula. This is the only subspecies to enter every mainland state except Western Australia, but some authors voice the opinion that the Inland Carpet Python may in truth be a composite of several forms, and therefore deserve further ecological and taxonomic study.

Carpet Python *Morelia spilota macrospila*

This subspecies, described in 1909 from an unknown locality, is no longer considered valid.

Papuan Carpet Python *Morelia spilota ssp.*

The status of all New Guinea Carpet Pythons is controversial. Carpets occur in Papua New Guinea (PNG), around Port Moresby and Central Province, and across the Gulf of Papua in the seasonally-flooded savannas of Western Province, where their distribution crosses the border into neighbouring West Papua (formerly Irian Jaya or Indonesian New Guinea) to Merauke. There may also be isolated populations of carpets on the small savannas of Gulf Province, PNG, but in PNG this species does not seem to enter woodland or forest or inhabit the mountains to the north. It has not been found in the grassy valleys of the Highlands, nor in the coastal lowlands of Morobe, Madang or the Sepiks to the north. However, there are reports of carpets from northwestern Indonesian New Guinea, so presumably either habitat is suitable for their radiation to the far west or the snakes have adapted to different habitats from those inhabited in PNG. The New Guinea populations are fragmented and isolated, and their taxonomic status and relationships have yet to be determined with certainty.

In my experience, Papuan Carpets are unfriendly and inclined to bite repeatedly. They also decline all prey animals offered, from small mammals to birds and lizards. Large

"I have found Carpet Pythons to be the most common python in the more arid areas around Port Moresby. However, in the twenty years I have been visiting PNG I have seen a distinct drop-off in the frequency that pythons can be found, and I fear that habitat loss through development, increased motor vehicular activity and active persecution by an increasing population may be threatening these snakes in this narrow coastal savanna strip. Certainly it is rare to find a Carpet Python in Port Moresby itself, whereas it was once a very common snake. I have found a few places in the outskirts where Carpets were common, locations where I used to release those specimens I captured in the town, but even these areas are no longer remote as dense kunai grass is cleared and roads are cut into the bush. Gone are the days when I could find eight Carpets together in a single abandoned mine workings."
Port Moresby and Sogeri, Central Province, PNG

"Late one evening I left the University of PNG and was walking back to my accommodation across town, carrying a cloth sack. I was approached by a local man, who decided to walk with me and engage me in overtly friendly conversation. Eventually, as we reached a more deserted part of town, he asked me what he had probably wanted to know all along – what was in the bag. Having expected this line of enquiry I told him he had three guesses and, if he guessed correctly, I would pass over ownership. He guessed three times, three valuable items of the type one would not willingly give to a stranger. I told him he was wrong on all three occasions but, as he had done so well, he could have a peep in the sack. I untied the drawstring and he looked in to find a large Carpet Python gazing back at him. Before I had retied the sack he had retraced the last 50m of our walk and disappeared around a corner."
Port Moresby, NCD, PNG

RARE AUSTRALIAN PYTHONS

Even though Australia is such a vast continent, it is still surprising to learn that large snake species like pythons managed to evade scientific discovery until the end of the 20th century. Two new species were identified in Northern Territory and Western Australia, and more may yet be hiding in the Outback.

Oenpelli Python *Morelia oenpelliensis*

Found in the sandstone escarpments surrounding Oenpelli in remote western Arnhem Land, Northern Territory, this is an extremely slender and slightly built python – it has even been suggested that it may be the most slender and elongate python in the world. The entire snake gives an impression of being drawn out, etiolated, even the head being long and slender, an effect further enhanced by its bulging, slightly forward-facing eyes. The Oenpelli Python is also one of the few python species capable of subtle colour changes, being pale pastel with slightly darker blotches at night, and darker, with the reddish or greyish blotches blending into the ground colour, during the day.

Habitat consists of steep, weathered sandstone escarpments and the dense forest at its base, similar to that inhabited by the Rough-scaled Python (*M. carinata*) further west (see below). This slender python feeds on a large proportion of birds, some of which may be caught in fruiting trees, but it is capable of subduing surprisingly large prey including wallaroos and small wallabies. It is also possible that lizards form a part of its diet, since they are abundant in its rocky habitat.

Although only described and known to scientists since 1977, the aboriginal inhabitants of its range are very familiar with this species, calling it 'nawaran' and using its image in their petroglyphs and paintings.

Range: Arnhem Land, Northern Territory, Australia • Max. length: 3.0–4.5m • Habitat: Sandstone escarpments and rocky outcrops • Prey: Mammals and birds • Reproduction: Oviparous, 4–9 eggs

Rough-scaled Python *Morelia carinata*

This species may be the python species with the world's smallest range, which lies within a 50-mile area encompassing the Mitchell and Hunter Rivers in the remote Kimberley region of Western Australia. Like the Oenpelli Python, the Rough-scaled Python is an inhabitant of rocky river gorges and associated monsoon forest. Also like the Oenpelli, it is a poorly known species, with fewer than ten known specimens.

At first glance its red-brown coloration and blotched patterning resembles a Carpet Python (*M. spilota*) or Centralian Python (*M. bredli*) but there are two immediately obvious differences. The Rough-scaled Python has extremely strongly keeled dorsal scales, especially on the body, less so on the head, neck and tail. Although this is a common characteristic of desert snakes, no other python in the world has keeled scales. It also possesses an enlarged round scale in the centre of the head, which further separates it from other pythons. The patterning also lacks any hint of black pigment, not even a scale-tip is melanistic.

BELOW: *The Oenpelli Python* (Morelia oenpelliensis) *from Arnhem Land in Northern Territory, reaches 4.5m but was only described to science in 1977.*

The diet of this python probably consists of birds; it has extremely long teeth which would penetrate the plumage easily, but small mammals and lizards should not be discounted as prey in the wild.

Several expeditions to the Hunter River gorge have resulted in specimens being collected under licence for captive breeding at the Australian Reptile Park, Gosford, NSW. This breeding programme has been successful and has so far produced seven clutches of hatchling Rough-scaled Pythons. **Range: Kimberley region, Western Australia • Max. length: 1.2–2.0m • Habitat: Sandstone river gorge and monsoon forest • Prey: Probably birds, possibly small mammals and lizards • Reproduction: Oviparous, 10–14 eggs • Similar species: Carpet Python (*Morelia spilota* spp.) and Centralian Python (*M. bredli*)**

" I joined John Weigel of the Australian Reptile Park on one of his expeditions to find Rough-scaled Pythons. We camped for ten days in a gorge, but it was not until Day 9 that John found a female Rough-scaled Python resting in a tree. The next day, as the film crew packed to depart, I heard John's friend Alf Britton calling from up the gorge. When I got to him he was wrestling a male Rough-scaled Python out of the mouth of a large Olive Python *(Liasis olivaceus)*. By the end of the trip, John had the second pair he needed for his captive breeding programme at ARP."
Hunter River Gorge, Kimberley, Western Australia

TREE PYTHONS
Many of the pythons of Australasia are terrestrial snakes, and although all can climb, only one species can truly be termed a 'tree python'. One of the most attractive snakes in the world, it demonstrates a startling similarity to a boa living in the Amazon Basin.

Green Tree Python *Morelia viridis*
This is probably the best-known python from the Indo-Australian region. It is certainly one of the most frequently photographed and written-about species, owing no doubt to its great beauty and desirability for both public and private collections. Originally described in the then catch-all genus *Python,* the Green Tree Python spent 120 years in its own (monotypic) genus *Chondropython,* a reference to the granular nature of its tiny body scales. Since 1990, the close relationships between the Green Tree Python and the Carpet Python complex (*Morelia spilota*) have been recognized and the species has been transferred to the genus *Morelia.* The loss of the familiar and popular generic name *Chondropython* has not prevented this snake's many fans from continuing to refer to it endearingly as the 'chondro'.

The Green Tree Python has a wide distribution. It is found throughout New Guinea below 2,000m, both West Papua and Papua New Guinea, and on many of the satellite archipelagos, such as Misool and Salawatti to the west, Aru to the southwest, Yapen, Biak and other islands of Geelvinck Bay to the northwest, Ferguson and Normanby Islands (d'Entrecasteaux Archipelago) to the southeast, Daru and the islands of the Torres Strait to the south, and a very small strip of coastal rainforest in northeastern Cape York Peninsula, Queensland, as far south as the Normanby River.

Since this python is also an extremely variable species, both in coloration and finite body proportions, many herpeto-culturists differentiate between different populations, especially those from islands, defining them as Aru, Sorong, Biak or Yapen variants or races. None of these names has any scientific validity, and there are no recognized subspecies.

Green Tree Pythons are covered in numerous rows of tiny body scales with even the familiar dorsal head scutes fragmented to the size of the body scales. Adults are generally green above and yellow below, with or without additional markings which may consist simply of scattered white or yellow scales or be as elaborate as a light blue vertebral line with small off-shoots of the same colour, combined with large attendant spots of yellow or white. Some of the captive-bred specimens are stunning in their appearance. Juveniles exceed the adults in the diversity of their liveries. Most are bright yellow with white spots and stripes edged with light brown, but they may be orange, brick-red or even almost black with startling yellow markings. Occasionally juveniles start out green, like the adults, but almost all turn that colour by their second year. This is known as ontogenetic colour change. One of the most amazing aspects of the patterning of juvenile Green Tree Pythons is the way the shape of the large round eye is disrupted by a stripe running from the snout, actually through the eye and back to the angle of the jaw. Combined with the vertically elliptical pupil, this patterning probably serves to break up the outline of the eye. The tail tip in both adult and juvenile is a different colour from the rest of the body, the juvenile at least using it to 'caudal lure' potential prey within strike range.

The vivid and contrastingly different juvenile and adult colour patterns of the Green Tree Python in Indo-Australia mirror those seen in the equally arboreal South American Emerald Treeboa (*Corallus caninus*, p.39), to the point that to a layman the two species are indistinguishable. Clearly the adults are camouflaged for life in the rainforest, but the purpose of the startling and seemingly highly visible coloration of the juveniles remains a mystery. The Green Tree Python and the Emerald Treeboa are the most frequently quoted examples of convergent evolution within the

RIGHT: *Juvenile Green Tree Pythons* (Morelia viridis) *are stunning snakes, yellow (or orange) with black or brown and white dorsal markings.*

OPPOSITE: *The rare Rough-scaled Python* (Morelia carinata) *inhabits river gorges in the remote Kimberley region of Western Australia.*

snakes. One of the easiest ways to distinguish between the Emerald Treeboa and the Green Tree Python involves examining the side of the head. In the Green Tree Python the majority of the supralabials, apart from the rostral and anterior two or three scales on either side, are entire and not scored by deep heat-sensitive pits, whereas in the treeboa all the supralabials posterior to the eye are deeply incised with pits. The snout of the treeboa is also longer and more pointed than that of the Green Tree Python.

Although the prehensile tail and body suggest the Green Tree Python is primarily an arboreal species, it is not uncommon to find them prowling on the ground at night. It is possible that, when they are encountered in compounds or crossing roads, they are hunting terrestrial mammals or seeking mates.

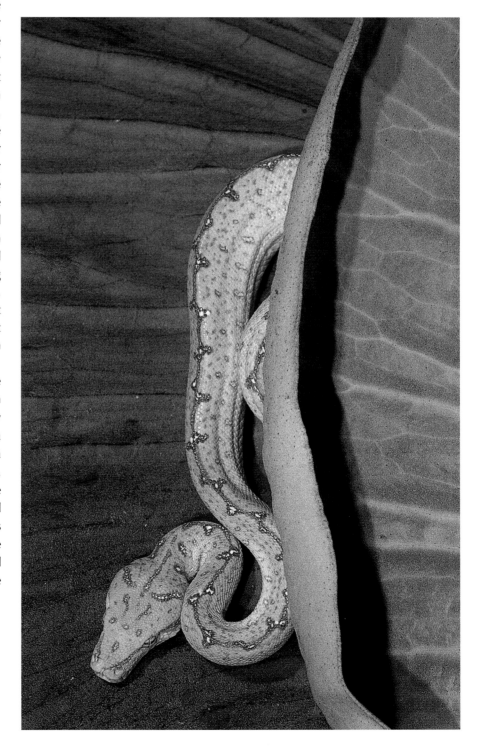

Juveniles are also found at night, coiled in low vegetation, even garden hedges, and they seem to prey on a higher proportion of small lizards than their larger relatives. It has not been determined to what degree, if at all, they take birds or bats, common prey of the Emerald Treeboa.

Range: eastern Indonesia, New Guinea and eastern Cape York Peninsula, Queensland, Australia • Max. length: 1.6–2.2m • Habitat: Coastal and rainforest but also gardens and secondary growth to 2,000m • Prey: Small mammals as adults, some lizards as juveniles • Reproduction: Oviparous, 6–32 eggs • Similar species: Emerald Treeboa (*Corallus caninus*)

" I have seen many Green Tree Pythons in Papua New Guinea, but the two specimens that stick in my mind most were not found by me. I was eating dinner in the restaurant attached to the lodge where I was staying when someone came in and said, in a loud voice and to the great interest of everyone else present, "Mark, the police are outside and they want to see you!" I went out to discover an armoured police vehicle and five Papuan policemen. Unsure of the reason for their interest in me, I was much relieved when they smiled and handed me a sack containing a beautiful adult female Green Tree Python they had collected on the road two hours to the north. The second occasion also involved the authorities. Based in the National Museum in Port Moresby I had a visit from the security officers from the Prime Minister's residence down the road, and they presented me with the most striking female Green Tree Python I saw in all my visits to PNG."

Jais Aben, Madang Province, and Port Moresby, NCD, Papua New Guinea

ABOVE: *Although superficially similar to the Emerald Treeboa (Corallus caninus) of South America, the Green Tree Python (Morelia viridis) differs in that most of the supralabials (upper lip scales) lack thermo-sensory pits.*

OPPOSITE: *An adult Green Tree Python in typical sleeping posture, body looped with head in centre.*

SCRUB PYTHONS

Two names have been widely used for this large Indo-Australian python, the term 'Scrub Python' appearing most frequently in the Australian, and sometimes American, literature, a reference to the semi-arid savanna-woodland inhabited by some populations. The alternative common name of 'Amethystine Python', which is used more often in British literature, and the scientific name *Morelia amethistina*, are references to the iridescent sheen that is visible when sunlight falls upon the body scales. This is a common feature in nocturnal snakes and often reflected in their names, hence Rainbow Boa, Iridescent Earth Snake, Sunbeam Snake etc, and may be a form of disruptive patterning, breaking up the outline of the coils in daylight, like a hologram, to confuse a foraging predator.

The Scrub or Amethystine Python was long considered a single, widely-distributed, Indo-Australian species consisting of the nominate New Guinea-eastern Indonesian subspecies and a Queensland, Australia subspecies, described in 1933, but a recent and significant study of the Scrub Python complex (Harvey *et al*, 2000*) not only elevated the Queensland population to full specific status, but also identified three new species from the island to the west of New Guinea. What was once a single species now comprises a five-species complex. The authors of the study also suggested that additional species may yet be described from the northern and southern New Guinea and Bismarck populations of *M. amethistina*, a hypothesis I fully support having observed the diversity of Amethystine Pythons in Papua New Guinea. I will use the term 'Scrub Python' for all those species not now included within the original name *M. amethistina*.

The five species within *Morelia amethistina* (*sensu lato*) were delineated, in part, by differences in their DNA. Fortunately for the python enthusiast and the fieldworker, the authors of the 2000 study also used morphological characteristics in their species definitions, differences in head scalation and aspects of the patterning, so that it is also possible to identify the five species by close physical examination. Since the finite scalation differences between the species are too complex to be included here, the interested reader is referred to the original paper with its fine illustrated figures of the head scalation. All five species are included below, but it should be understood that the New Guinea Amethystine Python probably contains three or more as yet undescribed species.

The Scrub Pythons are all relatively large snakes, although

some data are lacking on the three new species. They are fairly elongate with powerful, muscular bodies and long heads and prehensile tails. Primarily nocturnal, like all pythons, they are active on the ground but also extremely adept at climbing, their body form being perfect for an arboreal existence. Prey, therefore, can be very diverse and includes not only large and powerful ground-dwelling mammals, such as bush pig or wallabies, and large birds like chickens, but also tree-dwelling species like cuscus, sugar gliders, tree kangaroos, fruit bats and birds. There are reports of Scrub Pythons frequenting large fruit bat colonies.

* Harvey, M.B., Barker, D.G., Ammerman, L.K. & Chippindale, P.T., 2000, 'Systematics of pythons of the *Morelia amethistina* complex (Serpentes: Boidae) with a description of three new species'. *Herpetological Monographs* 14:139–185.

New Guinea Amethystine Python *Morelia amethistina*

At the time of writing this taxon still comprises Amethystine Pythons spread over a significant area and the authors of the 2000 study are almost certainly correct in their suggestion that *M. amethistina* may still contain three species. There appears to be a northern New Guinea race that occurs from Sorong at the extreme west of the Doberai Peninsular (Vogelkop) to Jayapura, from where it continues into northern Papua New Guinea (PNG) in the Sepik region. This is described as a pale to medium brown snake with dark patterning, beginning as a pair of bold transverse neck bars, continuing strongly onto the body but absent from the posterior third and the tail, and the anterior supralabials (upper lip scales) having bold black edging. Within this race there exists a form lacking any patterning beyond the presence of the two dark neck bars.

A southern New Guinea race occurs in the Merauke region of southern West Papua, and across the border into Western, Gulf and Central Provinces, PNG. The authors of the 2000 study also attributed the island populations from the Aru and Kei Islands, in the Arafura Sea to the south of Indonesian West Papua, to this form, while noting that the Biak Island population, from northwest of New Guinea, appeared to show closer similarities to the southern populations than to the geographically closer northern race. The southern race is generally a medium to dark brown snake without neck bars but with pale patterning throughout the entire body length, and the supralabials unmarked, or only faintly marked with dark pigment.

The status of Amethystine Pythons from northeastern PNG, Madang, Morobe, the Huon Peninsula, appears to be less easily defined and in need of greater study, while southern

The Amethystine Python (Morelia amethistina) *is a large New Guinea species which preys on wallabies.*

The Amethystine Python is probably a complex containing several species. This unicolor specimen is very different from the typical specimen opposite.

populations from Western Province, PNG, have been described as forest phase (dark brown) or savanna phase (sandy brown). Although the northern and southern races appear to be geographically separated in West Papua (Indonesian New Guinea), it seems as though they may exist in sympatry, or at least in very close proximity, in PNG.

The authors of the 2000 study also suggested that the Amethystine Pythons from the Bismarck Archipelago to the east of New Guinea, which comprises the large islands of New Britain and New Ireland and numerous smaller islands and islets, may also represent taxa separate from the mainland races. They described a specimen as unpatterned but with 'a pinkish taupe' in life. Since this is a region of considerable endemicity, with many species of snakes and lizards confined to individual islands or groups of islands, there is every chance that more than one species from the *M. amethistina* complex will eventually be described from here.

However, a major problem exists with regard to the defining of the taxon *Morelia amethistina* and the apportioning of names to other New Guinea populations. The type specimen described as *Boa amethistina* by Schneider in 1801 was lodged

in the Berlin Museum, but is now believed to have been lost, possibly during World War Two, when many zoological collections were destroyed or disrupted. Unfortunately, Schneider did not provide a type locality for the specimen so it cannot even be allocated to the northern, southern or Bismarck populations based on geographical data. Therefore, should *M. amethistina*, as it now exists, become further fragmented, it is not known which population should inherit the original name and which should be described as new taxa.

Although these are large and powerful snakes, capable of devouring wallabies and other relatively large mammals, amethystine pythons are not invulnerable. They have predators too, not least other pythons such as the snake-eating Papuan Python (*Apodora papuana,* p.124).

Range: New Guinea and Bismarck Archipelago • Max. length: 4.0–6.0m • Habitat: All habitats from savanna-woodland to swamp and montane rainforest to 1600m • Prey: Mammals, rats to wallabies, also birds • Reproduction: Oviparous, 5–21 eggs

"In 1990 I was collecting venomous snakes for an Oxford University venom research and snakebite project, and had placed an advert in the *Times of PNG*, asking to be alerted through

my publisher's Port Moresby office if someone saw a Taipan or Papuan Blacksnake. On one occasion I was out following up a call when another call came in about a large snake in a tree. This was clearly a python, and my publisher informed the caller that I would contact him on my return. One hour later the caller and three friends drove up my publisher's drive in a pick-up truck, a small tree protruding out of the back with a 2.0m Amethystine Python coiled in the upper branches."
Port Moresby, NCD, Papua New Guinea

" I was called to a large snake in the roof of a sawmill which turned out to be a 3.0m Amethystine Python. I talked to the mill-owners and explained that the snake was probably doing them a great service, feeding on rats, and was able to convince them to allow it to stay. They knew it was not venomous, but it was a 'snake' ! Pythons are often persecuted for no reason other than that they are snakes."
Alexishafen, Madang Province, Papua New Guinea

" We were engaged in a search for a large monitor lizard known as Salvador's monitor or the 'tree crocodile' *(Varanus salvadori)* for a documentary of this elusive reptile. As we travelled down the Binaturi River in two small boats, I saw a large snake swimming casually towards a large entanglement of vegetation that protruded far out into the river. Anxious to capture the snake, whose patterning I did not recognize, we approached with as much stealth as possible.

I was concerned that the boat would spook the python and it would dive, never to be seen again, so I entered the water quietly and swam towards the coils, which by now had almost reached the overhanging vegetation. I could not believe my luck as I closed my hand on the body of the python somewhere on the anterior section – I could not see its head. I had it, it would not now escape me. That was true, I had it, but it also had me because it immediately coiled its posterior body around my legs and tightened up so that I could no longer swim, and it seemed to have anchored its tail somewhere deep down below because I felt myself being winched under the water. Somewhat alarmed, I called for assistance from the crew, asking them to extend a long snake grab so that I might pull myself to the boat. Misunderstanding my needs the director threw the grab to me and it sank without trace.

Eventually they understood my predicament and brought the boat alongside so I was able to climb aboard, coils still firmly wrapped around my legs.

The specimen turned out to be a rather unusually tiger-stripe patterned Amethystine Python measuring some 4.2m. The snake grab was retrieved by a local diver who said the river bottom at that point was over 6.0m."
Weam, Western Province, Papua New Guinea

Australian Scrub Python *Morelia kinghorni*

Australia's longest snake, with average maximum lengths of 3.5–5.0m and occasional larger specimens culminating in a 1948 report of an 8.5m specimen, the Australian Scrub Python was described in 1933 in honour of the noted Australian Museum herpetologist James Roy Kinghorn (1891–1983). It is found primarily in the coastal rainforests along the eastern side of Cape York Peninsula, where it basks in the tree canopy or on rocky outcrops, to as far south as Townsville.

This is a pale to medium brown snake, with bold dark brown

markings that begin as a pair of neck bars and continue as bars and blotches running the full length of the body and tail, and unmarked supralabials. Patternless specimens are unknown, but females are reported to be darker than males and their snouts are shorter, giving the impression of a broader head.

Male *M. kinghorni* are reputedly aggressive to one another in the breeding season, engaging in aggressive biting and combat for the attentions of the female. Such behaviour is known for other species, such as the Reticulated Python (*Python reticulatus*), where the wounds inflicted may be so severe as to cause death.

The status of the pythons on the Torres Strait islands, between Queensland and New Guinea, is open to question, since some authors consider them to be *M. kinghorni* while the authors of the 2000 study state that at least some are *M. amethistina*. Since some of the Australian-owned islands are only few kilometres off the shore of Western Province, PNG, such strong links are very likely and the separation between the two taxa must occur nearer to Cape York.

Range: Eastern Cape York Peninsula, Queensland, Australia • Max. length: 4.0–8.5m • Habitat: Most habitats from montane rainforest to coastal scrub and swamp • Prey: Mammals, from rats, fruit bats and wallabies to bush pigs, and birds from bee-eaters to chickens • Reproduction: Oviparous, 8–20 eggs

Halmahera Scrub Python *Morelia tracyae*

The Halmahera Scrub Python is believed to be the most diverged member of the *M. amethistina* complex. It may be confined to the northwestern peninsular of Halmahera, a glove-shaped island resembling a small Sulawesi, which it shares with the Asian Reticulated Python (*Python reticulatus*), another elongate python and another species harvested locally for its skin.

Named for Tracy Barker, one half of a respected Texan python breeding couple, *M. tracyae* is a brown snake with dark postocular stripes, transverse neck bars and broad, darker brown bands across the body, which may or may not meet over the back on the anterior part of the body. A defining characteristic appears to be the presence of a red iris to the eye, when all other

The Australian Scrub Python (Morelia kinghorni) *of Queensland is probably the largest of the amethystine-scrub python complex.*

Photo by David G. Barker, VPI

Photo by David G. Barker, VPI

members of the complex possess a gold or black iris. This species is reputed to frequent fruit bat roosts and feed on fruit bats. **Range: Halmahera, northern Maluku (Moluccas), eastern Indonesia • Max. length: not known, 2.8m (type specimen) • Habitat: Evergreen rainforest • Prey: Presumed to be fruit bats, probably other mammals and possibly birds • Reproduction: Oviparous, clutch size unknown • Similar species: Reticulated Python (*Python reticulatus*)**

Seram Scrub Python *Morelia clastolepis*

Described from the islands of Seram and Ambon and suspected to occur on neighbouring islands, the Seram Scrub Python differs from its closest relatives in that it lacks the dark postocular stripes and transverse neck bars common in other

species in the complex. Some specimens also possess subocular scales, which separate the supralabials from the eye, and these scales are absent from all other members of the complex. Two colour phases exist, grey with black eyes and brown with gold eyes, with patternless specimens also known. Little is known of the natural history of this species although there is a report of one preying on a cuscus, a prehensile-tailed arboreal marsupial. **Range: Seram and Ambon, southern Maluku (Moluccas), eastern Indonesia • Max. length: 1.5–3.8m • Habitat: Evergreen and semi-evergreen rainforest • Prey: Mammals, small-medium marsupials • Reproduction: Oviparous, clutch size unknown**

Tanimbar Scrub Python *Morelia nauta*

The southwestern-most member of the complex, the Tanimbar Scrub Python is given the Latin name for 'sailor', since the Tanimbar Islands have never been joined to another land mass and the python must have arrived by rafting. This is the smallest and most slightly-built member of the complex, and also the one with the most pronounced pointed snout. In coloration it is a variable species with patternless and patterned specimens, but most of the patterned, darker specimens possess rows of cream spots down their flanks. **Range: Tanimbar archipelago, Maluku (Moluccas), eastern Indonesia • Max. length: not known, 1.7m (type specimen) • Habitat: Moist deciduous forest with some coastal semi-evergreen rainforest • Prey: Probably mammals and/or birds • Reproduction: Oviparous, clutch size unknown • Similar species: Lesser Sundas Python (*Python timoriensis*)**

MONTANE PYTHONS

Pythons seem to be most abundant in low-lying habitats, and there are parts of coastal Madang, Western or Central Provinces, PNG, where one might encounter four or five species in one night. The Highlands of New Guinea are less well endowed with pythons, but there is at least one gem, a truly montane python, found there which does not extend its range into lowland coastal habitats.

Boelen's Python *Morelia boeleni*

The Boelen's Python, or Black Python as it is sometimes known, is probably the python most associated with the island of New Guinea. It is one of the most desirable of all pythons, but also one of the most difficult to maintain and breed in captivity. Boelen's Pythons are not lowland snakes, like most if not all other pythons, but highland animals with a dislike of hot, arid conditions. They inhabit the cool, humid, low-light rainforests between the 1,000m contour and the tree-line, where forest gives way to Papuan highland grassland.

The University of PNG probably failed to keep their specimen alive because Port Moresby is located in a particularly dry and arid part of southern coastal PNG, whereas the National Museum just down the road was accidentally more successful. The museum has a central open area where they maintain native fauna and set into its wall they had installed tall cages that could also be viewed from inside the museum. They tended to keep displays of PNG pythons in these aluminium-framed cages but, unfortunately, or perhaps fortunately, the cages were not so well constructed as to be

ABOVE: *The Tanimbar Scrub Python* (Morelia nauta) *inhabits a small group of isolated islands to the southwest of New Guinea.*

OPPOSITE TOP: *The Halmahera Scrub Python* (Morelia tracyae) *shares its Indonesian island home with the Reticulated Python* (Python reticulatus) *of Southeast Asia.*

OPPOSITE BOTTOM: *Head of a Seram Scrub Python* (Morelia clastolepis), *a species which inhabits Seram and Ambon, between New Guinea and Sulawesi.*

watertight and when it rained in the inner courtyard they leaked badly. I believe this was why the large pair of Boelen's Pythons kept there survived for so long, at least until the female ate the male!

Boelen's Python was named in honour of Dr K.W.J. Boelen, a government surgeon at Enarotali, in what was then Dutch New Guinea, who obtained the type specimen of this newly discovered python for the Rijksmuseum in Leiden. It is a robust species, stout-bodied with a broad and powerful head, a physique suggesting it adopts a terrestrial existence as an adult, although highlanders claim it is also extremely arboreal. More slightly-built juveniles are certainly more adapted to life in the trees. In coloration this species could not be confused with any other. The dominant colour is black, or blue-black, overlaid with the iridescent sheen shared by many other nocturnal snakes. The underside is immaculate white, cream or yellow and on the anterior portion of the body this contrasting light pigment extends forwards and upwards onto the flanks in a series of diagonal bars that stand out strongly against the

black background. This contrast of black and white continues as a series of bold bars onto the supralabials, the only pigment on the entire snake that is not blue-black or yellow-cream being the grey of the eye. The Boelen's Python is an extremely striking species as an adult, though juveniles are quite different, being red-brown above with only the faintest hint of the lateral pale bars.

This is probably the least studied New Guinea python, both in the wild and in captivity, and there is still much to be learned about its maximum length, prey preferences, habitat preferences and reproduction that can only truly be discovered by thorough fieldwork. Even its recorded distribution is patchy, with a scattering of montane records from the Wissel Lakes in West Papua through to the Highlands of PNG and the high mountains above Port Moresby. There is only one known offshore locality, on Goodenough Island in Milne Bay Province, PNG.

The Boelen's Python is the most protected reptile in PNG and cannot be owned by a non-national person. Technically, even owning a piece of shed skin could be considered to be breaking the law and for a time this regulation even included a ban on filming or photographing the species. In fact, the species is probably neither rare nor endangered, just rarely encountered.

ABOVE: *Head of a Boelen's Python* (Morelia boeleni) *with its sharply contrasting black and white lip scales, grey iris, and iridescent 'oil-on'water' scale sheen.* OPPOSITE TOP: *A juvenile Boelen's Python, yet to develop its stunning adult livery.* OPPOSITE BOTTOM: *A Lesser Sundas Python, a complex and still imperfectly understood species.*

Range: New Guinea • Max. length: 2.5–4.5m • Habitat: Montane rainforest above 1,000m • Prey: Probably mammals and birds • Reproduction: Oviparous, 14 eggs

" In 1990 I spent two weeks working with the BBC Natural History Unit on a two-part documentary, *New Guinea – An Island Apart*. I was anxious that birds-of-paradise, cassowaries and tree kangaroos would not 'steal the show' and so proposed some sequences involving interesting reptiles, including one featuring Boelen's Python. I borrowed a large specimen from the National Museum live collection, and had agreed to reimburse the museum a sizeable financial sum if I lost it. We drove to Varirata National Park and I asked the director if he wanted to film the snake in some ferns. Instead, he led us into a dark valley and indicated he would like to film the python swimming across a dark forest creek until it submerged. Worried it would escape, I was permitted to move through the water, just out of shot, to affect a recapture. It took about seven takes to get the shot. I was extremely relieved when the director said "wrap" and I was then able to return the python to the museum. Sadly, the sequence was never used. **Varirata National Park, Central Province, Papua New Guinea."**

Photo by David G. Barker, VPI

SUNDA ISLAND PYTHONS

The Sunda Islands are a link between the Oriental and Australasian regions and home to species, including pythons, originating from both zones, ie. Reticulated Pythons, *Python reticulatus*, and Freckled or Water Pythons, *Liasis mackloti*, respectively. However, they also exhibit endemicity, with species occurring here and nowhere else.

Lesser Sundas Python *Python timoriensis*

Of all pythons, this species must have the most bewildering history of nomenclatural confusion, beginning in the years preceding its actual discovery. In 1829 four pythons from Timor and Semau islands were deposited in the Leiden and Paris Museums, pending their description. The first name attributed to them, in 1837, was *Python amethystinus*, an existing species that we now know as *Morelia amethistina* (p.140), a species complex that probably does not occur in the Lesser Sundas. In 1844 the three Leiden specimens were described as a new species, *Python timorensis* (corrected to *P. timoriensis* in 1846) but in the same year the single Paris specimen was named as *Liasis mackloti*, a species that today forms part of an Indo-Australian complex with *L. fuscus* (p.122). It was subsequently argued, over 120 years later, that the name *Liasis mackloti* should take precedence, since it was the more accepted and established name. But what of *Python timoriensis*?

In 1876 another python was described from the Lesser Sunda islands, but only as a geographical variety of the Amethystine Python. Three years later the variety was described as a new species, *Liasis petersii*, based in part on new material from the island of Flores, but this name never found favour and in 1893 the species became known as *Python timoriensis*, causing confusion with the earlier use of the name for the python now known as *Liasis mackloti*.

There is a further complication, in that this python may not actually occur on the island of Timor. Most of the reliable records and museum specimens come from the Lesser Sunda

island chain to the northwest of Timor, from Alor in the east, to Flores in the west. There is reportedly a museum specimen from the island of Lombok further to the west, but no records from Sumbawa or the Komodo islands in between. Although the type specimen came from Kupang, southwestern Timor, that is no guarantee that the species occurs on the island (see *Vini peruviana* below) and no additional specimens appear to have originated from there in the intervening 130 years.

If *Python timoriensis* does not occur on the island of Timor, the common name 'Lesser Sundas Python' is more appropriate than 'Timor Python', yet the latter persists as the most frequently-used common name, possibly out of ignorance. This does not mean that the scientific name should be changed, since the primary purpose of the Latin binomial is to define one species as separate from all others, whether or not it conveys accurate information about that species. Indeed, there are many instances of names not accurately describing the appearance or origin of species, such as the yellow and black dart-poison frog from northern South America, which was described in 1864 as *Dendrobates leucomelas* (*leuco* means white, *melas* means black) because the preservative had changed the yellow pigment to white. Other examples include the blue lorikeet *Vini peruviana*, described from specimens that arrived in Paris from Peru in 1776, but which originated from their native Tahiti, and the Anthill Python, *Antaresia perthensis* (p.119), which does not occur within 600km of Perth, Western Australia, even though this was given as the type locality in 1932. The problem is that,

ABOVE: *The Lesser Sundas Python* (Python timoriensis) *is found from Alor to Flores but probably not actually on Timor.*

because of the confusion with the name *Python timoriensis* prior to the discovery of the species now bearing that name in 1876, this particular scientific name does not even seem to accomplish its primary purpose.

In physique, the general gracile body form and elongate head of *P. timoriensis* resemble the physical proportions of an Amethystine Python (*Morelia amethistina*) but also those of a young Reticulated Python (*P. reticulatus*), a widespread Asian species which reaches its eastern limits in these islands (see p.88). The tail of *P. timoriensis* is shorter, and possibly less prehensile, than that of *M. amethistina*, and only a single supralabial contacts the eye in contrast to two in the latter species. *P. timoriensis* is a red-brown to yellow snake, overlaid with a darker brown blotched or cross-barred patterning, more fragmented than in *M. amethistina* and lacking both the dark postocular stripe and transverse neck bars. The undersurfaces, belly, throat and lips are bright yellow or white.

Range: Lesser Sunda islands (Alor to Flores, possibly Lombok, unlikely Timor), Indonesia • Max. length: 1.0–1.8m • Habitat: Dry and moist deciduous forest with some montane rainforest and grassland • Prey: Probably mammals and birds • Reproduction: Oviparous, 4–6 egg • Similar species: Amethystine Python (*Morelia amethistina*) and Reticulated Python (*P. reticulatus*)

Pacific Boas

The Australasian region is the realm of the true pythons, while it is Latin America that is dominated by the true boas. Three true boas (genera *Acranthophis* and *Sanzinia*) also occur on Madagascar in the Indian Ocean (pp.108–10), while the remaining five species, in genus *Candoia*, are found in the equally remote southwestern Pacific.

However, boas are not the only 'American' reptiles to occur on the wrong side of the Pacific. The Americas are also the centre of diversity for the true iguanas (Iguanidae), with 31 species represented, three species occurring in the Galapagos Islands (genera *Amblyrhynchus* and *Conolophus*), 960km west of Ecuador, and two species, in the genus *Brachylophus*, inhabiting Fiji and Tonga, 10,500km further to the west. The Fijian-Tongan iguanas are most closely related, not surprisingly, to the Galapagos iguanas, and the ancestral Fijian-Tongan stock was thought to have rafted across the Pacific from the Americas on the Southern Equatorial Current. It was also assumed that the Pacific boas had followed a similar route, also originating from Caribbean stock, prior to the formation of the Panamanian isthmus and the closure of the Caribbean-Pacific corridor.

However, more recent studies suggest an Oriental origin for the Pacific boas. The genus may have been in the Pacific for over 40 million years, time enough to evolve to the degree we see today. A clue to their origin may lie in their presence from the eastern Samoan archipelagos, through the Solomons, Bismarck and Admiralty Archipelagos and thence through northern New Guinea to as far west as the Maluku archipelagos of eastern Indonesia. They also occur as far south as the Loyalty Islands, off New Caledonia, as far north as the Belau (Palau) archipelago, but they are not recorded from the southern savannas of New Guinea or from Australia. It may not be readily realized that New Guinea was not a single landmass in the past. The southern half formed part of the northward moving Australian plate, but elements known as 'terranes' came in from the northeast and collided with northern New Guinea along its plate boundary to form first the Highlands, and then, later, the Maluku archipelagos, the north coast of New Guinea and the Admiralty and Bismarck archipelagos. If the ancestors of *Candoia* were riding on those later terranes they would have reached the length of northern New Guinea but not the south, nor Australia.

Bibron's Bevel-nosed Boa (Candoia bibroni), *a highly variable species found from Samoa to the Solomon Islands and south to the Loyalty Islands.*

PACIFIC ISLAND BOAS

Until 2001 this widely distributed and physically diverse genus *Candoia* contained only three species, the 'A–B–C boas' *C. aspera*, *C. bibroni* and *C. carinata*, with the slender arboreal *C. bibroni* the most basal or primitive member of the genus, and the stout, terrestrial *C. aspera* the most derived or advanced. The species exhibits a great deal of overlap in distribution, with a long-tailed, slender arboreal species and a short-tailed, stout terrestrial species often occurring in sympatry.

A recent major revision (Smith *et al*, 2001*) of the *C. carinata* complex resulted in that single and highly diverse species being split into three separate species, with ten subspecies between them. At the time of writing, the genus *Candoia* contains five species and 14 subspecies. Most species exhibit sexual dimorphism, the males being much smaller than the females. Males also possess cloacal spurs, but these are greatly reduced, or may even be absent, in females.

* Smith, H.B., Chiszar, D., Tepedelen, K. and Van Breukelen, F., 2001, 'A revision of the bevelnosed boas (*Candoia carinata* complex) (Reptilia: Serpentes)'. *Hamadryad* 26(2): 283–315. Note: the authors proposed the name 'bevelnosed' boa for species in the *C. carinata* complex but in my opinion this name is equally applicable to *C. bibroni*. I also prefer to use geographically relevant common names where they provide more information than patronyms, and I also differentiate between arboreal treeboas and terrestrial ground or viper boas.

Bibron's Bevel-nosed Boa *Candoia bibroni*

The eastern-most and most primitive member of the genus, *C. bibroni* is an arboreal snake that primarily inhabits forests but which may also be found in coastal mangrove and in cultivated areas. This is a slender species with a prehensile tail and an elongate, angular head not unlike that of the more western *C. carinata*. Patterning is extremely variable, ranging from dark grey to yellow-orange or rosy-pink, overlaid with blotches or stripes.

Prey consists largely of skinks, but geckos, bats, rats and nestling birds are also taken. There are suggestions that the southernmost population, on the Loyalty Islands, was established deliberately by 16th-century Polynesians, as a source of food, or later as a biological control for rats. According to some sources this snake is eaten in some part of those islands today. Two subspecies are sometimes recognized. **Range: Samoas, Fiji and Tonga, Vanuatu, Loyalty Islands (east of New Caledonia) and eastern Solomon Islands • Max. length: 1.3–2.0m • Habitat: Forest and coastal mangrove •**

BELOW: *A slender Schneider's Bevel-nosed Boa* (Candoia carinata) *from Papua New Guinea. Note the white saddle over the cloaca at the base of the tail.* OPPOSITE: *The narrow head of the Schneider's Bevel-nosed Boa probably limits its prey to small lizards.*

Prey: Lizards, small mammals and birds • Reproduction: Viviparous, 2–33 neonates • Similar species: Paulson's Bevel-nosed boa (*C. paulsoni*)

Schneider's Bevel-nosed Treeboa Candoia carinata

The original *Candoia carinata* contained a confusing array of slender, long-tailed, predominantly arboreal boas and stout-bodied, short-tailed ground dwellers which were variously named short-tails and long-tails, or allocated the subspecific titles of *C. c. carinata* and *C. c. paulsoni* respectively. Almost everyone knew this was a complicated species in dire need of re-organisation, but most attempts to understand it failed, until the Smith *et al* revision of 2001, which split the species into three and much reduced the scale of *C. carinata* as a species. Today *C. carinata* still comprises two subspecies, from mainland New Guinea and the Indonesian Malukus (Moluccas), and the Bismarck Archipelago to the west.

These are extremely slender, almost etiolated snakes, little thicker than a pencil, with long prehensile tails and equally drawn-out slender heads. Coloration tends to be grey or brown, and while most grey specimens are blotched or spotted with black, many of the brown specimens are striped. A common and easily discerned characteristic of the specimens I have examined has been the presence of a yellow-cream dorsal just anterior to, and a white ventral spot just posterior to the cloaca. This boa also seems to be capable of colour changes as specimens darken and lighten considerably at different times.

Owing to the diminutive size of the females the litter size is much smaller than the former subspecies now known as *Candoia paulsoni* (below). Prey seems to consist primarily of small lizards (skinks or geckos) since most mammals would be too large for all but the largest specimens to tackle.

Range: New Guinea, Indonesian satellite islands and the Bismarck Archipelago • Max. length: 0.5–0.7m • Habitat: Forest, and coconut, coffee and cocoa plantations • Prey: Small lizards, possibly frogs • Reproduction: Viviparous, to 6 neonates • Similar species: Belau Bevel-nosed Boa (*C. superciliosa*) from Palau Archipelago

" I was pursuing a skink of the genus *Carlia* through the vegetation when the fleeing lizard darted under a low sapling with thin branches protruding only a short distance from the ground. I glanced under the bush and saw an adult Bevel-nosed Treeboa in ambush position, coiled on the lowest branch, with head and neck angled downwards at 45 degrees. This slender treeboa was a common occurrence in the coconut plantations, usually found at a height of 1.5–2.0m in the cocoa and coffee trees between the rows of palms, and my assistants and I found many specimens."

Karkar Island, Madang Province, Papua New Guinea

Paulson's Bevel-nosed Ground Boa *Candoia paulsoni*

Formerly the 'short-tailed' subspecies of *C. carinata*, this species of bevel-nosed boa is probably the most complicated, with six subspecies and a very fragmented distribution comprising three separate divisions. The eastern division encompasses the Solomon Islands from Santa Cruz Island in the east to Bougainville and the small islands to the east of New Ireland and contains two subspecies, one from the Solomons and the islands off New Ireland, and one from Bougainville and Buka Islands. The species is absent from the large islands of the Bismarck Archipelago (New Britain and New Ireland) but occurs again in Papua New Guinea, the central division, which extends southeast to the d'Entrecastaux Archipelago. The Woodland and Misima Island boas are considered unique and given subspecific status, not surprisingly since these islands are also home to other rarities including small venomous forest snakes of the genus *Toxicocalamus* (Elapidae). The western division is located far to the west and centred on the Indonesian island of Halmahera, but with records also from the northeastern arm of Sulawesi and neighbouring islands.

C. *paulsoni* is a fairly stout-bodied snake which grows much larger and produces larger litters of neonates than *C. carinata*. It is also usually either red to red-brown, or off-white to cream, with a dorsal pattern that usually consists of a dark zigzagging ventral stripe. The large white cloacal spots of *C. carinata* are absent from

Paulson's Bevel-nosed Boa (Candoia paulsoni) *was originally a subspecies of* Candoia carinata *but its body is much stouter and its habits more terrestrial.*

C. *paulsoni*. Being a larger, more robust species, *C. paulsoni* may take larger prey than its relative and includes small mammals in its diet. It is an inhabitant of forests but also cultivated land, and is primarily terrestrial, although it climbs well.

Range: Solomon Islands, eastern and northern Papua New Guinea, and Halmahera and northeastern Sulawesi, Indonesia • Max. length: 0.8–1.3m • Habitat: Forest and cultivated land, plantations etc • Prey: Lizards and small mammals, including rats and possibly bats • Reproduction: Viviparous, 30–50 neonates • Similar species: Bibron's Bevel-nosed Boa (*C. bibroni*)

New Guinea Viper Boa *Candoia aspera*

The New Guinea Viper Boa is an extremely stout-bodied, short-tailed snake that is sometimes mistaken by Papua New Guineans for a death adder (*Acanthophis* spp.). This confusion may be behind the unsubstantiated rumours of 1.0m death adders from the Markham River valley. On several occasions I have been presented with large death adders in sacks, only to find a large Viper Boa instead. The strongly-keeled body scales, fragmented head scales and blotched brown patterning all assist in both the crypsis of this forest-floor species and its resemblance to a death adder.

A terrestrial species that probably never climbs, this is believed to be the most advanced or derived member of the genus *Candoia*. Prey may be fairly diverse, since there are many terrestrial frogs, lizards and small mammals within its size-range.

Scale counts and other differences, such as the number of dorsal spots or the colour of the iris, have been used to distinguish the New Guinea population from the Bismarck population and some authors recognize two subspecies.
Range: New Guinea, excluding southern savannas, Indonesian satellite islands and the Bismarck Archipelago • Max. length: 0.6–1.0m • Habitat: Rainforest and coconut plantation to 1,300m • Prey: Frogs, small mammals and lizards • Reproduction: Viviparous, neonates • Similar species: Death adders (*Acantophis* spp.)

" The Viper Boa can be exceedingly common. It is certainly the snake species I have encountered most frequently when searching coconut huskpiles for the venomous New Guinea Small-eyed Snake *(Micropechis ikaheka)* and it is not uncommon to find three or four boas in a single huskpile. When uncovered it does not make any attempt to escape, its only reaction being to 'ball-up' in the defensive manner of other small to medium-sized boas and pythons, with its head tucked in the middle. This behaviour has earned it the local name of 'sleepy snake', but not every specimen acts in this manner. I was once called to collect a very large female that was holding at bay three plantation workers armed with coconut-cutting knives. I suspected they had been goading the boa into her frenzied striking, but they had not injured her in any way. I was not sure they would have been so generous had she landed one of her strikes on target. The strangest place I have found a Viper Boa was inside a New Guinea Small-eyed Snake, the latter being an ophiophagous species.
Karkar Island, Madang Province, Papua New Guinea

The non-venomous New Guinea Viper Boa (Candoia aspera) *is frequently mistaken by locals for a highly venomous death adder* (Acanthophis laevis).

Further Reading and Bibliography

It is not feasible to list every national field guide and every historical scientific paper covering boas, pythons and basal snakes. Nor it is feasible to include every full colour herpetological article on the captive care and breeding of pythons and boas, nor every taxonomic paper, species description, range extension or complete revision. The list below is therefore confined to fairly recent and available regional or general publications on the subject, which will guide the reader towards more specific national, generic or species-related sources of information.

New Holland also produces a range of pocket-sized photographic guides to the reptiles of Southern Africa, Australia, South and Southeast Asia (see details on jacket flap).

Several important taxonomic revisions to a new anaconda (Dirksen & Böhme 2005), two new reticulated pythons (Auliya et al 2002), discussion of water pythons (Rawlings et al 2004), three new scrub pythons (Harvey et al 2000), and a revision of the bevel-nosed boas (Smith et al 2001), are cited at the relevant places in the species accounts.

GENERAL AND INTRODUCTION
Greene, H.W. (1997) *Snakes: The Evolution of Mystery in Nature*. California University Press.

Pough, F.H., Andrews, R.M., Cadle, J.E., Crump, M.L., Savitzky, A.H. and Wells, K.D. (2004) *Herpetology* (3rd edition). Pearson Prentice Hall, New Jersey.

Ross, R.A. and Marzac, G. (1990) *The Reproductive Husbandry of Pythons and Boas*. Institute of Herpetological Research.

Zug, G.R., Vitt, L.J. and Caldwell, J.P. (2001) *Herpetology: An Introductory Biology of Amphibians and Reptiles*. (2nd edition). Academic Press.

CHAPTER ONE – THE AMERICAS
Crother, B.I. (1999) *Caribbean Amphibians and Reptiles*. Academic Press.

Dirksen, L. (2002) *Anakondas*. Natur und Tier Verlag. (in German).

Henderson, R.W. (2002) *Neotropical Treeboas: Natural history of the* Corallus hortulanus *complex*. Krieger Publishing.

Kivit, R. & Wiseman, S. (2005) *The Green Tree Python and Emerald Tree Boa: care, breeding and natural history*. Kirschner & Suefer Verlag.

Manthay, U. and Grossmann, W. *Amphibien & Reptilien Südostasiens*. Natur und Tier Verlag. (in German).

Murphy, J.C. and Henderson, R.W. (1997) *Tales of Giant Snakes: a historical natural history of anacondas and pythons*. Krieger Publishing.

Petzold, H-G. (1995) *Die Anakondas*. Westarp Wissenschaften. (in German).

Stafford, P.J. and Henderson, R.W. (1996) *Kaleidoscopic Tree Boas: The genus* Corallus *of Tropical America*. Krieger Publishing.

Tolson, P.J. and Henderson, R.W. (1993) *The Natural History of West Indian Boas*. R&A Publishing.

CHAPTER TWO – EUROPE AND ASIA
Arnold, E.N. and Ovenden, D.W. (2002) *Reptiles and Amphibians of Europe* (2nd edition). Princeton University Press.

Fredriksson, G. (2005) 'Predation on Sun Bears by Reticulated Python in East Kalimantan, Indonesian Borneo' *The Raffles Bulletin of Zoology* 53(1): 165–168.

Groombridge, B. and Luxmore, R. (1991) *Pythons in South-East Asia: a review of distribution, status and trade in three selected species*. CITES.

Malkmus, R., Manthey, U., Vogel, G., Hoffmann, P. & Kosuch, J. (2002) *Amphibians and Reptiles of Mount Kinabalu (North Borneo)*. ARG Gantner Verlag.

Scott Keogh, J., Barker, D.G. and Shine, R. (2001) 'Heavily exploited but poorly known: systematics and biogeography of commercially harvested pythons (*Python curtus* group) in Southeast Asia' *Biological Journal of the Linnean Society* 73: 113–129.

Silva, A.de (1990) *Colour Guide to the Snakes of Sri Lanka.* R&A Publishing.

Smith, M.A. (1943) *Fauna of British India: Reptilia and Amphibia Vol.III Serpentes.* Taylor & Francis.

Stuebing, R.B. and Inger, R.F. (1999) *A Field Guide to the Snakes of Borneo.* Natural History Publications (Borneo).

Whitaker, R. and Captain, A. (2004) *Snakes of India: The field guide.* Draco Books.

CHAPTER THREE – AFRICA AND THE INDIAN OCEAN ISLANDS

Broadley, D.G. (1983) *FitzSimons' Snakes of Southern Africa.* Delta Books, Johannesburg.

Glaw, F. and Vences, M. (1994) *A Fieldguide to the Amphibians and Reptiles of Madagascar.* Zool. Forsch. und Museum Alexander Koenig, Bonn.

Henkel, F-W. and Schmidt, W. *Amphibians and Reptiles of Madagascar, and the Mascarene, Seychelles and Comoro Islands.* Krieger Publishing.

McCurley, K. (2005) *The Complete Ball Python: a comprehensive guide to the care and breeding and genetic mutations.* ECO Publishing.

Spawls, S., Howell, K., Drewes, R. and Ashe, J. (2002) *A Field Guide to the Reptiles of East Africa.* Natural World, Cape Town.

CHAPTER FOUR – AUSTRALASIA AND THE PACIFIC OCEAN ISLANDS

Barker, D.G. and Barker, T.M. (1994) *Pythons of the World Vol.1 Australia.* The Herpetocultural Library.

Cogger, H.G. (2000) *Reptiles and Amphibians of Australia* (6th edition). New Holland.

Greer, A. (1997) *The Biology and Evolution of Australian Snakes.* Surrey Beatty & Sons.

Kend, B.A. (1997) *Pythons of Australia.* Canyonlands Publishing.

Kivit, R. & Wiseman, S. (2005) – see under CHAPTER ONE – THE AMERICAS.

Maxwell, G. (2003) *The Complete Chondro: a comprehensive guide to the care and breeding of the green tree python.* ECO Publishing.

McCoy, M. (1980) *Reptiles of the Solomon Islands.* Wau Ecology Institute h/b 7.

Mense, M. (2006) *Rautenpythons* Morelia bredli, Morelia carinata *unde de* Morelia-spilota-*complex.* Natur und Tier Verlag. (in German).

O'Shea, M. (1996) *A Guide to the Snakes of Papua New Guinea.* Independent Publishing.

Shine, R. (1991) *Australian Snakes: A natural history.* Cornell University Press.

Torr, G. (2000) *Pythons of Australia: A natural history.* Krieger Publishing.

Wilson, S. and Swan, G. (2003) *A Complete Guide to Reptiles of Australia.* New Holland.

Index

Page numbers in *italics* denote illustrations; those in **bold** denote featured species

A

Picture Credits

All photographs by the author except as follows:

T. Allan/FLPA: page 21
A.N.T Photo library/NHPA: pages 122, 140
Anthony Bannister/NHPA: page 107
David G. Barker, VPI: pages 77, 103, 132, 133, 143, 144 (top),
    145, 147
Mark Bowler/NHPA: page 51
Jonathan Campbell: page 37 (bottom)
James Carmichael Jr/NHPA: front cover, pages 1, 2, 7 (top right),
    102, 138
Mark Carwardine/NHPA: page 64
Indraneil Das: pages 69, 70 (both), 71 (right)
Lutz Dirksen: page 57
Gerry Ellis/Minden Pictures/FLPA: page 22
Nick Garbutt/NHPA: pages 109, 111
Drew Gardner: page 92

Ken Griffiths/NHPA: pages 20, 118 (both), 130, 131,
Wolfgang Grossmann: page 73
Daniel Heuclin/NHPA: pages 34 (left), 44
Dr Gunther Köhler: page 60
Jean-Louis Le Moigne/NHPA: page 53
Bill Love/NHPA: pages 42, 46, 59 (bottom), 62, 87, 91, 104,
    126–127, 129 (top). 147 (bottom), 152
Mike McCoy: page 115
Chris Mattison/NHPA: pages 8, 92
Jany Sauvanet/NHPA: spine
Kevin Schafer/NHPA: pages 32, 39 (bottom),
Jeroen Speybroeck: page 68
Karl Switak/NHPA: pages 47 (bottom), 52, 59 (top), 63, 108,
    135
Laurie J. Vitt: page 36
Steve Wilson: page 114

Acknowledgements

The author would like to thank his fellow herpetological photographers, especially Dave Barker and Wolfgang Grossmann, who worked hard to find images of rare specimens at short notice, but also Jonathan Campbell, Indraneil Das, Drew Gardner, Gunther Köhler, Mike McCoy, Jeroen Speybroeck, Laurie Vitt and Steve Wilson. Thanks also go to my editor, James Parry, and to my partner, Bina Mistry, who once again has accepted that an author's days are long and frequently eat into 'personal time'. Finally, I would like to thank Alex Harris of Midnet, based at West Midland Safari Park. Armed with DiskWarrior, he single-handedly saved Chapters 1 and 4 when they were lost to a Macintosh hard disk meltdown. Without his technical know-how you might not be holding this book right now.

Macrostomatan Alethinophidia

- Boidae (Boinae) (Boas)
- Boidae (Erycinae) (Burrowing Boas)
- Tropidophiidae (South American Dwarf Boas and Woodsnakes)
- Ungaliophidae (Central American Dwarf Boas)